One Foot
in the Finite

One Foot in the Finite

Melville's Realism Reclaimed

✦

K. L. Evans

NORTHWESTERN UNIVERSITY PRESS
EVANSTON, ILLINOIS

Northwestern University Press
www.nupress.northwestern.edu

Printed in the United States of America

10 9 8 7 6 5 4 3 2 1

Library of Congress Cataloging-in-Publication Data

Names: Evans, K. L., author.
Title: One foot in the finite : Melville's realism reclaimed / K. L. Evans.
Description: Evanston, Illinois : Northwestern University Press, 2018. | Includes bibliographical references and index.
Identifiers: LCCN 2017028641 | ISBN 9780810136137 (cloth : alk. paper) | ISBN 9780810136120 (pbk. : alk. paper) | ISBN 9780810136144 (e-book)
Subjects: LCSH: Melville, Herman, 1819–1891—Criticism and interpretation. | Realism in literature.
Classification: LCC PS2388.R37 E94 2018 | DDC 813.3—dc23
LC record available at https://lccn.loc.gov/2017028641

CONTENTS

PREFACE AND ACKNOWLEDGMENTS

It is no longer practicable (was it ever?) for a literary critic to become absorbed in a subject as remote as the logic of language and to pursue this subject for more than a decade to the detriment of her health, bank account, and family standing. Yet I found myself unable to stop doing what I was doing, what might charitably be called a study of language conceived as a companion volume to Melville's *Moby-Dick*. The idea that the most companionable book in all American literature requires additional support would invite jeering if we did not so often misread Melville's evident preoccupation with language and meaning—his faith in the integrity of language as a means for communicating truth, which brings him into conflict with anyone for whom language is a flexible set of conventions, man's way of foisting meaning onto things. One clue that critics have misunderstood Melville's account of meaning in language is that he is repeatedly taken to endorse the very relativism to which he was implacably opposed.

To take the most optimistic view, then, this book's dual allegiance to literature and to provocative reexaminations of the nature of language—by Wittgenstein, in particular—may help readers turn away from what in the realm of Melville criticism remains wide of the mark.

My title, comically, gives no sign that this book is an extended study of Wittgenstein's writing. But Wittgenstein plays a vital role in this book because his work in logic makes possible its central thesis—namely, that "we have a choice over our words, but not over their meaning," as Stanley Cavell writes in *The Senses of Walden*. For Wittgenstein (as for Cavell), it is because words have meaning beyond our ability to give them meaning that it is possible to keep our bearings as speakers of language. As his sharpest readers have made clear, Wittgenstein rescues language and thereby the possibility of discourse when he shows how the meaning of a word, the thought it expresses, isn't contrived by the speakers of language but is rather sedimented out of practical life—the life we enjoy not as mere operators of a system of signs but as experiencing, feeling persons.

Of course, when Wittgenstein recognizes our special human capacity to "experience the meaning of a word" (a sensation identified as "the familiar physiognomy of a word, the feeling that it has taken up its meaning into itself, that it is an actual likeness of its meaning"), he is not reinforcing the belief that private impressions or sense-data serve as the starting point of a word's meaning. A considerable part of Wittgenstein's investigation is directed toward offloading the idea that language is a device for representing either private mental states or their presumed extramental correlates. Instead of thinking that some "inner" experience is essential to the feeling that a word is "an actual likeness of its meaning," Wittgenstein shows how words get their meaning through "intercourse with other people," as Wittgenstein's student and friend Rush Rhees writes. It is because our capacity to experience the meaning of a word is deeply intertwined in our social relations and socially devised practices—the wide and ever-changing variety of interpersonal dealings that make up what Wittgenstein calls a "form of life"—that Wittgenstein says meaning lies in use.

It follows that one of the strangest misappropriations of Wittgenstein's writing has been to make his attentiveness to the subjective states of language speakers serve a very different argument about the subjectivity of meaning. The inference is quite the reverse for Wittgenstein, a philosopher who carefully attends to the human practices that shape the use of language for the purpose of further exploring how language belongs to our lives—how, as Cavell says, "we learn language and the world *together*." As Rush Rhees holds, Wittgenstein's farthest-reaching conclusion is that the experience of meaning isn't some discrete subjective phenomenon but a multilayered intersubjective *feature* of this life with words.

Though it is not always recognized, Wittgenstein nimbly constructs a case for the possibility of meaning in language. This becomes feasible, Bernard Harrison deftly helps us to understand, after Wittgenstein both denies the existence of a direct referential relationship between words and things and at the same time dispels the view that language is self-referential, the meaning of its signs established by nothing more than the history of language. In other words, it is faithfulness to the conditions of language as such that the exacting computations of Wittgenstein's *Tractatus Logico-Philosophicus* or the cumulative philosophical remarks of his *Philosophical Investigations* are designed to achieve. By this interpretation Wittgenstein offers a philosophically rigorous account of meaning in language, one that is unusual in that it does not refuse to attribute meaning to individual words, even while it does energetically dispute any view which holds meaning to be an independent phenomenon, as if our words carry around with them a single unassailable meaning, or as Wittgenstein writes, "as if the meaning were an aura the word brings along with it and retains in every kind of use." This makes Wittgenstein required reading for literary theorists wishing to talk about texts that are redemptive or as Cavell says pledged to the "rescue of language"—that are designed to allay the feeling that our lives and our language betray each other.

What I hope to make clear is why *Moby-Dick* is an arresting example of such work. Read in sympathy with the spirit in which it is written (a spirit, we should say, quite out of keeping with the main current of European and American thought) *Moby-Dick* is not only breathtakingly different from anything else on the scene, then or now. It is also an investigation of the interrelations of language and concrete, earthly life as illuminating and provocative as Wittgenstein's. Like Wittgenstein, Melville was incapable of conducting his investigation pedantically or dully. But more to the point, Melville's book can galvanize into action those theorists who remain unimpressed or unmoved by the proposal that signifieds (as in Saussure's semiology) are concepts that are arbitrarily related to words or signifiers. In *Moby-Dick*, in contrast, the view that the word "whale" refers to something out there in the world isn't open to question.

By this hint about Melville's realism, as I will call it, I do not mean that for Melville the term "whale" refers to some entity posited as enjoying an existence independent of any linguistic, conceptual, or otherwise constitutive activity of the human mind. Rather, I mean that for Melville the term "whale" is no mere arbitrary counter whose meaning (or lack of meaning) can be left for the speakers of language to determine as they please. As Patricia Hanna and Bernard Harrison argue in *Word and World: Practice and the Foundations of Language*, words seem like arbitrary counters "only if we consider them in abstraction from the modes of insertion into our lives which confer upon them all the meaning they possess." To Hanna and Harrison the thought this suggests is that words are cultural artifacts *and* that words have a kind of objectivity—that these two positions are not the polar opposites they are commonly taken to be.

Indeed, in *Moby-Dick* the whole notion of objectivity is reconceived—which accounts for why Melville's book is so beneficial for readers hoping to move beyond the debilitating skepticism of postmodernist thought. For Melville is a realist not only in the literary but also in the philosophical sense. Like many of Plato's dialogues, Melville's writing reveals a concern with the intelligibility of language or the possibility of understanding. Like Plato, Melville worries about the conditions for meaningful discourse, the conditions on which the possibility of understanding depends. What needs to be recognized, though, is that for the realist philosophers who have these concerns, "the possibility of understanding is not simply the possibility of communicating," as Rush Rhees points out. "It is the possibility of distinguishing waking from nightmare." For Plato the point is that unless there is meaning in our words—unless there is something which can be understood (or misunderstood)—then nothing that is said can be understood and discourse is impossible. That Melville constructs his whaling narrative so as to make a case for this view is the reason I call his book philosophical as well as literary.

The question of whether a work of literature can simultaneously be a work of philosophy is a recurrent one, trotted out on any occasion in which philosophers wish to declare literary artists presumptuous in their claims and foolish in their aspirations, and artists wish to return the disservice (or lodge their own set of objections) by announcing that art is art, and should not be expected to make specific claims. It is generally safer to say that philosophical arguments play a role in works of literature only in passing or by chance, and that such works are valuable in their expressive function without regard to the intellectual capacities of their authors. As Stephen D. Ross explains in *Literature and Philosophy* (without subscribing to this position), "the role of the philosophical literary critic is often to express as philosophical—in language suitable to philosophy—views and attitudes which are found in works of art in a totally different form, and which are therefore not quite philosophical. The interpretation makes them so." Views are presented in the work of literature but not in assertive form; it is the task of the critic to turn the embodiment of a philosophical position into explicit philosophic claims. Nevertheless there are some writers—and Melville is one of them—who show how an artist *qua* artist can make legitimate claims to particular insights. Melville doesn't just display theoretical positions; he supports them, in a manner much like making an argument for them. And as Ross notes there is something glorious about writing that not only succeeds in literary terms but that contains and develops ideas of great philosophic worth.

In *Moby-Dick* Melville plays out elemental conflicts (why, for example, "The running battle of star and clod / Shall run for ever, if there be no God") in dramatic form—that is, by bringing together voices intellectually and morally at odds with one another in a tale that surprises, disorients, delights, and is told, as Howard Jacobson writes, "vertiginously, by a narrator it would not be wise of you to trust." Yet one of the readiest complaints about Melville's whaling narrative is that its action is interspersed with wearying passages of technical and encyclopedic matter, and that its characters habitually hold forth on issues more in keeping with Melville's own interests, and thus as a result seem not so much characters as the central means by which the novel's overriding concerns are somewhat hollowly revealed. As such charges suggest, confusion about what Melville's book confronts intellectually makes it is hard to see what kind of book it is. *Moby-Dick* falls into the category of books I. A. Richards called "machines to think with"—works of fiction whose function is to "fine-tune our mental capacities," as Joshua Landy writes, imaginative books that with time and sustained engagement can "hone our abilities and . . . help us become who we are." For Melville is not satisfied with portraying *some* people out at sea, with their problems and setbacks. Melville's book is about *man* (as Ross characterizes books of literature and philosophy), which is only to say that the problems of the people in his whaling narrative are our problems, just as their solutions and range of options mirror our own.

Naturally, there are numerous ways in which the intellectual concerns of Melville's book might be framed, but there is a rather particular, to some extent irreplaceable, set of people who have helped me as I have framed them here. First on that list is Bernard Harrison, to whom I wrote in 2008 after completing the original version of this book. It is a sign of this eminent philosopher's astonishing magnanimity that his response to my out-of-the-blue missive (essentially, "I'm okay on Melville but can you make sure my reading of Wittgenstein isn't rubbish?") was initially, "Yes, but first I have to read *Moby-Dick*," followed three weeks later by a fifteen-page response to my manuscript (which understood at once what I was aiming at), followed, over the years, by any number of personal communications and more formal letters championing my project and immeasurably improving my understanding. Not only this book but my whole grasp of the concepts of meaning and of understanding, and of how Wittgenstein exegesis can influence literary studies, or how a novelist can be a moral philosopher, or indeed what fiction is *for*—how, as Harrison says, the description of imaginary events and situations can illuminate something worth calling reality—is inconceivable without his influence. That this incomparably clever man is also impossibly decent, kind, and generous has proved one of the great comforts of my adult life.

Other remarkable Wittgensteinians who have transformed my ideas (and who in the same way reveal that rare blend of intellectual rigor, humility, mettle, and perspicacity Wittgenstein's best readers invariably possess) include David Charles McCarty, whose long essay "The Philosophy of Logical Wholism" is a masterpiece of Wittgenstein scholarship; Danièle Moyal-Sharrock, who has tirelessly worked to have the "therapeutic" nature of Wittgenstein's writing moved off-center in Wittgenstein studies; H.O. Mounce, who stresses Wittgenstein's evident connections with the tradition of classical realism, and likewise Silvana Borutti and Fulvia de Luise, who have done much to draw out the consonances between Wittgenstein and Plato; and Hugh Knott, a rare bird of a philosopher who passes his days as an ecologist.

In the end, I needed as careful a check on my presentation of Melville as on my understanding of Wittgenstein, and this invaluable intervention came in the form of Samuel Otter. I count myself extremely lucky to be the recipient of his penetrating, comprehensive critique and generous encouragement. Without Sam's expert pruning this book would have been much longer and no better. Speaking of savvy interventionists, I am also particularly grateful to Branka Arsić for plucking me out of a rich pool of Melvilleans to co-edit a volume, and by this means teaching me a very great deal about any number of things. Her passion, intellectual courage, and dedicated work ethic make her a model Americanist and vital ally. In a rough couple of years, Michael Snediker's scholarship and friendship were enchanting. And indeed Melvilleans of all stripes—the prominent scholars mentioned in these pages and many more—have schooled and enlightened me; I can't think of a better society of readers to learn from. Last but certainly not least, I give thanks for Kenneth Dauber, who introduced me to Melville and Wittgenstein and is more than anyone responsible for my formal and moral education. Ken brought me into being as a reader, and not only that; he lights up a room, and I am immeasurably glad to have lived my life in his orbit.

This book owes a special debt to Neil Hertz, who read and charitably commented on the long introduction, doing much to improve it. Likewise Rebecca Brown, Sam Chambers, Richard Deming, Antoine Traisnel, and John McGowan, who all read my book's unusual overview in draft and wisely drew attention to some of its blind spots. Rachel Cole offered a meticulous line reading of the introduction and chapters 1 and 3, and her unassailable judgment has in numerous instances refined my prose and more generally boosted the book's quality. As it was transitioning from one kind of book into another, a reorienting conversation with George Shulman—and participation in his dynamic political theory discussion group—proved vital. The heroic Mario von der Ruhr aided this project from its conception. Joel Bettridge remains the best friend a person could have, and it doesn't hurt that he's so smart. (Any author attempting to be courageous needs a co-conspirator—and Joel is unrivalled in that capacity.) At a crucial juncture Rhian Williams read my whole book and suggested no changes. Because I know her to be as conscientious as she is discerning, this was a thrilling response. No less valuable have been the expert readers to whom I sent the finished manuscript: Michael Puett,

Johannes Voelz, and Charlie Altieri. (And though I only read Altieri's charged and enlightening *Reckoning with the Imagination: Wittgenstein and the Aesthetics of Literary Experience* after this book was in production, it still proved an influence, so persuasive do I find its arguments.) More gratitude to the tolerant and talented intimates who made it possible to finish this book without going completely mad: there's a crowd, but special thanks to Sarah Walston, virtuoso therapist and confidante extraordinaire. During the final weeks of writing I was a participant at The School of Criticism and Theory, hosted by Cornell University, which—under the princely directorship of Hent de Vries—was exactly the right place to be. (Especially since it brought me to Theresa Carmody.) Also at Cornell, English department chair Roger Gilbert offered a warm welcome during my extended term as Visiting Scholar. Masha Raskolnikov and Tom Campanella made me feel quite loved.

My most prized hours are those spent teaching, and the astonishing young people who regularly kept me on the edge of my seat—who listened, and prodded, and collaborated, and exulted, and could be heartbreakingly funny—range from my first undergraduates at the University of Redlands to the last class I taught at Yeshiva University, in which every one of the all-women participants studying Wittgenstein's *Tractatus* was wickedly smart and (thank God) determined to do her own thinking. That I cannot mention all of these students here does not mean that I have forgotten any of them. For their contributions to the richness of those years, and for their dedication to assembling a community of peers to be productive and disruptive with, I must single out Deb DeLaurell, Ellie Jones, Kristen Steslow, Molly Stroud, Emily Thomas, James Harvey, Brenna Sheffield, Izzy To, Nichole Verreras, Sarah Medved, Gila Kletenik, Mijal Bitton, Jina Davidovich, Daniela Aaron, Dani Lent, Channa Gila Ovits, Rachel Raice, Rachel Benaim, Becky Frankle, Lauren Burstein, Hannah Dreyfus, Esther Cohen, Leah Goldberg, and Elizabeth Sussman. Claudia Ingram is responsible for ushering me into the teaching profession, and her unfaltering support throughout the years has kept me afloat. A paragon of sympathy is Claudia, she of the lion heart.

I'm indebted to wise and kind Henry Lowell Carrigan for bringing this book to Northwestern University Press, as well as to the very able team who saw it through publication: Greta Elizabeth Bennion, Anne E. Gendler, Maggie Grossman, Marianne Jankowski, Trevor Perri, and J.D. Wilson. In Mike Ashby I had a copy editor as sympathetic and intuitive as he is meticulous. To Haaris Naqvi, editorial director at Bloomsbury Academic, I owe thanks for granting permission to reprint my chapter "Gospel Cetology," first published in *Melville's Philosophies*, edited by

Branka Arsić and K. L. Evans (Bloomsbury, 2017). I'm also grateful to W. J. T. Mitchell for introducing me to Antony Gormley, and for Antony's very generous permission to use one of his suggestive drawings for the cover.

My family members—all of them—have borne most of the weight of this project. They have at least supplied what every Melvillean requires: time, strength, cash, and patience. Infinite patience, really, of the kind modeled by Shel Hershinow, and unflappable goodwill. This book would not have been possible had my father Ian Evans not provided a place to write it in. My scholarly husband David LaRocca did not devotedly read every word that I wrote; more essentially, he spent countless hours taking first one child and then another to the park, or around the block, or on manufactured errands, so as to afford his writing wife some peace. There is little glory in such a gift but to me it was incalculably precious. Finally, this book is lovingly dedicated to my brilliant hardworking mom, Lorna Hershinow, who propped me up through the years I spent writing it, and also to my darling daughter Ruby, who felt hardest the loss of those years.

One Foot
in the Finite

Introduction

✦

Melvillean Mimesis

Moby-Dick is vast and astonishing, a whale of a book, its superabundance testament to the wide orbit of its author's interests. We must therefore say that Melville's book exists for various reasons. But one of them, and I think one of considerable importance, is to find a place in the list of philosophical investigations into the relationship between the mind and the world. To the oldest of problems Melville's whaling narrative contributes an original and unexpected solution. I have worked to throw light on that solution—assuming that it has been hard to see not because Melville lacked philosophical astuteness but because *Moby-Dick* is primarily a work of imaginative literature. Thus I write as though I am speaking to someone who is already familiar with *Moby-Dick*, already "boldly launched upon the deep," but someone unsatisfied by our view of Melville as a spiritual wanderer, as in Hawthorne's well-known sketch: a moody, honorable quester who "will never rest until he gets hold of a definite belief" and never does.[1] Such exaggerated portrayals have obstructed our view of Melville's philosophical achievement.

I begin by rescuing the term "mimesis" in relation to Melville's writing. For Melville imitates real life in his whaling narrative—and draws a valuable distinction between the art of imitation and what is merely an attempt to copy from, document, or reflect sensible life. Misunderstanding mimesis (failing to honor the difference between writing that simply mirrors the world and writing that develops pictures of imaginative worlds real enough to engage audiences and solicit our corresponding imaginative activity) has led to a tradition in Melville studies of splitting *Moby-Dick* in two—of thinking Melville's whaling narrative adheres to and enforces a strict distinction between the world we conceive and the world we have practical dealings with. Taking one of *Moby-Dick*'s primary tasks to be the recovery of the world from this sundering, I assert the novel's radical wholeness, its depiction of what is neither the noumenal nor the phenomenal world but a third level of reality, one that stands between the individual mind and nature. *Moby-Dick* portrays the third realm—not the ghostly realm in which all things real are naught but imponderable thoughts, as the skeptic concludes, but the bright and gleaming intelligible world in which we find ourselves.

Moby-Dick also affords philosophical insight on the subject of *how*, exactly, fictionalized narratives in particular have the capacity to present, as Melville writes, even "more reality, than real life itself can show."[2] This understanding is ever more indispensable. For although the eighteenth century was profoundly excited by the idea that works of fiction could examine and illuminate something worth calling reality, and though, as A. D. Nuttall reports, this excitement lasted well through the nineteenth century and still rises, unbidden, in the untheoretical reader, twentieth-century criticism has acted largely to strip readers of their trust in what Aristotle identified as the robust possible relation between fiction and the truth.[3] Instead of associating great works of fiction with what Melville calls "short, quick probings of the very axis of reality," many readers no longer take seriously the possibility that mere words, however cunningly arranged, can represent real life in all its complexity.

And yet real life—matters of common, interpersonal experience, fit to be discussed and examined in a shared language—is depicted everywhere in *Moby-Dick*, even when Melville is telling tall tales. *Moby-Dick*'s chief example of real life is the state of affairs captured by the term "whale": this, Melville seems to insist, is not the stuff of subjective fantasy but objective reality. Indeed, philosophical investigation into "what it *is* to be an objective reality, rather than a subjective fantasy," as the philosopher Bernard Harrison writes, is a constituent element of Melville's whaling narrative.[4] Melville's readers are compelled to start thinking about the relation between fiction and the truth since Melville's great achievement is to have written a story that feels factual regardless of its obvious artistry, or despite the presence of a narrator who draws attention away from the tale to accentuate the way it is told. *Moby-Dick*'s scenes are so carefully and concretely imagined, the writing has such vigorous life and freshness, readers feel convinced that there is something more than just made up or chimerical about the concept "whale"—that this general notion is sufficiently deserving of the label "real" to drive out the worry that it is a mere projection of the human mind.

For this reason I associate Melville's narrative mode with literary realism and include *Moby-Dick* in the tradition charted by Erich Auerbach. Few other American authors have understood as profoundly or practiced more consummately the writing Auerbach describes in *Mimesis: The*

Representation of Reality in Western Literature and its precursor *Dante: Poet of the Secular World*. The realist tradition as Auerbach identifies it is upheld by writers who adopt the ordering, interpreting spirit of the Middle Ages by trying to find the formal element of any thing or action (who seek an answer to the question, How does God see the earthly world?) but who nevertheless offer a rich sense of historical immediacy and the temporal aspects of existence—who preserve experiential life in its "unique, contingent, ephemeral this-worldliness."[5] Realist writers use selective details to produce the imaginative worlds or *pictures* of the world that, as we become attuned to the way these invented worlds have been constructed, allow readers to work out what we care about. Realism by this measure is in keeping with the central task of art, which isn't to explain the world but to intensify our individual relationships with it—and as Charles Altieri notes "there is no intensifying a world that readers will not take as a plausible one."[6] Literary realism doesn't document everyday objects and situations. It is determined rather by a writer's way of narrating. The power to make cooked-up or fictional events vivid and distinct—"so clear and palpable," Auerbach writes, "that the question of their likelihood arises only on subsequent reflection"—unites the works in this tradition.[7]

Thus the realism on significant display in *Moby-Dick* is not what Henry James disparagingly called "dingy realism," the faithful redescription of everyday life. The mimesis of a Melvillean scene cannot be mistaken for what one nineteenth-century author calls "pen photography," writing that conflates the imitation of reality with the mere transcription of phenomena.[8] The expectation regarding realism in this narrow sense is that the persons, places, and things the writer depicts are built up out of observed detail; also that there is nothing to these naturalistic observations over and above what is being shown, except perhaps the way they are tied to what happens in the narrative, how its plot unfolds.

Melville, on the other hand, writes realism in which the idea of truth is not replaced *tout court* by verisimilitude. Like the type of story James does happily recommend to readers, *Moby-Dick* is "perfectly a romance, and yet it is profoundly real. It is a piece of the finest polish, and yet it bristles with 'sensations'; it is at once the work of a master of style, and of a consummate story-teller."[9] *Moby-Dick* is the kind of book James calls "simply beautiful." Melville made an appreciable investment in reliably documenting the sensible objects of his place and time, which is the reason his writing has earthly particularity, why it is so convincing and lifelike. At the same time, Melville's story certainly confirms the view that "a work of art should be lighted with a ray of idealism," as James notes:

that artists must extend their vision to include immutable patterns of which individual persons and things are imperfect copies.

In *Moby-Dick*, Melville treats the world of forms as well as the world perceptible to the senses. This seeming disjunction has given rise to a misunderstanding: that what Melville attempts is two different kinds of books, rolled into one. Yet what readers encounter again and again in the passages of Melville's whaling narrative is much more unified. Darting through the novel and transforming its scenes is the whale: a figment of discourse or creature of the fertility of the mind through which concrete, temporal life is robustly preserved.

In Melville's narrative the whale is an example—maybe *the* example—of how concepts come into being. Concepts (like "whale") are puzzling because they are not part of the natural world, the world of physical objects and forces in which human beings are immersed, and yet they are not denizens of the subjective, essentially private "inner" world philosophers since Descartes have associated with the world of ideas. Though the whale that figures centrally in *Moby-Dick* is otherworldly or nonsensible, a "phantom," as Melville writes, it is *not* merely an idea or something that exists in the mind. Melville is accordingly a realist in the classical sense, too—that is, someone for whom our concepts (and their linguistic expressions) are not highly subjective. As Melville uses his whaling narrative to illustrate, the concept "whale" is not private but public. In *Moby-Dick* Melville plays up the fundamental difference between ideas and concepts and makes clear why, in contrast to ideas, our concepts are intersubjectively accessible and objectively real.

Melville thus contrives a fully material account of the thinking subject. He introduces a capacious and dynamic view of subjectivity—one that doesn't adhere to traditional notions, following Descartes, of the boundaries forming isolated private persons. As I aim to show, Melville's writing in *Moby-Dick* connects him to new materialism, as it has come to be known, with its attendant promise to redefine human life by breaking down the boundaries that separate us from all other things.[10] (Descartes taught us to think of the body, of our bodily situation in the world, as inessential to mind. This preconception dies hard, which is why the new emphasis on materiality is exceptionally useful in revealing how much of mental life is contingent upon material life.) But *Moby-Dick* must also be located in the context of a much older inquiry into the relationship between thought and the external world. For the reason that his whaling narrative investigates the relation between a linguistic construct or concept (the word or general name "whale") and a situation outside in the world (what Melville calls "the living whale in his full majesty and significance"), we should understand Melville's writing to be organized around a central philosophical concern: the question of whether, and by what means, the human mind can credit itself with access to reality. Because Melville offers an optimistic and compelling answer to this question, there is reason to call him a realist. However, what such realism bespeaks is, as Auerbach suggests, a certain refusal to separate what can be seen or heard from what can be intuited or understood. Realists as Auerbach identifies them vividly demonstrate the intimacies, rather than discrepancies, between appearance and truth.

The whale in *Moby-Dick* is a conceptual object, a thing or event structured not in itself but in the way that it is recounted. (Wittgenstein calls such objects "facts in logical space.")[11] In Melville's book this essentially symbolic object is depicted with what Auerbach calls "a completeness, a concentration, an actuality" which it didn't achieve on earth and "assuredly never revealed to anyone else."[12] Like Dante, the first great realist writer, Melville gathers "the human world in all its breadth and depth" into the structure of a lasting, unassailable order from which the confusion of earthly affairs ("not concealed or attenuated or immaterialized, but preserved in full evidence") might be scrutinized and considered.[13]

To picture real life is not to copy life; this is important to understand, because in order to bring about visions of reality a writer must imitate something that cannot be perceived. Homer achieved this in his epic poems when he conceived of characters whose imagined principle of unity (as the ancient critics called an individual's unique combination of physical and spiritual qualities) manifested some larger feature of a common if not universal human condition. Homer's implementation of the Heraclitean maxim that "a man's character is his fate"—the poet's invention of Achilles or Odysseus, Helen or Penelope "by heaping up acts and sufferings that were all of a piece"—was enormously valuable to imaginative storytelling, as Auerbach reports, because what can be represented in poetic terms "is not that good things happen to a good man and brave things to a brave man, but that the fate of Achilles is Achillean."[14]

Homeric imitation, which the ancient critics called "mimesis," is thus "not an attempt to copy from appearance; it does not spring from observation."[15] Homeric imitation "is no mere copy of life," and not only because the events Homer narrates are mythical. For Auerbach, the inestimable value of Homer's poetry lies in the fact that the three-dimensionality of his characters, his characters' "living presence," doesn't originate in naturalistic observation. It originates in the poet's conception of character—in the way "an act revealing a man's nature, or, one might say, his nature as manifested in a first act, unfolded naturally and inevitably into the sum and sequence of that man's kindred acts, into a life that would take a certain direction and be caught up in the skein of events which add up to a man's character as well as his fate." Only *after* the poet's conception is established does naturalistic description set in, as Auerbach notes, and "there is no need for the poet to summon it; it comes to him quite spontaneously."[16] Homer's characters are beings that have no validity of their own, in other words, or that find their measure not in themselves but in the many scenes in which they speak and move.[17] And, precisely because Achilles or Odysseus are creatures of pure textuality, beings whose living presence originates in the way their fate follows from their unity, the poet is free to render his "plastic manifestations" in rich color and detail.[18] Indeed, such figures even seem to gain in concrete presence from the poet's rigorous rendering.

What heirs to Homeric imitation portray are therefore not living men and women but beings of the imagination, beings conjured in a work of art. Auerbach calls them "figures." Such beings are *not* persons, even when they bear a resemblance to autonomous individuals down to the most extreme particularities of their sensuous beings, because, as Auerbach reasons, they have their ground and limit in "the very definite event that is being related."[19] So, in *Don Quixote*, Cervantes's knight is a man who stands there complete, in all his sensual fullness, only because his distinctive, particular, earthly side is fully encompassed by the "event" that is being related—the confusion of a man whose class has lost its function, "whose life is running meaninglessly out," or "whose life is hardly better than a peasant's but who is educated and who is neither able nor permitted to labor as a peasant does."[20] By engineering a concordance between Don Quixote's distinctive personality and the event that is being related (social order crumbling; the state of affairs in which people are affiliated with a class they cannot emancipate themselves from but to which they belong as mere members, without wealth and without high connections), Cervantes assembles his picture of real life.

Accordingly, what I call "Melvillean mimesis" or Melville's representation of reality in *Moby-Dick* does not depend on Melville's sharp observation of the sensible world, though Melville's whaling narrative does offer readers an unprecedented sense of historical immediacy and the manifold aspects of earthly existence in mid-nineteenth-century America. Naturalistic observation plays a part in the construction of Melville's scenes, augmenting the writer's imagination and enriching it. However, the mimesis of a Melvillean scene derives from Melville's way of writing, a narrative mode that, rather than putting constraints on the powers of imagination, allows writers to "mobilize and thicken experience," as

Altieri writes, to build models of complex human concerns and investments "by sheerly verbal means."[21]

This book draws attention to Melville's dual status as writer of fiction (of narratives lit with "a ray of idealism") and shrewd spectator of the visible, palpable world but does not enlist the argument that Melville at times abandoned the conventions of the fictive mode in *Moby-Dick*, or that Melville did not produce a book of fiction but a book that mixed fiction, autobiography, travel narrative, and aesthetic treatise, as is often suggested. Rather, I make the case that Melville's preeminent work of fiction offers Americans a chance to think differently about literary realism. *Moby-Dick* invites readers to disambiguate realism and subsequently to recognize a parallel between Melville's style of narration and the one adopted by Shakespeare or, prior to that, by Dante—the first writer in the modern world to insist that readers follow him, as Auerbach argues, "into the extreme particularity of the real situation that he conjures up."[22]

Among readers of literature, the term "realism" is now almost as uncertain and perplexing as it was when Auerbach directed his very great powers toward removing its ambiguity—perhaps because many subsequent literary theorists have been less agile than Auerbach in their attempts to address realism in its philosophical context. One consequence of this confusion is that we continue to blur the distinction between realism as an attempt to hold a mirror to the natural world or to everyday life and the complex and sophisticated realism rightly associated with the work of Dante and Shakespeare, Woolf and Joyce. Because such writing denies the copying function, we clearly need more adequate means of connecting events in fiction with events in the outside world.

Charles Altieri modernizes realism in his *Reckoning with the Imagination: Wittgenstein and the Aesthetics of Literary Experience*. Here is one of Altieri's typically crisp efforts to put on notice those who use the term lazily: "Traditionally we treat realism as a rhetorical mode emphasizing what can be seen through language rather than what language in the form of the space of reasons can do on its own to supplement experience. Realism is a rhetoric binding us to how people typically construct worlds by negotiating everyday objects and situations. For many readers, and writers, this rhetoric seems to put heavy constraints on the powers of imagination. But think again of what realism becomes in the hands of a Tolstoy or George Eliot or a principle revived by means of experimental efforts in James Joyce or Virginia Woolf. Here realism is best seen as a mode of displaying collective feeling for a shareable world rather than a rhetoric setting limits on literary representation."[23]

Again, then, Melville isn't struggling to defend what Plato denied: that simply by describing or recounting the world around him the writer can imitate real life. Instead he is contributing to the view that even in highly stylized narratives or narratives that include fantastical elements a powerful light can be cast on life as it is lived and experienced. Ultimately the triumph of literary realism, its most salient characteristic, is what it contributes to our sense of the objective reality of certain events, events ordinary people are customarily able to discuss and examine, when for instance we talk about being bereaved or orphaned, or experiencing the effects of exorbitant pride, or finding our friends unexpectedly charitable or mean-spirited. As Bernard Harrison points out, what terms like "orphaned" or "mean-spiritedness" bespeak is not, of course, the inhuman, extracultural reality studied in the natural sciences. But neither can the occurrences captured by such terms be easily dismissed as creations of mind.

That is the guiding premise of this study of Melville's capacity to depict real life in an invented narrative. For as I see it the great accomplishment of Melville's whaling narrative is the massive obstacle it presents to the passage or progress of Cartesian dualism. (And subsequently the obstacle it presents to Cartesian skepticism.) Descartes burdened subsequent Western thought with the idea that the world contains two radically different kinds of thing—material objects and minds—and furthermore that the material world is accessible in common to numerous observers but that conscious states, thoughts, the acts of a mind, are personal, individual, and highly subjective.[24] Melville, though, belongs to a select number of thinkers and writers for whom the two Cartesian realms, "outer" (or public) and "inner" (or private, subjective) "fail to exhaust the contents of reality," as Harrison reasons. The main problem with Descartes's type of dualism is that everything nonmaterial is labeled "subjective," or assigned to the essentially private world of personal fancy. But what, then, is the whale? When we consider the sense of the term "whale"—not, that is to say, the *natural objects* to which this word refers but the *conceptual object* Melville calls "the living whale in his full majesty and significance"—what is clear is that the whale cannot plausibly be allocated to either Cartesian category.

Melville's whaling narrative thus demonstrates the need for a "third realm," as literary critic F. R. Leavis calls the realm "which is neither public in the ordinary sense nor merely private."[25] Late nineteenth-century logician Gottlob Frege, who also held that "a third realm must be recognized," explains that anything belonging to this third realm "has it in common with ideas that it cannot be perceived by the senses, but has it in common with things that it does not need an owner so as to belong to the contents of his consciousness."[26] More recently critic Sharon Cameron, thinking expressly of the American literary tradition, has called for the recognition of a new, third ontological realm, one that confounds the difference between the "inner" and "outer" worlds.[27] Cameron's petition evolves from and is in keeping with Stanley Cavell's reorienting claim that the founding writers of the American literary tradition explicitly challenged attempts by both the classical empiricists and by Kant to account for how phenomena can be made to accord with mental representations. Cavell's philosophical reconsideration of Melville's famous contemporaries Ralph Waldo Emerson and Henry David Thoreau leads to the galvanizing conclusion that America's most consequential philosophy can be found in the "metaphysical riot of its greatest literature."[28] In this literature Cavell finds all but explicit the idea that the place we inhabit "is itself a world, as it were a Third World of the spirit."[29] In other words, talk of a third realm is itself a challenge to the usual means of explaining how sense impressions can come to furnish the mind with ideas. Critics like Leavis and Cameron have championed the notion of a third realm precisely because it does not presuppose assent to Lockean and Cartesian notions of "the mind" as an entity separate and distinct from physiological processes. What if, as Branka Arsić wonders, our contemplative practices actually emerge from, rather than simply reflect, our attachments to the world?[30] Critics who advocate the necessity of a third realm do not think of knowledge as the assemblage of accurate representations of natural objects or believe mental processes simply reflect or mirror nature.[31]

Now, in *Moby-Dick* the whale is certainly an occupant of the third realm, the realm of what is neither purely material nor merely subjective. But I suggest that Melville's whaling narrative advances an even more radical claim, namely that *all* things configured in a possible horizon of sense, a network of relations—that is, in language—occupy the third realm.

For Melville, learning that our concepts (for instance, the concept "whale" but by extension all our concepts) are neither things nor ideas is a revelation, one that opens up the external world for us. This discovery wouldn't have been possible, however, had Melville not endeavored in *Moby-Dick* to present more reality than real life itself can show or to produce a great work of realism. For as I will demonstrate, seeing Melville as a realist does not push the view of language held by those who think of language as a transparency, a way of naming something that comes prior to it.[32] The current and what I take to be impoverished understanding of the realist enterprise (wherein language is used to describe extralinguistic entities whose nature is agreed to be in no sense constituted by language) has no traction in a discussion of Melville or of any writer on whom the difficulty of writing presses. One hope of the present work, accordingly, is to refind in the terms "realism" or "mimesis" the percipient, transgressive connotations they once held.

Coming to grips with realism as a mode of displaying collective feeling for a shareable world, as opposed to the more conventionally rendered "faithful redescription of everyday life" (realism understood in a theoretically rigorous sense, as an attempt to understand the nature of discourse, of how in our life with language we make the world intelligible to ourselves) supports the view that the establishment of American literature required exacting philosophical labor. This labor Stanley Cavell recognizes as our founding writers' effort to redeem language and thereby reconceive human existence.[33] Language requires redemption when our lives appear detached from the signs we use to interpret them—when "the very language of our parlors" would seem to "degenerate into *palaver* wholly," as Thoreau writes, and "our lives pass at such remoteness from its symbols, and its metaphors and tropes are necessarily so far fetched," that it seems "only the savage dwelt near enough to Nature and Truth to borrow a trope from them."[34] For the writers of the American renaissance, in particular Emerson and Thoreau, the literary redemption of language is commensurate with recovering the presence of concrete objects in general names.[35] It is the attempt to "win back . . . possession of our words," as Cavell says, to draw connections between the formation of abstract concepts and the living record of human historical experience; and, as I argue, the redemption of language is a central theme in Melville's *Moby-Dick*.

This book therefore addresses two audiences: students of Herman Melville and students of philosophy—particularly those compelled by philosophy's continual desire to "respond to the questions that human beings ask themselves regarding their own life," as Pierre Hadot writes.[36] To the first group it offers a suitably complex theoretical framework in keeping with Melville's aesthetics circa 1850 and thus custom-made to tease out the philosophical narrative embedded in Melville's whaling narrative.[37] To the second group it offers *Moby-Dick* as a substantial manifestation of what, in the current critical climate, typically remains at the level of abstract hope—namely, a mode of life that closes the fissure between the comprehending mind and the affective body. For as I understand it, the immense contribution of *Moby-Dick* is its recovery of experience—not what Emerson calls the empiricists' "paltry" idea of experience (experience as the *basis* of our conceptual schemes, or, as Locke would have it, the chief means of achieving an alignment between inner and outer matters; a sensible solution to the epistemological problem of representation) but experience as it is richly conceived in the American literary tradition beginning with Emerson's *Nature* and cresting in Melville's *Moby-Dick*.[38] "Experience" for these writers is a name for our evident ability to grasp thought (the capacious and mutable *sense* of any word) as the result of, not despite, our residence in the physical, tangible world. This distinctive conception of experience has the advantage of honoring our attachments to the material world without being materialist—without denying that nothing exists *except* matter and its movements and modifications.[39]

Here, then, is an outline of what is to come. In the remainder of this introductory essay I acquaint readers with Melvillean mimesis, as I understand it, and try to make this account equally serviceable to philosophers new to Melville and Melvilleans unaccustomed to certain philosophical disputes, particularly over the logic of language. To that end I hope what I have produced is neither literary criticism nor philosophy but an exchange in which these autonomous but internally related disciplines participate as each other's other, as Stephen Mulhall writes.[40] Staged as seven interrelated sections or unfoldings, this dialogical introduction offers a guided tour of the larger project. I lay out what is at stake in this study as well as its literary and philosophical points of reference. I return to and meditate on these vital texts and arguments in more detail in the subsequent chapters. My general aim is to prompt a philosophical reading of *Moby-Dick*—to find key critical concerns in the text, as Elizabeth Duquette writes, rather than simply importing them from elsewhere.[41] Reading *Moby-Dick* philosophically is, in turn, in the service of a larger ambition—showing how the human mind can credit itself with access to reality. For "Leviathan is not the biggest fish," as Melville writes to Hawthorne after finishing *Moby-Dick*. "I have heard of Krakens."[42]

In chapter 1, "The Case against Melville," my target is the widely held notion that Melville failed to unite his incompatible impulses in *Moby-Dick*, particularly in regard to his choice of narrative mode, and thus that the book is half romantic fiction, half transcription of fact. Here I challenge the axiom that *Moby-Dick* is not a wholly fictionalized narrative, in the process offering a deep recapturing of fiction's power from those who would see fiction—which, after all, consists of nothing more than descriptions of imaginary events and situations, set down in words of the writer's own choosing—replaced by more direct conduits for critical discourse.

In chapter 2, "Melville's Reconstructed Realism," I suggest that it has been a mistake to push the thesis that in *Moby-Dick* Melville laments the ontological chasm between mind and matter (that is, that he admits and bemoans the profound difference between nonspatiotemporal thoughts and spatiotemporally bound thinkers). For in answer to the question,

Is a whale something we imagine or something we observe? Melville's response is, "Neither"—because knowing is a struggle in which we grapple, like Ahab, with the world and its naturally occurring phenomena, a world that ultimately transcends our cognitive powers and refuses to be exhausted by them. As *Moby-Dick* makes clear, a whale is the consequence of human invention operating upon the materials of brute nature in ways that introduce new entities into the world. The implication in *Moby-Dick* is that meaning *always* evolves from the combination of human ingenuity and fidelity to the facts. Far from being caught on the horns of a dilemma, as many Melvilleans have argued, Melville shows how the sensible world and the human mind are inextricably bound up with each other in the creation of meaning.

In chapters 3, 4, and 5, "Gospel Cetology," "The Third Realm," and "God's Servant," the central chapters of the book, I make sense of *Moby-Dick*'s startling conclusion—by which I mean not the demise of the *Pequod* and its crew but the resolution of the philosophical puzzle that gives Melville's book its momentum. What is the relation of our words or concepts to those aspects of reality irreducible to mental representations? What connects our words to the states of affairs our words pick out?

The problem—what Melville calls "the Problem of the Universe"—is that the conceptual objects to which our words refer ("the living whale in his full majesty and significance," when the word is "whale") cannot be found in the natural world. Or as we might also put it, the mind grasps thoughts, not things. In consequence, it is unclear how the things we *think* are constrained by sensible life. Happily there is a reading of *Moby-Dick* that brings clarity. I argue that Melville's whaling narrative accounts for why thought is not alienated from practical life. Melville's narrative spells out why our conceptual schemes don't cut us off from the material world. The pressing epistemological issue of how we can acquire knowledge of what is external to the private, "inner world" of the mind can be set aside, Melville shows, when we come to understand that our concepts are objective and public—that they are *outside* the mind.

In *Moby-Dick*, Melville shows how our concepts are tools for handling reality. But this point must wait on an investigation of Melville's curious realism.

The Great Art of Telling the Truth

Hawthorne's report that Melville "can neither believe, nor be comfortable in his unbelief" encapsulates what is for many readers the source of Melville's singular appeal: his impulse for paradox. Had he been less drawn to apparent contradiction, Melville's writing would not likely seem "both immediate and primordial," as Newton Arvin said admiringly of *Moby-Dick*, "both local and archetypal, both journalistic and mythopoetic."[43] But the notion that Melville's books embrace competing urges has been given disproportionate weight in his critical estimation. We have forgotten that a paradox is not a genuine contradiction. Believing Melville's impulse for contradiction to be his chief contribution to literature or to the history of ideas has adversely affected the estimate of his most famous work, for what might have been prized as *Moby-Dick*'s capacity to heal the rift between the literal and the allegorical, body and mind, self and world, is reduced—immeasurably reduced—to the idea that the true innovation of Melville's writing is its power to reconcile disparate and seemingly incompatible points of view. Hence John Bryant's observation, about the centennial of Melville's death, that "if Melville has in our day achieved the rank of greatness, he is 'great' largely because of his diversity: the diverse responses he continually inspires and the diverse uses to which he may be put." Bryant sounds the voice of a generation when he declares "greatness" as applied to the author an "outmoded concept. It smacks of enforced canonization, authoritarian preachment, and an ideological insistence upon the elevation of a single mind above all others. Melville, then, is not so much great as he is full."[44]

As a result it isn't simply outmodishness that makes me say Melville *is* great or governs my worry that the myth of Melville's fullness has unjustly diminished his reputation as one of the "masters of the great Art of Telling the Truth."[45] For if calling him "full" pays tribute to the fine Melvillean habit of leaving nothing and nobody out, or of rejecting the comforts of any settled creed, it also rejoices in the immoderation, the prodigious excess, of an aesthetic credo constructed out of opposing forces. Calling Melville "full" extends the claim made by many contemporary scholars that his work contains diametrically opposed views "either balanced against one another or interfused."[46] It assumes there *are* mutually exclusive outlooks that Melville consecutively or in chorus takes up and so celebrates his aesthetic achievement by repeatedly drawing attention to what is contradictory in his aesthetic sensibility. A very odd kind of approbation ensues, from which Melville emerges as a devoted writer of romance who now and then simply transcribes the natural world; a man whose "spiritualizing nature," as Sophia Hawthorne names it, purportedly nourished a vein of corrosive, impinging doubt; a reader of "old books" whose feeling for classical philosophy never troubles his essentially modern view.

Rather than allow that the contradictions associated with Melville's most subtle and complex narratives may be a deliberately created impression—in other words, an essential component of his elaborate effort to combat dualism—readers who think Melville full emphasize the polarity of such contradictions in order to promote their eventual, inevitable union. Calling him full turns Melville into someone with whom everyone can identify—to whom adequate responses are as varied and numerous as the uses to which his work can be put—for the reason that in his writing incompatible outlooks are thrown into harmonizing equipoise. Calling him full effectively immortalizes Melville's power to suspend contrasting views in "tense repose."[47]

That prospect, however, is satirized by Melville in chapter 73 of *Moby-Dick*, when he recounts the unhappy condition in which a right whale's head is hanging to the *Pequod*'s larboard side and a sperm whale's head is hanging to its stern: "As before, the *Pequod* steeply leaned over towards the sperm whale's head, now, by the counterpoise of both heads, she regained her even keel; though sorely strained, you may well believe. So, when on one side you hoist in Locke's head, you go over that way; but now, on the other side, hoist in Kant's and you come back again; but in a very poor plight. Thus, some minds for ever keep trimming boat. Oh, ye foolish! Throw all these thunderheads overboard, and then you will float light and right." By calling these hoisted heads "Locke" and "Kant," Melville pokes fun at metaphysicians hoping to counterbalance empiricism with rationalism. Not that he was unsympathetic to the plight of that encumbered vessel, launched as he was upon his own brand of ontological heroics, but Melville's suggestive contrast between a ship at even keel because of the counterpoise of two whale heads (though "sorely strained, you may well believe") and a ship that floats "light and right" because both heads have been thrown overboard signals his deep dissatisfaction with any makeshift sensibility, any regularizing balance between competing forces, like rival inquiries into how we come to know the world from the evidence of our senses. As it happens the philosophically interesting thing about Melville isn't that he can "for ever keep trimming boat," as he writes, or go back and forth from one side to the other, but that he thinks it finer to cut drag and sail free. As his analogy reveals, the desirable state of true buoyancy isn't achieved through reasoning that, by counterbalancing two sides of a long-running dispute, in effect levels the scale. Accordingly, the harder we insist on Melville's ability to take up both sides of a debate, the harder it is to see his real achievement.

And yet the return of a Melville who is great rather than full need not depend on the author's ability to know—before writing—his own mind, or on an idea of literary greatness decried by Melville in "Hawthorne and His Mosses" as the "blind, unbridled admiration" heaped upon some authors, the consequence of repeated veneration of certain careers at the cost of others.[48] That is because greatness in literature is not simply an indication of superiority. It is more rightly grasped as a gauge of how effectively a writer is able to depict spiritual *and* sensible reality, in this way enabling the imitation of real life. In *Moby-Dick*, Melville shows himself to be a master of the art of telling the truth when he resurrects an event, the whale, that remains undecidable in its own terms and yet whose identity can be affirmed.[49] This view of greatness can't find footing, however, so long as Melville's most outspoken readers continue to be uninterested in the way purely imaginative works of literature offer views impossible to find other than in imaginative literature, and unconvinced, in any case, that Melville was able to write purely imaginative books—books of fiction—or even that he wished to.[50] Given how many readers accept what Nina Baym has called Melville's sense of fiction's inadequacy (and hence his departure from the conventions of the fictive mode, a departure that would moreover seem to throw into question the value and reach of imaginative literature) there are grounds for worrying that resistance to Melville's special status on the basis of his greatness comes from critics for whom the idea that purely imaginative literature has something to teach us seems to have run its course.

And so in this book I haven't disguised my affinity for critics who consider *Moby-Dick* both a tremendous literary achievement and one of those rare works of fiction that throw light on matters of still lively interest, matters of moral, social, and political concern, critics whose frequently incompatible views are linked by what Edgar Dryden calls their unstated "admiration and respect for the work itself—presuppositions that justified one's own attempt to clarify its meaning."[51] My prevailing interest in *Moby-Dick* itself, in the mystery of its lure and of its deep satisfactions, predisposes me toward critics willing to supply, on the basis of evidence drawn from Melville's text, an account of the author's object in writing it. (An author's "object" shouldn't be confused with his intentions. Distinguishing between an author's object and his intentions is particularly valuable in literary criticism for the reason that the notion of intention clearly looks beyond the text to the supposedly inaccessible consciousness of its author, whereas the notion of object is an entirely textual one.) It is the hope of redirecting readers back to Melville's *object* in writing *Moby-Dick*—*Moby-Dick*'s governing logic—that gives my book its basic shape. By restricting discussion to only one of Melville's many works I do not mean to suggest that *Moby-Dick* can on its own represent

Melville's philosophical commitments, but rather that when we attend to this book's governing logic, the intellectual reason for its existence, we encounter arguments revelatory for not only Melville studies but also literary studies more generally.

The notion that Melville *has* a clear object in writing *Moby-Dick* has not yet found favor with his readers. The view more traditionally championed is that Melville sees every issue as debatable, that he takes up both sides in any dispute, or that in Melville's books we see evidence of the thinker Hawthorne famously described as endlessly "wandering to-and fro," the man who "can neither believe, nor be comfortable in his unbelief."[52] As I argue, the proposition that dogged Melville from the beginning and that now goes unquestioned is that he writes with a divided mind, or that even when what he successfully pulls off is not the paradoxical either-or but the paratactic both-and, it is without quite meaning to, as if Melville's principal creative gift is heedlessness. This sureness about Melville's penchant for the irreconcilable seems to underlie most questions and most thinking in Melville studies; it has become the axis around which the study of Melville rotates. As a result—and in conjunction with a particularly aggressive distrust of the way imaginative writers make meaning, a disheartening development for readers of literature—it has been difficult for Melville's critics to think of him as altogether intellectually accountable for the extraordinary things that go on in his books. This, too, has thrown me into the path of critics who show an unabashed interest in his books' independent philosophical status, critics like Ronald Mason, whose groundbreaking *The Spirit Above the Dust* (1951) was one of the first attempts to cast a study of Melville in the form of a critical estimate of his books. That I came to Mason's writing late in my own study of Melville only reinforces the great irony of scholarship, which is that no matter what you are able to think and say, it will be forgotten. And then someone will say it again, never knowing that it had been said before.

Poet of the Secular World

In *The Spirit Above the Dust* Mason laid the foundation for anyone who wishes (as I do) to disagree with the proposition, now very nearly an assumption, that Melville's sensitivity to cultural and economic tensions in mid-nineteenth-century America and his eagerness to contribute to the formation of national consciousness troubled his commitment to literature—that Melville chafed at the requisite difference between the full range of a writer's imagination and the day-to-day lives of his countrymen, or that Melville's attempt to produce literature in the 1850s led him to question the very conventions of literature itself.[53] Because he wished to contribute actively to the process by which his nation took shape, Melville is said to have helped reinstate what the critic Jonathan Arac calls "national narratives," stories of the nation's beginnings and its potential future. In their perceived ability to advocate social, economic, and political reform, national narratives represent for many critics a step up from their literary counterparts, and Melville is understood to have anticipated their energizing effects. Yet what I mean to suggest is that without the benefit of Mason's shrewd observation that Melville was "the only American writer of genius effectively to sink the confining consciousness of nationalism in the wider context of the human soul"[54]—that Melville's exceptional creative achievement was to turn every subject that concerned the nation into a concern for humanity—we too easily concede that Melville ultimately gave up literary narrative, as Arac argues, that Melville desired to transport his views into the world of politics and practice more directly than fiction is dreamed of permitting.

In *The Emergence of American Literary Narrative, 1820–1860*, Arac makes a distinction between midcentury "literary narratives," of which Hawthorne's work is the great exemplar, and "national narratives," which instead of introducing fictional intermediaries "encourage readers to identify the narrating presence with the author, who in each case holds a clear ideological position on matters of national consequence."[55] National narratives by these means draw large numbers of readers into debate on important contemporary issues. In literary narratives, on the other hand, immediate and controversial issues seem to diminish next to more eternal matters of the human heart.[56] Moreover, because they create imaginary worlds that stand free from the world of everyday life—because they are an expression of the writer's *mind* rather than a direct representation of actual things and events—literary narratives require a certain kind of reader, one who understands that in order to reach a level of profundity or true insight, the author of a book of fiction "claims a certain latitude, both as to its fashion and its material," as Hawthorne writes in his preface to *The House of Seven Gables*. This "he would not have felt himself entitled to assume" had he professed to be writing the kind of book that "seeks a minute fidelity . . . to the probable and ordinary course of man's experience." Hawthorne warns readers for whom his book's story line or the authenticity of its account of the world threatens to overshadow his object in writing it that the form of his narrative is literary—that it is what Hawthorne would call a "romance." Like Defoe in his preface to *Moll Flanders*, he chiefly recommends the work "to those who know how to Read it, and how to make the good Uses of it, which the Story all along recommends to them."[57] Uniting the writers of literary narrative is the hope that readers will, as Defoe says, "be much more pleas'd with the Moral, than the Fable; with the Application, than with the Relation, and with the End of the Writer, than with the Life of the Person written of."

One problem with American literary narrative as framed by Arac, consequently, is that "it may require special talents to acknowledge it."[58] Literary narrative is said to ignore the ordinary reader, or not count as reading the capacity to follow a story's plot or admire some of its attractions. However, the bigger problem with writing like Hawthorne's is that it entails what Arac calls the "literary compromise," where the writer's desire to express spiritual truths in effect prohibits him from speaking out on issues affecting contemporary American life.[59] Arac contrasts the "political quietism" of Hawthorne's literature, which finds its precedent in writing that, like Wordsworth's, recounts the "growth of a poet's mind," with narratives that encompass "the full and free expression of the nation's mind," as Parke Godwin declares in an article in 1854 for *Putnam's* magazine, or in which America's cultivated writers, the "literary men of the nation," are "free to utter their wisest thoughts" on any subject that concerns them. Though Hawthorne writes what Edgar Allan Poe admiringly called "an Art-product alone," Godwin looked for an American literature "not in belles-lettres alone, nor in art alone, nor in science alone, but in all of these, combined with politics and religion."[60] In contrasting Parke's hopes for American literature with Poe's, Arac draws attention to literature's paradoxical quality, or distinguishes the reality unique to literature from all *lived* reality. And like Godwin he finds a regrettable difference between narratives that contain in a fictional tale an intense exploration of the poet's mind and narratives that contribute to national consciousness via a writer's freedom to speak directly on subjects Arac calls "public" or "political"—that demonstrate interest group politics as taken up by the members of a community. Arac points out that the rise of the literary narrative in mid-nineteenth-century America is connected to the Romanticism of earlier generations in Germany and Britain and that "in both of these cultures, the basis for what is now understood as 'literature' was laid through the sharp sense of an absent public sphere."[61] For Arac, American writers of literature proper follow the example set by the likes of Wordsworth and Coleridge in that they "turned from public life." Or as he notes even more finally, literature as fiction said nothing that bore on the world the way national narratives did; "that is, the literary work acts as a one-way valve, drawing the materials of the world into its own world, from which they do not return."[62]

Perhaps for this reason Arac names Melville's predominantly literary narratives *Moby-Dick* and *Pierre* "experiments" and describes literary narrative's emergence only to introduce its eventual "dead end," when reputedly national narratives like Melville's *Israel Potter* "succeeded in pleasing readers and provoking thought on important contemporary issues."[63] An admittedly ungenerous interpretation of Arac's thesis—that "amidst the political and economic crises from the mid-1850s into the Civil War and Reconstruction, readers and writers alike began to doubt the experiment of literary narrative"—is thus to conclude that the real problem with literature is that it exists outside partisan politics. In correspondence with this view of literature's failing, its ability to inspire little more than what Arac calls the "interpretive energy of the sensitive spectator," Melville surfaces for him as a writer who intuits the catalyzing effect on a nation's "transformative energies" of narratives that renounce the traditional distance between fictional other worlds and national life.[64] Even when he brings forth literary narratives, Melville incorporates into them elements of national narratives for the reason that he, too, was dissatisfied with literature's limited powers.

Despite Arac's credible portrayal, however, I wish to point to the appreciable difference between, on the one hand, thinking Melville had to abandon literature in order to say something that bore upon the shared public world, the way Arac does, and, on the other, thinking Melville *took up* literature for that purpose, as I believe Ronald Mason assumes. The difference hangs on how oppositely each critic views the relationship between literature and reality. To put this opposition more simply than it deserves, Arac argues that literature proper turns away from reality or from the concerns of everyday life in order to develop a freely imaginative space. This argument contributes, at least, to the idea that the main function of literature in our lives is to distract us from the business of living. Then again, there has always been a way to think of literature as developing a freely imaginative space, a fictional space, for the purpose of facilitating readers' turn *toward* reality (and as such, everyday life)—only with the added benefit of something sufficiently worth calling "insight" into "the human condition."[65]

A literary critic must choose between these rival positions. Either literature that is fiction is in direct competition with reality, in which case it hasn't the power to upset the edifice of a reader's everyday existence, to invite the reader to reconsider the practices and associated presumptions he or she ordinarily takes for granted, or, by presenting "another world, and yet one to which we feel the tie," as Melville writes, by depicting a world at once related to and removed from the world we inhabit, fiction is uniquely designed to "open a space," as political theorist George Shulman says, "between the given world as we are conditioned to perceive it and possibilities of living otherwise."[66] Fiction seen in this light offers a community the chance to rethink what Shulman calls its "core axioms, constitutive practices, and fateful decisions." According to this view, the point of conjuring fictional worlds elsewhere is, as Shulman says, to "illuminate enigmas closer to home."

By offering this bare-bones juxtaposition of two different ways to think about fiction, I mean not only to highlight the advantages of the second but also to indirectly criticize Arac's notion of a public sphere. After all, the idea of a protected space in which political participation is enacted through the medium of talk, an area of social life to which all citizens have access or in which individuals can come together to freely discuss and identify problems in society, is by now difficult to imagine or describe in plausible terms. As literary critic Donald G. Marshall noted some while ago, "to say that the public sphere is the realm of politics is to invite the illusion of understanding, for the 'political' here is something different from the particular and always transitory issues in which it presents itself to men and women."[67] In short, there is no sphere proper to politics, no protected political domain.[68] Indeed, when the "politics" of which Godwin speaks does appear in art, we can expect from that art a level of parochialism or the kind of unabashedly direct or moralizing writing that is itself testimony to the absence of a *wide* sphere of cultural influence, since the writing's claim on public attention is inextricably related to the distinguishing traits of its author. Tying a work's overall political impact to the persuasiveness or accumulated experience of a single person, to its author's "mere personality," is a problem because, as Marshall tartly observes, "insight into the public affairs of human beings cannot be authorized by reflections of childhood."

In conclusion we should say that there is something essentially paradoxical about literature, but not because the projected reality of a text gets set against real life. Literature's paradoxical quality lies rather in what Rancière calls "a logic of perseverance in its being." For "literature lives only by the separation of words in relation to any body that might incarnate their power. It lives only by evading the incarnation that it incessantly puts into play."[69] To put this in terms a nineteenth-century writer would understand, the author of *literature* is not able to depend on the usual substitute for an inadequate imagination—autobiography. Even so, as Wordsworth surely demonstrated, taking leave of the real world is frowned upon. The imaginative writer's unwillingness to merely copy daily life, concomitant with his profound interest in it, is the source of literature's paradoxical quality. It is also the starting point for what Aristotle thought of as fiction's robust relation to the truth, its engagement with reality.

This proviso of literature explains why readers who take up a purely imaginative work of literature do indeed "drop real life," as Melville writes in *The Confidence Man*, "and turn, for a time, to something different."[70] But because what they look for in a work of fancy is "at bottom, even more reality, than real life itself can show," the expectation Melville expresses is that readers turn to fiction in order to see *more truthfully* reality as it confronts them. In Melville's formulation, "reality" and "real life" are arranged in a way that highlights their difference but not their opposition. Instead of associating literature proper with a one-way valve, "drawing the materials of the world into its own world, from which they do not return," Melville advances the idea that books that do not seek a "severe fidelity to real life," as he says, echoing Hawthorne—that keep firmly in place the distance between art and life, that require the reader's strenuous analytical activity or that depend on the reader's greater investment in the "end" or purpose of the writer than in the lives of his characters—offer the most effective means of grasping something that has real existence or must be dealt with in real life. Melville's likeliest assumption is that reality is not something it's possible to grasp empirically or by way of the senses; in consequence, the writer wishing to depict real life must produce fiction.

The Living Whale in His Full Majesty and Significance

Thus it is crucial that we understand Melville as an author who never quits his preoccupation with actual existence, whose considerations rarely become too abstract and impalpable, who doesn't hesitate to draw upon or address the events that affected the shape of his life or that he chanced to live through—and yet whose experimental flights of the imagination convert every direct experience into creative art, or who produces only *conceptual* works in which the writer's highest creative powers are exercised.

In *Literary World* of November 22, 1851, editor and Melville friend Evert Duyckinck found the problem with *Moby-Dick*, as well as "one or two other of Mr. Melville's books," to lie in the "double character under which they present themselves. In one light they are romantic fictions, in another statements of absolute facts."[71] But we must have no doubt whatsoever that Melville's books are through and through a product of his creative ingenuity—not least because failing to grasp that the "double character" of his mature works is a deliberate contrivance puts readers correspondingly out of touch with Melville's reason for writing them. This objective Melville speaks of in terms of truth telling, the special province of fiction.

It is precisely because Ronald Mason has not come to doubt the experiment of literary narrative that I find his remarks on Melville so valuable. For there is a class of writer and reader, and with this class Melville sides, who "want novelty" from books of fiction, as Melville writes in *The Confidence Man*, who want the new sights and sensations only a highly subjective viewpoint provides, but who "want nature, too," who want to see what hasn't been brought into being by human consciousness or the human mind. What these writers and readers want to glimpse in fiction is reality, that is to say, the domain to which "experience is the only guide," as Melville writes, but a poor guide, since "no one man can be coextensive with *what is*."[72]

That fiction writers are specially equipped to generate pictures of *what is* (existing states of affairs like what Melville calls "the living whale in his full majesty and significance," essentially symbolic arrangements that, like ideas, can't be perceived by the senses and, like things, are not an invention of mind) is what Melville vouchsafes when in "Hawthorne and His Mosses" he aligns his writing and Hawthorne's with that of Shakespeare and "other masters of the great Art of Telling the Truth." As Melville would have it, showing "what is"—for example, what Ishmael calls "the true form of the whale as he actually appears to the eye of the whaleman when in his own absolute body the whale is moored alongside the whaleship so that he can be fairly stepped upon there"—falls to the writer of fiction, who, it follows, isn't satisfied simply by describing the readily perceivable world. Only by offering a concordance of the sensible and the conceptual—by showing at once the appearance and the significance of things—can writers tell the truth.

That truthful writers must show the significance of things is the idea set forth in Aristotle's *Poetics*, where the philosopher states very clearly that a writer doesn't just represent real life as it comes to him, in its apparent order and disunity, but creates events and situations superior to actual events and situations. And yet, as Melville's writing demonstrates, the writer wishing to tell the truth cannot afford to be careless with his observations, either. As he labors to show "what is," he cannot neglect the view his senses afford him. For Melville, the imaginative mind is both constrained and galvanized by the hard reality of the physical world.[73]

This indeed is the claim that gets a little more spelling out in Melville's whaling narrative. The idea Melville lays down authoritatively in *Moby-Dick* is that writers are capable of telling the truth when they learn to see with one eye, as it were, the *conceptual objects* named by the words in our language and *the world of natural objects* in which, in consequence of our own embodiment, speakers of language are immersed. For as Melville would have us remember, there are things with which man comes forcibly into contact that are *not* the objects of intellectual intuition, not creatures of the noumenal realm.

We can say Melville represents reality in *Moby-Dick* because even when his whale is transfigured, it keeps its distinct earthly particularity. Melville's whale is an extraordinary consolidation of the sensible and the conceptual. But in *Moby-Dick* Melville does more than prove once again that poetic or figurative writing is a more exalted medium than natural history while also constructing an imaginative reality that is shaped by and in accordance with the material world. He creates a work of literary theory, one that considers in full the relation between thought (and its linguistic expressions) and "what the world is like"—that examines with some meticulousness the connection between signs, like "whale," and things signified, "the living whale in his full majesty and significance," in Melville's distinctive phrase.

As I understand it, "the living whale in his full majesty and significance" is Melville's signature expression for the whale's intelligible form, the whale understood in its fullest sense—understood imaginatively, that is, but also accurately. The expression is supposed to call to mind the challenges of artistically re-creating the whale in prose (for as Emerson warns, the writer who lacks accuracy is a mere fabulist, while the scrupulous data gatherer who has lost sight of the end of all his inquiries is a pedant).[74] But the phrase also lends emphasis to the idea that however much its meaning has been informed by natural objects, the word "whale" does not name anything in nature.

The idea that our signs cannot possibly stand in direct relationship to empirical reality has long been a source of concern. In *The Foundations of Arithmetic* (1884), Gottlob Frege glosses the conundrum that has from the beginning troubled logicians when he shows how any sentence that makes meaningful use of the word "whale" *says nothing at all* about any one whale in particular. Even supposing a whale is before him, the speaker's proposition ("That whale is white!") still says nothing about *it*. What Frege draws attention to is that, "as a general principle, it is impossible to speak of an object without in some way designating or naming it; but the word 'whale' is not the name of any individual creature."[75]

And of course *that* point is the one God makes to Job, in what is at once the most electrifyingly humbling and enlightening of monologues. "Will you catch the leviathan with a fishhook?" God asks, scathingly. "Will merchants bid for his carcass and parcel him out in shops?" Whatever the whaler may catch and the merchant may peddle, what the word "whale" names is the thing *God* created: not only the whale in every stage of its existence, including those whales that are extinct and those that have yet to emerge, but also something other than what can be readily perceived. What God would have man comprehend is that he has a sense of the vast, illimitable quality of the whale because the word or sign "whale" discloses or promises this quality. In the book of Job, what God forces Job to concede is the significant difference between the world of things verifiable by observation and experience and the states of affairs our words name: *what is*, aspects of reality like the living whale in his full majesty and significance.

The Jobian lesson might also be put this way: the solidity of things derives from an eternal permanence. For if we take things as *only* finite, their solidity paradoxically vanishes.[76] God's remarkable speech to Job thus helps us decipher Plato's endorsement of what he calls the realm of Ideas or eternal forms. Because hypothesizing the world of forms (or holding with the notion of a realm of objects that transcend—i.e., are not answerable to—experiential knowledge) does teach us to think about the difference between those objects that can be readily perceived, such as whales hoisted bodily into the air or distributed at the market, and those that cannot—the continuous aspects of reality or *postulated* objects words like "whale" analogically imply.

There is reason, in other words, for Melville's signature phrase to recall the mode of expression that characterizes the Old Testament—a book, as G. E. Lessing reports, rewardingly full not of definitions but of hints and allusions. "By a 'hint,'" Lessing writes, "I mean that which already contains any germ, out of which the, as yet, held back truth allows itself to be developed. By allusion I mean that which was intended only to excite curiosity and occasion questions. As for instance, the oft-recurring mode of expression, describing death by 'he was gathered to his fathers.'"[77] As Lessing makes clear, hints and allusions operate in distinct contrast to repeatable formulas, generalizing definitions, or any other indices of the doctrine that essence is prior to existence. What Melville's conspicuous use of the phrase "the living whale in his full majesty and significance" points toward, I'm suggesting, is his supposition that "whale," like "death," names *a social experience still in process*. What "whale" names isn't a thing in the sensible world, or a thing in the mind, but a thing-in-language. "Whale" names a *hypothesized* object, a conceptual object postulated to ground and explain relations of qualitative identity and resemblance among individual material objects.

Like other good readers of the book of Job, Melville has learned to rethink the view that our linguistic expressions acquire meaning by being set in conventional relationships of association with perceivable objects. But he hasn't gone so far in the other direction that he thinks what "whale" names is invented or superadded, or that the order we find in things is the order we ourselves put in them.[78] Rather, he has come to understand (as God wished Job to understand) that a linguistic expression only ever alludes to an as yet held-back truth.

Surprisingly, this spiritually enlightened view of language is what puts us back in touch with the material world since it alerts us to the importance of feeling and experience—as opposed to reason or the power of the mind to form judgments—in the way our concepts come to have meaning. So, as readers of *Moby-Dick* discover, a whaler need never learn what a whale "is" in order to follow the instruction to "sing out for him!" But as the whaler learns to follow the instruction—as his responsiveness and careful attention to natural objects increases those objects' amplitude and resonance—he enlarges his comprehension of what a whale is. He boosts and intensifies his knowledge of what is grasped by someone who understands the concept "whale."[79] The interesting point here is that the whaler's ability to obey the instruction "sing out for him!" suggests that even in a world in flux a whale can have an abiding significance and affective presence, and without anyone having established its intrinsic nature, the set of qualities a whale has by necessity or without which it loses its identity.[80] This is worth noting, for it countenances a surprising conclusion: that it is possible to jettison the idea that every named object has an intrinsic nature (in this way appeasing critics for whom talk about an object's "universal" or "eternal" form perpetuates injurious notions of its perfect, unchanging, wholly unattainable *quintessential* form) but stay subtly alive to the cogency of Plato's theory of forms. That is what Melville pulls off in *Moby-Dick*.

We know Melville's belief in the objective reality of any object we can think about or name (what Plato would call its *eidos*, or "eternal form") isn't essentialist, in any case, because the *writer* who wishes to show "what is" must register the affective experience of being in the world. That is something we learn from reading Wordsworth, as the critic Rhian Williams submits. Williams deftly encapsulates a fertile strain of Wordsworth scholarship when she shows how Wordsworth's "earnest desire to write with and of nature" (suffered by the poet as an "awful burthen") prompts him to chronicle not his natural surroundings, however affecting, but what anthropologist Kathleen Stuart calls the "varied, surging capacities to affect and be affected" that "give everyday life the quality of a continued motion of relations, scenes, contingencies, and emergences" or that "catch people up in something that feels like *some*thing."[81] That his poems register *affective experience* accounts for why the things Wordsworth enduringly evokes, like the "rocks, and stones, and trees" of one of his known "Lucy" poems, prove "difficult to substantialize as a noun or a name," as Geoffrey Hartman writes—why they seem to exist "without imagistic or narrative detail," as if extant but "untouchable."[82] It explains Matthew Arnold's original insight that the poems generate "useful knowledge" of those things that are not "definite and ascertained."[83] Finally, Wordsworth doesn't just mirror the things he encounters in nature, and that is the reason Wordsworthian rocks, stones, and trees exhibit what Hartman has called a "ghostliness in nature," the haunting occurrence or "being there" of things-while-they-are-being-lived, things literally in motion.[84]

The category of experience that Wordsworth's poems represent, and to which something's fixed or stationary condition does not speak at all, thus has to do with what Raymond Williams calls "practical consciousness of a present kind," of "what is actually being lived, and not only what it is thought is being lived."[85] In order to emphasize the public or collective character of that which transpires "at the very edge of semantic availability," as he says, Williams identifies consciousness of what is actually being lived as "structures of feeling."[86] And he notes that however personal, private, or idiosyncratic they may seem, structures of feeling are "social" because what they really evidence (additions, deletions, and modifications over a *wide* range) is something quite general. This specifically affective element of consciousness may be identified as something that happens—for instance, what, in his poems, Wordsworth calls a stone or a tree—but because this nuanced interface of thought and feeling is a living process broadly experienced, it is also conjecture based on ample or sweeping (and so eclectic, heterogeneous, jumbled, miscellaneous) evidence. In Wordsworth's poetry a stone or a tree is not a thing but what Raymond Williams calls a "cultural hypothesis," a notion continually under construction; an idea derived from actual attempts to understand the affective elements of consciousness, collectively regarded and needing always to be returned, interactively, to the available body of evidence.[87]

As a result, and even though Wordsworth often "grasped a wall or tree" in order to recall himself from the "abyss of idealism to the reality," as he writes, his poetry transcends the kind of "reality testing" in which man infers the existence of things from the existence of *particular* things.[88] That is, the objects that occupy the poet are not like the objects that occupy the scientist, objects that can be verified by observation or experience. Rather, what the poet has to do with are postulated objects—the documenting of which is, as Williams writes, "the true source of the specializing categories of 'the aesthetic,' 'the arts,' and 'imaginative literature.' "[89] If "what is" can be captured by writers (who, since Plato, have understood that a sentence is "like no object in the world")[90] it is in part because writers' explicit expectation is that their words name *cultural hypotheses*, a priori ideas the consequences of which must be submitted to the yardstick of experiment so that their value can be tested—those starting points for further investigation known to us as "walls," "trees," "rocks," and so on.

For Melville or for the writer hoping to portray undiminished reality—hoping to include in the depiction of perceptible life the *conceptual* subject matter Plato prizes above all else ("the representational tension of language," as philosophers Silvana Borutti and Fulvia de Luise report, "most certainly at the heart of the problematic of *mimesis* developed in the *Republic*")[91]—this means conceding from the start that the words in our language do not name things. Rather, words name the special kinds of objects Wittgenstein, in a neat turn of phrase, calls "facts in logical space."

In his *Tractatus Logico-Philosophicus*, Wittgenstein calls the special objects or postulated objects (what the signs of our language *signify*) that all together make up the world "facts in logical space." He observes that the world "divides into" these facts. He makes clear that what we call "the world" *is* all these facts—that, in Wittgenstein's distinctive expression, "the world is the totality of facts, not of things."[92] Wittgenstein's facts in logical space are objects it isn't possible to explain the meaning of by showing how they conform to any element of the natural world, objects that have no existence in nature because they have no existence prior to the institution of the systems of convention that call them into being. What Wittgenstein calls facts in logical space, in other words—Tractarian objects—are things-in-language, configurations of sense.

Because such "facts" do not exist on the Euclidean plane we can think of them as opaque, to take up a visual metaphor. Or as Wittgenstein argues in his study of sign language, they are unsayable. We can "only speak *of* them." The sentences of our language can only say *how* these facts are, not *what* they are.[93]

Nevertheless these facts in aggregate are the world. In the Tractarian notion of "world," therefore, *there is no object that has not been elevated to its form*, or has not become a form object.[94] The surprise, for anyone who follows this logic, is that *form objects* are what we are talking about whenever we talk. They are our "rocks, and stones, and trees," our "whiteness" and our "whales." And to return finally to our initial proposition—that, as Melville notes, readers "want novelty" from books of fiction, but they "want nature, too"—in the end it is *this* world, the world Plato calls "real" because it is the world of things our words *signify* ("the world raised to a kind of ideal of itself," as Kenneth Dauber says)[95] that the realist writer must imitate.

The Logical Identity of Sign and Thing Signified

An object, as C. S. Peirce broadly defines it, is in a general sense any entity—for example, "the pyramids, Alpha Centauri, the number seven, a disbelief in predestination, or the fear of cats."[96] What readers and writers who want "more reality, than real life itself can show" have discovered is that objects can be seen in works of imaginative literature as they cannot be seen in daily life. When writers are not false but faithful to the objects they depict, we say that their art imitates reality. However, this feat requires that writers not deploy words the way Plato worried they would: as if there were a direct referential relationship between the meaning-bearing elements of language and some class of entities envisaged as corresponding elements of the sensible world. That is what Melville means to emphasize, in "Hawthorne and His Mosses," when he notes in the essay that "if I magnify Shakespeare, it is not so much for what he did do, as for what he did not do, or refrained from doing."[97] What Shakespeare does *not* do is imagine a direct referential relationship between a word and its referent, some thing in the natural world the word denotes. Denying the relationship between a meaning-bearing element of language and some corresponding element of the sensible world is in fact the defining characteristic of writing that, like Shakespeare's, Melville identifies with "the great Art of Telling the Truth."

Melville's view of writing that imitates real life thus takes shape alongside Plato's critique of imitative art, which, as Erich Auerbach argues, did not destroy the representation of reality in art but on the contrary gave it a new impulse and a new aim, for it was Plato who "introduced philosophy into art and laid the foundation for a more profound and at the same time more accurate perception of events," Plato who taught artists and lovers of art to "reflect on the presence of the Idea in the appearance of things and to yearn for it."[98] Without the philosopher's prompting, artists would not have been set the task of striving, by the imitation of an object's appearance, to arrive at its true essence, the group of properties without which it would not be what it is—and thus of discovering the insufficiency of essences when measured against the beauty of Ideas.[99]

The artist who wishes to imitate real life in writing thus had better recall the vast examination of the possible, efficacious use of words that commences in the *Cratylus*, when Plato's Socrates legislates against the possibility of a perfect correspondence between words and things, and culminates in the *Phaedrus*. This particularly knotty dialogue contains Socrates's invective against writing (in contrast to the dialectical movement of discourse), or more exactly his warning about words inscribed in ink as compared with words "written in the soul of the learner." Socrates's view in the *Phaedrus* is that truth is unachievable in written texts, which represent existing events the way motionless portraits represent living people.[100] Ultimately this dialogue raises disquieting questions about the value of writing, which is branded inadequate for the transmission of the "more precious things" (*timiotera*), an expression that, in the context of its use in the *Phaedrus* and in *Letters VII and VIII*, suggests those things that are given in language but cannot be said in it—*what is*, or what the words we routinely employ actually signify. By the "more precious things," Plato means the imperceptible but intelligible objects that make discourse possible—for example, not the referent of the word "whale" but what Frege would call the term's *sense*, the thought the term expresses.[101]

The question, then, for the writer who is a good reader of Plato—which Melville was—is whether the most precious things can take shape or find expression in a written work. *Is* it possible for the writer to depict the continuous aspects of reality, alongside what he is able to perceive? This is precisely the question Melville answers affirmatively in *Moby-Dick*.

In *Moby-Dick*, Melville endorses fiction's capacity for representing an aspect of reality beyond the one that we can see, an aspect of reality even more real than the one we see. But he shows how this is possible only when what the writer imitates isn't the immediate object of sense perception ("for if it were," Auerbach argues, "the work of art would not be more beautiful than the immediate object") but what Auerbach calls "the image in his soul." When the writer learns to imitate *the image of the object in his soul*—"which is nothing other than the immanent Idea, the Idea actualized in the formed particular"—the art of imitation is given a new philosophical justification.[102]

And yet in suggesting that the writer is able to imitate reality when what he imitates is the object's *intelligible form*, the image of the object in his soul, it is worth admitting that such language can be vexing. It is for this reason that I have included Wittgenstein's way of talking about form objects or hypothesized objects, the postulated objects Wittgenstein calls "facts in logical space" in order to accentuate their standing as neither pure form nor pure matter but configurations of sense. Wittgenstein's "facts in logical space" are not "ideas" and they are not "things"; they are the *things signified* by the signs in our language.

Wittgenstein's first book of logic, *Tractatus Logico-Philosophicus*, is an important resource for serious readers of *Moby-Dick* because Wittgenstein's contention in this book is that what ought to interest philosophers isn't the connection between signs and things but between signs and *things signified*. As Wittgenstein writes in one of his orienting notes, "The obscurity *obviously* resides in the question: what does the logical identity of sign and thing signified really consist in? And this question is (*once more*) a main aspect of the whole philosophical problem."[103]

What Wittgenstein calls the "logical identity" of sign and thing signified—the fact that sign and thing signified share what philosophers call a relation of identity—consists as he says in "its not being permissible to recognize more or less in the sign than in what it signifies."[104] For Wittgenstein, the logical identity of sign and thing signified ought to be deeply bewildering, it ought to be the obscurity to which the philosopher devotes himself, because what anyone trying to follow the logic of language must explain isn't the perfect correspondence between, for example, the word "whale" and whales caught and sold (for that affinity is the result of an arbitrary specification) but between "whale" and *the living whale in his full majesty and significance*. What explains *that* correspondence? As Wittgenstein points out, the obscurity that ought to taunt and attract the philosopher is the same obscurity that attracts and taunts the poet: the logical identity of sign and thing signified, or what Wittgenstein calls the "internal" agreement in the sentences of our language.[105]

The logical identity of "whale" and "the living whale in his full majesty and significance" (or as Wittgenstein puts it, the impossibility of recognizing more or less in the word "whale" than in what it signifies) is the obscurity Melville investigates in *Moby-Dick*. For what Melville determines to contend with in his whaling narrative isn't the relation between words and things in the physical world, which after all doesn't concern him, being a *writer*, but between words and what they signify. In *Moby-Dick*, Melville turns the full force of his attention on what philosophers call the paradox of identity.

Identity is a paradox, as philosophers from Plato to Wittgenstein have pointed out, because "to say of *two* things that they are identical is nonsense," as Wittgenstein writes. "If 2 × 2 were really the *same* as 4, then this proposition would say no more than a = a." If identity is a relation, in short, it must hold between two *distinct* objects.[106] Or as Melville understands his challenge in *Moby-Dick*, he must show the relation of identity between the words man uses and, markedly different, what is. Because—as the book of Job would have us recall—if there is a relation of identity between the word or concept "whale" (which is evidently a creation of the human mind) and true being, the living whale in his full majesty and significance, then *this* relation is what the writer hoping to imitate reality must make plain.

When Truth Requires Just as Much Bolstering as Error

Melville's writing in *Moby-Dick* consequently alerts readers to the most suppressed recollection in contemporary literary criticism: the relation between *signs* and *things signified* (rather than signs and things) is what provides the basis for mimetic art. What the modern mimetic writer "imitates" isn't a word's referent but its meaning, the posited object or form object for which there is no readily perceivable correlate in the physical world.

And isn't this the lesson of *Moby-Dick*'s symbolism? The symbolic writer doesn't just depict the given or immediate object but something more literally in motion, the object's meaning as it is actively lived or felt. The task of the symbolic writer is to represent things-in-language, configurations of sense. Or to say again my working premise, Melville is able to successfully imitate reality because what he imitates in his whaling narrative isn't a natural object but a postulated or hypothesized object, the image of the object in his soul, the immanent Idea.[107]

In the case of *Moby-Dick*'s central symbolic object, the great whale itself, Melville imparts this imaginative vision by way of numerous preparatory passages in which the whale is "first hinted at, then reiterated in countless small details," as Ronald Mason reports (passages whose cunning "can be too readily overlooked, either in irritation at their superficial incongruity or in impatience at the continued delay of the start of the whaling-voyage proper"), before being expanded and elaborated, exalted and condensed, in great set pieces of rhetoric like chapter 9, "The Sermon," or chapter 42, "The Whiteness of the Whale."[108] Because in order to imbue his phantasm whale with the required degree of tangibility, to impart "a little more necessary body to the inevitably nebulous idea of whales and whaling in the mind of the average reader," Melville had to ensure that his readers were as intimately and reflexively acquainted with the whale as he himself was.[109] He had to manufacture the kind of familiarity usually born of physical ardor and years of grinding labor. For as in all effective symbolic art, writes Mason, "in Kafka's intricate law-processes as in Dostoevsky's elaborately-fashioned police investigations," communication of the ultimate imaginative vision "is achieved in proportion to the degree of familiarity and palpability which the central symbol has been enabled to achieve."[110]

That is why, in *Moby-Dick*, it is the *detail* Melville is after. For it is by means of his meticulous and suggestive thick description, as it were, his beautifully controlled "hints touching the plain facts, historical and otherwise, of the fishery," that Melville will make his picture of the whale convincing, even though what he pictures is not a natural object but a form object, a cultural hypothesis or notion continually under construction.

Regarding technique, calling *Moby-Dick* a work of realism presupposes that the convincing quality of Melville's portrayal hangs on the assured use of technical detail his earlier writing had furnished him with—that Melville's capacity to successfully imitate reality grew out of his writing of *Redburn* and *White-Jacket*, those "remarkable intermediate books" Melville wrote between *Mardi* and *Moby-Dick*, or "between the experiment with the symbol and the control of the symbol."[111] For as Mason also notes,

> The elaborate preparations which were necessary to put the reader in possession of sufficient store of fact and tradition to carry the weight of the subsequent spiritual tragedy must have been massy and laborious work for Melville. It does not read so. His constructional skill had learned much from his failure in *Mardi* and from the necessary discipline ordained upon him in *White-Jacket*, where huge masses of technical detail had to be given shape and meaning and life. He uses it with matured cunning in *Moby-Dick*, alternating his passages of bare cetology with sudden incidents of intense action or unusual suggestiveness.[112]

Accordingly in the two books after *Mardi*, Melville is "doing more than he is willing to admit to himself," as Mason says. "He blasts and sneers at *Redburn* for beggarly trash and seems to have no higher opinion of *White-Jacket*," but "he need not have been so harsh. For the accumulated detail of *Redburn* and *White-Jacket*, pedestrian and artless as it may have seemed at the time (and to Melville himself more than anyone), was being used unwittingly but inevitably to build up a sure foundation on which the immense ambitious symbol of *Moby-Dick* could rest."[113] In *Moby-Dick*, Melville's formidable task is to communicate to readers largely unacquainted with his chosen milieu not only the profound imaginative significance that the whale has for him but also an accurate understanding of a highly specialized trade. And as Mason notes, in the result "he accomplished this with honor; and established his book in the process as a handbook of whaling that most vividly perpetuates for its readers a largely-superseded stage in the history of the great industry."[114]

But concerning Melville's larger project, his poetic urge to represent reality or show the identity between sign and thing signified, to depict the thoroughly material yet thoroughly spiritual world from which there is no escape, it is Melville's instinctive or reflexive choice to build up a sure foundation on which the symbol of *Moby-Dick* could rest that permits him to make visible what in *Moby-Dick* Ishmael calls "something like the true form of the whale as he actually appears to the eye of the whaleman when in his own absolute body the whale is moored alongside the whale-ship so that he can be fairly stepped upon there."[115] Because he chooses to imitate the *conceptual* object "whale" (a prospect, as we will see, for which exacting observation of the material world is compulsory), Melville employs affect to suggest a perceptible, tangible entity without ever referring to it definitely, or without disputing the fact that the whale is one of the world's "undeliverable, nameless perils," that it is at bottom an "overwhelming idea."

Melville's herculean effort to construct this glimpse of *what is* thus constitutes the awful or considerable burden the author has cause to mention in *Moby-Dick*'s chapter 45, "The Affidavit." Here, either because he anticipates his readers' confusion at the sheer weight of technical detail the construction of his vast whale requires or because he, too, is growing weary of manufacturing familiarity with an object about which, for obvious reason, most readers have only the vaguest notion, Melville offers the kind of poignant apologia with which all his most challenging writing is interspersed. Before submitting a vivid realization of both the perils of the whale fishery in general and the particular perils of the sperm whale fishery, Melville writes, "I do not know where I can find a better place than just here, to make mention of one or two other things, which to me seem important, as in printed form establishing in all respects the reasonableness of the whole story of the white whale, more especially of the catastrophe. For this is one of those disheartening instances *where truth requires full as much bolstering as error*. So ignorant are most landsmen of some of the plainest and most palpable wonders of the world, that without some hints touching the plain facts, historical and otherwise, of the fishery, they might scout at Moby-Dick as a monstrous fable, or still worse and more detestable, a hideous and intolerable allegory."[116]

In this passage Melville forever parts company with those who would see in his whale something to interpret for its veiled meaning and throws in with those writers who, like Wordsworth, relish the harder goal of showing what is open to view. He confirms that a certain kind of writing has the capacity to represent otherwise inexpressible objects. And he associates this fearsome undertaking—depicting "some of the plainest and most palpable wonders of the world," aiming directly at the concrete representation of transcendent substance (the imitative or mimetic art Auerbach ranks above any "far-fetched, pedantic interpretation of the sensory world")—with the discovery that "truth requires full as much bolstering as error."[117] He shows, in short, how the chief action of the mimetic writer is not to simply describe but to *build up* the objects of his attention. That is what Melville does in *Moby-Dick*, as Kenneth Dauber argues.[118] For Melville, building up the objects of his attention (in this way closing the disabling disconnection between the reality unique to thought and all *lived* reality) is indispensable to the project of showing the identity of sign and thing signified—what I have identified as the basis of the writer's power to imitate real life.

When I say that in *Moby-Dick* Melville imitates reality, then, what I mean is that the objects and events that figure in the writing are built up rather by the whole structure of explanatory narrative than by the bare fact of their standing in a denotational relation to some class of classically substantial entities. I mean that Melville's cast-iron certainty about the class of extant being *not* subject to caprice—whatever he would grasp to recall himself to reality—goes along with his equally firm conviction that any question regarding the precise nature of objects is not merely a question of no particular import, given that objects no longer afford the ultimate *explanans*, but, in truth, a foolish question.[119] I mean that rather than render abstract that which is sensible (in this way "drawing the materials of the world into its own world, from which they do not return"), Melville renders "sensible that which is abstract," as Joseph Joubert says of the true metaphysician, making "apparent that which is hidden; imaginable, if so it may be, that which is only intelligible; and intelligible, finally, that which an ordinary attention fails to seize."[120]

By the same token, what calling *Moby-Dick* mimetic emphasizes isn't the lack of correspondence but the *vital affinity* between what Duyckinck calls "romantic fictions" and "absolute facts." For Melville clearly understood that his symbolic vision could be achieved only if readers felt vividly at home in his constructed narrative—if the authenticity of his writing, as dependent on his inventive powers, his countless hours of reading and conversation and conjecture as on his years of travel, was able to evoke genuine responses in the mind of a sympathetic reader. "For on that reader's acquiescence, which it is the author's task to demand and receive, is constructed the enduring value" of Melville's symbolic novel, as Mason writes. If Melville's chosen symbols are accepted, then his book offers "a true record of experience, whether Melville lived through the incidents or merely thought them out for himself."[121]

Melville's decision to write a realistic book of fiction (or, as I've argued, the kind of book that ignores the illusory relation between words and things in order to demonstrate the extant relation between words and things signified) is consequently what anchors his writing to daily life or what rescues his book from abstraction. That is, Melville's refusal to think that the function of language is largely referential accounts for why, to "any Nantucketer," his novel offers a truer picture of a whale than, for example, Fredrick Cuvier's *Natural History of Whales*—why in comparison with his own whale "Cuvier's Sperm Whale is not a Sperm Whale, but a squash."[122] For what *Moby-Dick*'s realism hinges on, and thus what it calls attention to, is the logical identity of *signs*, for instance the word or concept "whale," the meaningful use of which grows out of the collective experience of humanity, the uncounted millions, both dead and to come, for whom the crew of the *Pequod* in some way stands, and *things signified*, the living whale in his full majesty and significance.

Unsurprisingly, the relation of identity between signs and things signified is nothing Melville thinks the writer is able to manufacture. It is, however, what he can register if he demonstrates what Geoffrey Hartman calls the poet's "complete respect for ordinary experience as well as for its extraordinary potential"—or humbly accepts that truth requires just as much bolstering as error.[123] When through extraordinary, humbling effort Melville effectively builds up the objects of his attention in *Moby-Dick*, what he is able to show is that a relation of identity *does hold* between the premonition man names "whale" and what in Genesis is called the "living thing that moveth," the great whale God created, the timeless evolving entity that, as Ahab points out, "hast seen enough to split the planets and make an infidel of Abraham."[124] Showing this relation has astonishing consequences because it shows, too, the affinity, the "myriad linked analogies," between what Ahab calls the "Soul of man," everything that is related to or is the creation of the human mind, and "Nature," what is neither responsive to nor the creation of our conceptual schemes, linguistic practices, and beliefs.

The Problem of the Universe

Having come full circle on the question of *Moby-Dick*'s realism or Melville's ability to convincingly imitate reality, we are perhaps better prepared to receive Ronald Mason's endlessly reorienting comment that Melville was "the only American writer of genius effectively to sink the confining consciousness of nationalism in the wider context of the human soul." Mason is speaking here to the moral depth of Melville's writing, his ability to configure what Auerbach calls life in its full complexity, man in his living historical reality.

For in keeping with his own talents and temperament, Melville writes for general, immediate, concrete comprehension, for the sensory apprehension of everyday things and events. He is directly concerned with the individual person and the individual incident. At the same time, Melville's writing often reveals a conception of human shortcomings and virtues that experience alone could not have given him. The distinctiveness of his poetic scenes, such as the scene in "The Cabin" in which Pip catches Ahab by the hand in order to follow him and Ahab gently sets the boy aside on the grounds that "there is that in thee, poor lad, which I feel too curing to my malady," thus has to do with Melville's power to make an iconic occurrence, the bond between a blind king and his wise fool, feel immediate and concrete, wholly adequate to time and place. Only think how, in "The Cabin," the historical record of mid-nineteenth-century race relations is forcibly inserted into the scene by Ahab's phrase "and a black!" In the wake of Pip's entreaty, his assurance that Ahab is not wholly lost but has lost only a part of him, the one lost leg for which Pip offers himself as replacement ("only tread upon me, sir; I ask no more, so I remain a part of ye"), Ahab names Pip the restorer of his faith in human trustworthiness: "Oh! spite of million villains, this makes me a bigot in the fadeless fidelity of man!—and a black! and crazy!—but methinks like-cures-like applies to him too; he grows so sane again."[125] In his treatment of the sublime and eternal, that is to say, Melville doesn't scorn everyday life or the sensorily realistic but shows that he is riveted by it, that in fact it is his prevailing interest in the specific detail of everyday life and his practical concern with the lives of individuals that inspire and make possible his conception of the elevated or sublime.

This is the reason we call *Moby-Dick* lifelike, even when what Melville describes has never been seen or is not plausible. In Melville's novel readers are not forced to turn their attention away from but *toward* sensory occurrence. We do not, as Jonathan Lear says, "leave the human realm behind" but "get deeper into it—its smells, feels, textures, and the imaginary feelings we give to them."[126] That is, the "higher" or "deeper" truths that may be discovered in Melville's writing do not transcend material existence but, as Lear writes, "lie immanent to it." That is why even the most exalted descriptions and scenes are in Melville's hand rendered visually concrete. Reading *Moby-Dick* we see a man's whole life "become one watch on deck" when we encounter Ahab "either standing in his pivot-hole, or exactly pacing the planks between two undeviating limits,—the main-mast and the mizzen" as well as, through the night, standing in the scuttle for hours, "the unheeded night-damp gathered in beads of dew upon the stone-carved coat and hat," never going beneath the planks, neither touching his supper nor reaping his beard, "which darkly grew all gnarled, as unearthed roots of trees blown over, which still grow idly on at naked base, though perished in the upper verdure."[127] We feel ourselves, if cowardly in times past, now seated like Pip in Ahab's own screwed-down chair, burdened with required courage "as if thou wert the captain"; like Pip honorably sitting, as if under a spell, "against the transom, in the ship's full middle, all her keel and her three masts before him"; staying, though downhearted, till, as Pip says, "this stern strikes rocks; and they bulge through; and oysters come to join me."[128]

Which is only to suggest that as a compiler of events, Melville does not admit the antagonism between meaning and sensory appearance: he does not hold to the dualism of mind and matter or believe that no matter how things appear to us to be, how they actually *are* is surely another, essentially independent matter.[129] *Moby-Dick* verifies that Melville believes quite the opposite, actually, for rather than disregard his instinct for particularity or his desire to do justice to every aspect of earthly life as he knows it, in his story of the whale Melville pushes the thesis that every given object's distinct, perceptible uniqueness—its personality—is *encompassed in its ultimate fate*, or is important for the part it plays in the order (or forms of order) that exists independently of ourselves. Melville's desire to give a picture of the truth (to show, for example, what is grasped by someone who understands the concept "whale") does not therefore compete with his preservation of experiential life or preclude him from drawing his readers' attention to myriad examples from the world of his experience. No physical object or event is too ordinary for Melville to describe; the most commonplace, everyday experience has its function if it helps to give his thought concreteness. As *Moby-Dick* makes plain, Melville's desire to depict *what is* does not obligate him to adopt a contemptuous and dismissive attitude toward what can be readily perceived.

Indeed, Melville's spectacular success as a symbolic writer is indebted to his appreciation of material life—indebted, that is, to his refusal to treat as irrelevant the contingent or temporal form of any object's outward manifestation. That conceivably explains why twentieth-century critics' fever for separating Melville's story from its sensory base or encouraging readers to turn away from the sensory occurrence of the whale and toward its allegorical meaning proved so disastrous—why the critical explanation or interpretation of the text took on an increasing boldness and inanity. In the 1920s E. M. Forster called *Moby-Dick* a "prophetic song" about a man whose "knight-errantry turns into revenge." By the 1950s C. L. R. James was describing it as "the biography of the last days of Adolf Hitler." And by the end of the twentieth century, the novel was widely understood to be the story of a sadistic demagogue whose personal need for vengeance inspired a host of comparisons to both Osama bin Laden and George W. Bush.[130] Melville's highly wrought realist novel is thus distilled into a simple fable or cautionary tale. His whale is made into a hideous and intolerable allegory, and his rare, revolutionizing Captain Ahab (who, like all *original* characters, isn't just a product of his author's resourcefulness but is one in whom there is discernible something prevailingly "of the age," as Melville says)[131] is reduced to a hackneyed archetype of criminal leadership or species of madness nobody can really recognize but everybody knows how to judge.

Perhaps because they have refused to take proper notice of *Moby-Dick*'s realism, what these accounts fail to consider is the book's most extraordinary feature, what Ronald Mason calls its "limitless human sympathy," its seemingly inexhaustible willingness to address with compassion the vastest problems to which human imagination can extend itself. There is in other words a way of looking at *Moby-Dick* that misses entirely Melville's object in writing it. This Mason identifies as Melville's "search for the rediscovery of that innocence in the human soul of which contact with worldly experience has deprived it." Of this search Melville's books "make up a single, deeply impressive record," as Mason says.[132] But if there is much evidence of Melville's comprehensive and untiring development of his signature theme, of the courageousness of his attack upon it, what has become significantly *less* clear in the intervening years since Mason boldly confronted Melville's work is what, even in a rudimentary way, this theme involves—what it entails or what interesting philosophical possibilities it opens out.

My own goal consequently is to make the nature of Melville's object come alive for new readers of Melville's novel—readers for whom discussion of the human soul feels foreign or meaningless. Readers' disconnection from such talk is easily remedied, however. For as soon as we know *worldly experience* (what Shakespeare's Hamlet names "the thousand natural shocks that flesh is heir to") to be its adversary, we know *innocence in the human soul* to be the state in which man is not forced to make a choice between a realm of appearance and a realm of transcendent reality—not required to choose between a sensible and an ideal view of things.

This is an impossible, an intolerable choice, as Babbalanja complains in Melville's spiritual adventure *Mardi*, for "things visible are but conceits of the eye," and "things imaginative, conceits of the fancy. If duped by one, we are equally duped by the other."[133] There must as a result be a way not to make this choice. Engineering a way *out* of this dilemma is the driving purpose of *Moby-Dick*, the ambition to which Melville's every other ambition, political as well as literary, is roped—more his reason for writing in the first place than the subject of his writing.

Thus *Moby-Dick*, Melville's most massy and laborious novel, is also his most elegant. For here the increasingly tormented preoccupations and mounting eloquence of Babbalanja are given mature expression, and whereas in *Mardi* Melville packed in the whole range of his newly acquired philosophical consciousness, in the later more controlled work he trained his considerable powers of attention on the problem of modern life he thought most vital.

This Melville calls "the Problem of the Universe" and shows it to be the problem of a divided universe, one composed of two distinct realms. In *Moby-Dick*, awareness of the Problem is prompted by the recollection that "the soul is glued inside of its fleshly tabernacle," as Ishmael says. Or as Ahab puts it, that man is cursed with "that mortal inter-indebtedness which will not do away with ledgers. I would be as free as air; and I'm down in the whole world's books. I am so rich, I could have given bid for bid with the wealthiest Praetorians at the auction of the Roman empire (which was the world's); and yet I owe for the flesh in the tongue I brag with."[134] Of course it is Plato's Socrates who first communicates the problem of living in two worlds, the world of appearances and the world of forms. It is Socrates who examines the impediment to the soul of its mortal frame, "this which we now carry about with us and call the body, fettered to it like an oyster to its shell."[135] Two thousand years after Socrates names it, the problem is the same. For as Melville's near contemporary Maurice de Guérin reports, the answer to the question of what makes man "the most suffering of creatures" is that "he has one foot in the finite and the other in the infinite, and that he is torn asunder, not by four horses, as in the terrible old times, but between two worlds."[136]

Melville's split, severed Ahab offers even more concrete expression to this predicament, which philosophers after Kant identify as the problem of living in two worlds, the phenomenal world of human experience and the noumenal world of transcendentally real objects—a precarious situation that raises obvious questions about the limits of human knowledge. As Ahab discovers, his body tethers him to the world of particular things, the world in which he knows the white whale by its "wrinkled brow and crooked jaw." And yet his *understanding* of the whale or of any object depends throughout on generality. As the ancients observed, we are unable to characterize a particular object except as an instance of something more general. How then, as Ahab worries, are the objects of sense not mere appearances of something else—something that cannot itself appear?

Kant argued in the *Critique of Pure Reason* that the something else of which sensible objects are only appearances (and whose existence we must grant) cannot itself be known. Discontent thus blooms in the wake of Kant's "settlement," as Stanley Cavell calls Kant's attempt to limit knowledge to make room for faith. For in order to put flight to skepticism, "to assure us that we do know the existence of the world or, rather, that what we understand as knowledge is *of* the world," as Cavell writes, "the price Kant asks us to pay is to cede any claim to know the thing in itself, to grant that human knowledge is not of things as they are in themselves."[137] Dissatisfaction with the Kantian settlement is what Cavell finds explicitly expressed in the great romantic works of literature ("romantic war horses" like Coleridge's *Ancient Mariner* and Wordsworth's "Immortality Ode" but also and more strikingly Emerson's *Essays* and Thoreau's *Walden*), but as Cavell humorously notes, "you don't—do you?—have to be a romantic to feel sometimes about that settlement: Thanks for nothing."[138]

Granting that human knowledge is not of the noumenal realm deeply exasperates Ahab, in any event, and it is easy to see why. For the sundering Ahab feels more keenly than other men is that of the world of experience from the world of truth. To cut a long story short, Ahab ("faint, bowed, and humped," as though he were "Adam, staggering beneath the piled centuries since Paradise") shows why having only one foot in each world or having to lurch back and forth between the world of appearances and the world of forms only proves the extent to which "the human being now lives in *neither* world," as Stanley Cavell writes, "that we are, as it is said, between two worlds."[139]

What Mason's "innocence in the human soul" describes is thus a mode of existence fundamentally *unlike* the one in which there is a rigid barrier between the realm of truth and the world of human experience—that mode of existence in which, as Ahab exclaims, "the dead, blind wall butts all inquiring heads at last" and all "things real" are naught but "imponderable thoughts."[140]

And yet one of the striking features of *Moby-Dick* is that this divided state isn't what Ahab is felled by but what he *weathers*—what his "determinate, unsurrenderable willfulness" and the "fixed and fearless, forward dedication" of his glance prepare him to endure. In chapter 28, "Ahab," Ishmael reports being struck by "the singular posture" Captain Ahab maintains, an erect bearing procured by auger holes bored into the deck that stabilize his bone leg. The Captain's physical immovability thus corresponds to the "infinity of firmest fortitude" that marks his whole grim aspect. This fixedness offers stark contrast to a pensive young fellow willing to let his thoughts wander, as Ishmael sometimes identifies himself, the kind of "lad with lean brow and hollow eye; given to unseasonable meditativeness; and who offers to ship with the Phaedon instead of Bowditch in his head." Chapter 35, "The Mast-head," finds dreamy meditative Ishmael comfortably suspended on the mast-head, "a hundred feet above the silent decks" and sliding gladly into the kind of languorous mood in which the incidents of common life no longer seem interesting—the faraway, listless, indolent mood Ahab's rigid mien is calculated to safeguard him against.[141] There is a penalty for such entranced thought, for though Ishmael's task is to monitor the seas for any sign of whales his transcendentalizing unfits him for duty. As he recounts, "Let me make a clean breast of it here, and frankly admit that I kept but sorry guard. With the problem of the universe revolving in me, how could I—being left completely to myself at such a thought-engendering altitude,—how could I but lightly hold my obligations to observe all whale-ships' standing orders, 'Keep your weather eye open, and sing out every time.'"

Now, given the identification many readers of *Moby-Dick* are likely to make between Ishmael and Melville, or given the expectation that *Melville* subscribes to Ishmael's "unseasonable meditativeness," it is hard to see clearly Melville's critique of transcendentalizing young men. It is hard not to treat as a kind of ironic utterance Ishmael's admonishment to the shipowners of Nantucket not to enlist a fellow such as himself—one who does not feel sufficient "interest" in the voyage. The reason Ishmael gives is that "whales must be seen before they can be killed; and this sunken-eyed young Platonist will tow you ten wakes round the world, and never make you one pint of sperm the richer." Because readers' sympathies aren't lodged with the shipowners or their investments, we are prone to hear dry irony in Ishmael's warning that "nowadays, the whale-fishery furnishes an asylum for many romantic, melancholy, and absent-minded young men, disgusted with the carking cares of earth and seeking sentiment in tar and blubber." Nevertheless I think this construal would be misguided. For in "The Mast-head" Melville's sympathies aren't with the listless (though able-bodied) youths, "lost in the infinite series of the sea" and so keeping sorry guard, but with their upright, scarred, and seasoned captains, half hinting that these entranced youths "are so hopelessly lost to all honorable ambition, as that in their secret souls they would rather not see whales than otherwise." So long as a young whaler is contracted with or working under the terms of the "vigilant fisheries," in other words, he can't simply show contempt for but must learn to observe all whaleships' standing orders: that if you see a whale, you say so.

What stops Ishmael from reporting on the directly sensible is the conviction that the objects of sense are mere appearances. The certainty that human beings cannot know a thing "in its internal constitution, but only know its appearances" is what Melville christens the Problem of the Universe.[142] And yet it is worth noting that in *Moby-Dick* Melville intriguingly makes the Problem of the Universe the problem of the *young* man, withdrawn from the working world and given over to a life of reflection, what Ishmael calls a life of "sublime uneventfulness," in which "you hear no news; read no gazettes; extras with startling accounts of commonplaces never delude you into unnecessary excitements; you hear of no domestic afflictions; bankrupt securities; fall of stocks; are never troubled with the thought of what you shall have for dinner."

In "The Mast-head," Melville names these fledgling philosophers, in whose hands lay the destruction of the phenomenal world, "young Platonists." This suggests, to be sure, that antiquity offers the most compelling reason to turn away from everyday life—to turn from what can be readily perceived about the whale to the purifying idea of it. What happens to Ishmael or to the young Platonist is that he feels prohibited from actually *looking* at whales because he already believes that the reality is hidden from him. And if reality is hidden, then his everyday judgments about the material world are inconsequential. (For seeing as the young Platonist believes himself inescapably "short-sighted," Melville writes dryly, "what use, then, to strain the optic nerve?") For Melville, who wishes to represent real life in art—and for whom, as for Emerson, "no picture of life can have any veracity that does not admit the odious facts"—young Platonists are anathema because all that interests them are independent intellectual objects prior to or uncorrupted by experience.[143] Even so, by associating Platonism with sophomoric youth, Melville introduces an important difference between the distracted, inattentive fellows he fingers as the "many romantic, melancholy, and absent-minded young men, disgusted with the carking cares of earth" and philosophers proper, careful readers of Plato *and of much else.*

Young Platonists are to be pitied on two fronts. As aspiring intellectuals they have failed to recognize that "there is no such thing as a standard for the creative spirit," as the eponymous character of Melville's *Pierre* discovers—"that no one great book must ever be separately regarded, and permitted to domineer with its uniqueness upon the creative mind."[144] But much more worryingly, these listless youths are "learning to live by rehearsing the part of death." The young Platonist "is fitting himself for the highest Life, by thinning his blood and collapsing his heart." In short, the scholarly, disheartened youth—Hamlet is the literary original—learns to limit the knowledge his senses afford him in order to clear the way for reflection and reason. If such youths seem subsequently to go mad, perhaps that is because for every moment of acumen the suppression of empirical evidence supports—for example, Hamlet's seeing in his smiling uncle his father's murderer—is a foolish blindness it perpetuates: Hamlet's seeing frailty in Ophelia's evident love for him.

In "The Mast-head" Melville thus underscores the opposition that occupies him throughout: the difference between holding that man's vision is imperfect (an entranced feeling nourished and supported by an individual's withdrawal from ordinary life) and trusting in what Melville calls "the intense feeling of the visible truth."[145] In his letter to Hawthorne of April 16, 1851, Melville introduces the intense feeling of visible truth as a necessary alternative to the young man's feeling that experience is constituted by appearances and thus not to be trusted. In contrast to the choice the philosophizing youth imagines himself having to make between "things visible," as Babbalanja says, and "things imaginative" (in which, moreover, the imagination always triumphs), man's feeling of the visible truth enables him to regard earthly things and heavenly intuitions "with equal eye."[146] It lets him think his vision is *not* imperfect—that he can grasp reality (which is intellectual *and* sensual) on his own recognizance, as it were. To Hawthorne, Melville describes this intense feeling as "the apprehension of the absolute condition of present things as they strike the eye of the man who fears them not, though they do their worst to him." The man whose soul is innocent "may perish," Melville maintains, but real things do not elude him; they do not seem to him to be the "strange, half-seen, gliding" embodiments of his "elusive thoughts."[147]

Along these lines it is worth noting that "The Mast-head," which details the youthful man's craving to *escape* earthly life, is followed immediately by the chapter "The Quarter-Deck," which—particularly in Ahab's "All visible objects" soliloquy—lays out a seasoned man's determined attachment to that life. Accordingly, one likely possibility is that in *Moby-Dick*, the man whose soul is innocent is Ahab. In Ahab, Melville gives us this great gift of opposition, this rejoinder to Hamlet, a character just as self-consciously mad, no doubt, or in the same way the embodiment of extreme apprehension, but, perhaps because he's a blasphemous *old* man, a "swearing good" man in the final stages of his life, one who refuses to live as if rehearsing death. By this view, Ahab's hard-won innocence isn't belied by his overall antagonism.

Ahab, as I understand him, is a figure sincerely in pursuit of what William Blake called "achieved innocence," which is neither the naive innocence of the child nor the conditioned benumbing of the veteran. To be in possession of an achieved innocence is to have found one's way back to the value of subjective experience. In the terms set out by the great American romantics Emerson and Thoreau, it means finding in every word of our language an account of the history of individual things. For Ahab, it means recovering the presence of physical objects in the word "whale," recovering the experience of men lost (and men living!) in the word "whaleman."

However, in order to even consider the possibility of achieved innocence, and thus to conceive a means to express it, Melville had to make for himself a distinction between two frightening (but *not equally* frightening) prospects. The first is that sooner or later man's questions relating to God, free will, and fate will force him to confront the epistemological problem underlying all problems affecting the limits of reason. And yet as Melville confides to Hawthorne, "we incline to think that the Problem of the Universe is like the Freemason's mighty secret, so terrible to all children. It turns out, at last, to consist in a triangle, a mallet, and an apron,—nothing more!"[148] Melville's impulse is not to solve the problem of the universe but to dissolve it: to see as *not* exclusive and not inescapable the insisted-upon contrast between the "Soul of man" and "Nature."[149] Showing how Melville, in the writing of *Moby-Dick*, discovers an argument capable of disputing the contradistinction between what the Greeks called *nomos* and *physis* is the philosophical work of the present volume. However, Melville's suggestion that "there is *no* secret," or that what presents itself as an irresolvable riddle may simply have something to do with the presentation, alerts us to his recognition of the difference between the melancholic, entranced mood men are apt to bring upon themselves and the quite different and much more fearsome obstacle Melville calls "The King of Terrors."

In a journal entry of August 9, 1860, while aboard the clipper *Meteor*, Melville describes a gale during which "Ray, a Nantucketer, about 25 years old," fell from the main topsail yard to the deck, & striking his head foremost upon one of the spars was instantly killed. His chum, Macey (Fisher) of Nantucket, I found alone in the upper cabin sitting over the body—a harrowing spectacle. 'I have lost my best friend,' said he; and then 'His mother will go crazy—she did not want to let him go, she feared something might happen.' "[150] As Melville recounts, "It was in vain to wash the blood from the head—the body bled incessantly & up to the moment of burying; which was about one o'clock, and from the poop, in the interval between blinding squalls of sharp sleet. Tom read some lines from the prayer-book—the plank was sloped, and—God help his mother.—During the brief ceremony, made still the more trying from being under the lee of the reefed spanker where the wind eddies so—all stood covered with Sou-Westers or Russia caps & comforters, except Macy—who stood bareheaded." The next day, on August 10, Melville reports

> calm: blue sky, sun out, dry deck. Calm lasting all day—almost pleasant enough to atone for the gales, but not for Ray's fate, which belongs to that order of human events, which staggers those whom the Primal Philosophy hath not confirmed.—But little sorrow to the crew—all goes on as usual—I, too, read & think, & walk & eat & talk, as if nothing had happened—as if I did not know that death is indeed the King of Terrors—when thus happening; when thus heart-breaking to a fond mother—The King of Terrors, not to the dying or the dead, but to the mourner—the mother.—Not so easily will his fate be washed out of her heart, as his blood from the deck.

In this entry we hear again the warning Melville sent up, in "The Mast-head," to all the moody Childe Harolds, "perched upon the mast-head of some luckless, disappointed whale-ship." For "while this sleep, this dream is on ye, move your foot or hand an inch; slip your hold at all; and your identity comes back in horror. Over Descartian vortices you hover. And perhaps, at mid-day, in the fairest weather, with one half-throttled shriek you drop through that transparent air into the summer sea, no more to rise for ever."[151] The admonishment here isn't that death puts a verifiable end to the rationalist's flights of fancy. Rather, what Melville makes clear when he invokes the order of human events "which staggers those whom the Primal Philosophy hath not confirmed," is that there are proceedings we cannot protect ourselves from—from "Ray's fate" there *is* no protection, for those who mourn him—but that some things happen to us for which there are protective measures. In short, the very worst of what need *not* be suffered Melville connects to the cost of entertaining too long or to ill effect the "Problem of the Universe." And he names a reliable source of comfort or fortification, the intellectual equivalent of "Sou-Westers or Russia caps," something he calls "the Primal Philosophy." As Melville opposes the Primal Philosophy to the Problem of the Universe, or offers it as safeguard, it's incumbent upon his readers to ask, What kind of philosophy is this? And how does it reveal itself?

In his journals and fiction Melville characterizes the Primal Philosophy as a native or indigenous power, the mode of existence for which "the intense feeling of visible truth" forms the base, and as such a state of innocence, of man in his instinctive form not prior to but in the face of the dispassionate enmity of experience.[152] Though it commemorates a state of innocence, the Primal Philosophy requires therefore an education in seeing and feeling, a way of thinking and living less intellectual than practical, responsive—for the Primal Philosophy is not a primitive condition, fated to be surpassed by what Weber calls *Entzauberung der Welt*, the epoch of the "disenchantment of the world." Rather, it is what Borutti and de Luise, following Wittgenstein, describe as a characteristic feature of the awakening mind of man, a philosophico-poetic condition rightly associated with a certain *reenchantment* of the world, the feeling of wonder and amazement that transpires when speakers of language perceive themselves capable of sense—when our minds awaken, as Wittgenstein says, to the fact that phenomena come to have meaning for us.[153]

How the Primal Philosophy works in us is the matter Melville, in *Moby-Dick*, will make clear. But if there is a lesson to be drawn from "Ray's fate," it is that man is "the most suffering of creatures" because his reason alerts him to his fragility—to the unexpectedness and irrevocability by which a life may be snuffed out, by which it may be subject to that "speechless quick chaotic bundling of man into Eternity."[154] It *isn't* because, in the ordinary course of daily life, we feel ourselves torn between two worlds. It isn't because all things real seem like nothing other than imponderable thoughts. Someone who is careless with his everyday obligations in order to entertain this worry is overlooking the fact that doubt about identity, about who or what a person or thing exactly is, is generally prompted by an attempt to get to the bottom of some state of affairs—to ask the kinds of questions that enable someone to conspicuously define something for all time—and so represents a philosophical misfiring, an attempt to settle what cannot be settled like that.

Visible Truth

I have thus far labored to show why the indefatigable search in *Moby-Dick* is for "that innocence in the human soul of which contact with worldly experience has deprived it" and also why we should understand this state of innocence as the mode of existence in which one is not forced to choose between things visible and things imaginative. For those in whom the Primal Philosophy operates, how something is experienced and "what it is" are brought into line. What is more, and contrary to commonsense expectation, I have associated this philosophico-poetic condition with Ahab—at least, with the life he seeks, the life he desires.

The great irony regarding Ahab, after all, is that the power he spends himself to brandish—to feel the factual dimensions of his figurative expressions—is a power the speakers of language already ordinarily enjoy. Accordingly the question Melville uses his whaling narrative to answer is *how* this is the case. Precisely how do we (as Ahab would have it) recapture the presence of natural objects in names? Exactly how does practical life feature in and shape conceptual life? What is the connection between a sign and a situation outside in the world?

The question is a characteristically philosophical one. But as Melville exultantly discovers a way to answer it, in *Moby-Dick*—as he assembles his singular, ingenious account of the relationship between discourse and what it concerns—he draws on the knowledge instilled in him by his self-appointed task: to represent real life in writing. Had Melville not attempted his prodigious feat of poetic mimesis, that is to say, and so forced himself to solve the problem of how writers make imagined events convincing, he would not have been so well positioned to resolve the philosophical puzzle his novel confronts head-on.

What follows thus gives renewed attention not to Melville's endless versatility but to his inexhaustible sympathy; not to his disenchantment with fiction but to his great insight about language and consequently about both philosophy and literature; not to his doubts, easily mounted, but to his certainties, precariously secured. My goal has been to find in Melville's whaling narrative a suitably rich conception of realism—to find in Melville's writing overwhelming evidence of his characteristic commitment to giving concrete expression to the most precious things. That is the determination surging through *Moby-Dick* and filling it with a peculiar power.

Chapter 1

✦

The Case against Melville

There are evidently two if not three books in Moby Dick rolled into one.

—Evert A. Duyckinck, *Literary World*, November 22, 1851

Melville's genius is everywhere acknowledged; what is peculiar is the continuing wide acceptance of the "botched" nature of his books. That includes *Moby-Dick*, the novel that more than any other issuing from an American author is counted among literature's ultimate achievements. Readers prize *Moby-Dick* despite a feeling of apprehension, one they take Melville to share and even, by his own candor, generate, that the book is clumsily executed, an irregular if exceptional composition in which various kinds of writing crudely stitched together endlessly compete. Such misgiving lurks, anyway, behind critics' frequent reference to a remark in Melville's letter to Hawthorne of June 1851: "What I feel most moved to write, that is banned,—it will not pay. Yet, altogether, write the *other* way I cannot. So the product is a final hash, and all my books are botches."[1] Here Melville is taken to have encapsulated his predicament and offered an apt judgment. For apparently Melville's antithetical dreams of securing an audience and of writing in a way that was not accommodating but true introduced a curious incongruity into his books. In *Moby-Dick*, critics regularly suggest, this incongruity is evidenced by the novel's rough coupling of fact and fancy, its bewildering back-and-forth between what is on the one hand an essentially faithful representation of the physical world of whaling, awash with social-political commentary, and, on the other, an extraordinary mixture of all kinds of fiction, delivered in exalted, supercharged prose. Melville's perceived inability to unite his incompatible impulses has over time become *Moby-Dick*'s most familiar feature, and the conviction that Melville never entirely decided upon the direction or desired effect of his creation, never fully chose between conflicting representative modes, has given rise to the present estimation of him: a genius who couldn't or wouldn't choose between writing plausibly and writing truthfully; author of a book begun in one mood and ended in another; a brilliant, intrepid, anguished, self-destructive spoiler who *almost* wrote the great American novel.

Against this estimate I'd like to propose a different view of both Melville and his masterwork: a shrewder, less-divided writer, deliberately grappling with the precisely formulated demands of an ambitious project, and a more controlled, integrated book, one that meets these demands when it triumphantly illuminates the nature of literary expression—when it reveals fully and formally what literature is and can do. This construal takes *Moby-Dick* to be governed by an idea of literature, a reimagining of literature's essential role, in obedience to which the whole force of the novel is ultimately yoked. But if it is accurate, if *Moby-Dick* "is a work strong in the sense of the whole, unfractioned power of literary utterance," as Richard Brodhead has written,[2] then it should also be true that the book is *not* botched, not a jumbled concoction, not half one kind of narrative and half another. Melville's book is both more momentous and more enjoyable when we see how its disparate elements have been arranged in order to create an overall aesthetic impression. This, the narrative's special organizing principle or form, confirms that the work did not make itself and is not a copy of the world as it is experienced; rather than simply describe whatever he encounters, a self-conscious author has formulated a world of his own.[3]

The more clearly an author's orchestrating efforts are in evidence the harder readers will work to identify the controlling pattern and movement of his fictional world. Regrettably, the reverse is true as well. Readers who find scant indication of what Henry James calls the artist's "operative consciousness," the theory behind the fiction, will be unable to discover what a book is able to express, intellectually speaking—the *concern* of the text, as distinct from the novel's plot or its characters or their concerns.

The widespread conviction among his readers that Melville engagingly "writes on" in the absence of any strict organizing principle is thus related to the equally prevalent view that the real achievement of Melville's writing is its robustness or exuberance, not its philosophical lucidity. For where there is no elucidating relationship between the operative consciousness of the author and the world of the novel, there is no need to try to account for all a book's details in the hope of discovering its motivating logic. There is no reason to occupy oneself with the book's intellectual justification, its place in the world of thought.

This was the conclusion Brodhead reinforced when in *Hawthorne, Melville, and the Novel* (1973) he spoke less eagerly of Melville's operative consciousness than of his "imaginative presence." As Brodhead reasoned, Melville's procedure of "energetically creating parts rather than carefully orchestrating wholes," his "preference for writing without a plan," accounts for why the theory behind Melville's fiction is less evident than the *spirit* of his enterprise, the "exuberance of personal inventiveness and discovery" that informs his art. His belief that Melville did not have a clear sense of what kind of book he was writing leads Brodhead to suggest that the way the novel heightens readers' consciousness of Melville's imaginative process and the way it pits competing representational modes against one another come off "in spite" of the author's intentions, "not because of them."[4] As sympathetic a Melville critic as Brodhead can as a result approvingly quote Warner Berthoff's declaration, also designed as a compliment, that "the particulars of the work itself—themes, ideas, procedures, forms—come to seem to a degree incidental. We grow aware of something further, of a continuous imaginative presence and energy sustaining these particulars and positively generating them."[5]

Indeed, the particulars of Melville's work are bound to seem incidental if from the outset one refuses to believe that Melville is—by means of them—driving at something. Berthoff and Brodhead draw attention to Melville's energy, not his object, the intellectual reason for his books' existence, because for them Melville's object is irresolvable. Or rather, Melville's object in books like *Moby-Dick*, *Mardi*, and *Pierre* is self-serving, impossible to tell apart from that kind of "unique experiment in which an author attempts to give birth to his own creative self by giving form to whatever surfaces in his mind."[6] According to this view *Moby-Dick* is a brilliant accomplishment in Melville's career as a writer, but philosophically speaking it is a series of incompatible formulations, written without plan. Berthoff and Brodhead thus contribute to the assessment that "as a thinker, Melville was an inspired amateur," as Richard Chase asserted.[7] They continue the tradition of treating dismissively what in an early study Charles Anderson had disparagingly called Melville's "sailor metaphysics."[8] Brodhead confidently allows that "Melville loves to philosophize, but in the end his philosophical statements are less interesting for their intellectual content than for the animated activity of thinking they manifest."[9] Trying, through the careful examination of his text, to discover Melville's object is consequently not "the sort of appreciation that Melville's peculiar production requires."[10]

And yet it is an author's *object* that sets all his work in motion—what, on balance, is reached when his work's particulars have their desired effect. It is his object that is the secret of his attraction for other minds. As Matthew Arnold first reasoned, there is a significant difference between what Arnold calls an author's propositions (everything that gets said in a book, all its particulars) and an author's object, the book's motivating logic, without which none of its particulars are enlisted to any lasting effect. An author's object is of paramount importance because his propositions "pass by mankind at large like the idle wind, which mankind regards not; it will not even listen to a word about these propositions, unless it first learns what their author was driving at with them, and finds that this object of his is one with which it sympathizes, one, at any rate, which commands its attention."[11]

I mean therefore to point out the disadvantage in agreeing that *Moby-Dick* is less remarkable for what it achieves than for "the spiritedness" with which Melville "goes about creating his art," consequently stressing "not Melville's achievement but his example—an example of a prodigal and forceful imagination throwing its whole energy into an earnest attempt to articulate its own insights."[12] The disadvantage, as the current drift of Melville criticism makes clear, is that with little confidence in Melville's operative consciousness, readers hardly feel their obligation to discover his object, the intellectual justification in accordance with which every aspect of his invented narrative must arrange itself. Even critics in no doubt about Melville's philosophical acuity—the many readers for whom Melville's writing throws light on the most pressing debates in literature and philosophy, readers for whom Melville emerges as a thinker of genuine philosophical significance to the current critical agenda—appear unable to see or unwilling to say what, in *Moby-Dick*, Melville is driving at.

This reluctance to name *Moby-Dick*'s raison d'être seems unwarranted, however, given the author's emphatic declaration of his goal: to depict the material dimensions of the spiritual world, to enable those things that are conceptual and hence without corporeal form to stand corporeally (concretely, palpably) before him and before his readers.

The desired outcome of *Moby-Dick* is the representation of reality—"reality," by the measure Auerbach offers, meaning the realm in which something's outward appearance is not distinct from what Plato would call its Idea but contained in it and transfigured.[13] Melville's object in this novel is to represent the whale *sub specie aeternitatis* (from the viewpoint of eternity) without forsaking the entire earthly, historical record of his knowledge and experience.

There is reason, in other words, for critics involved in the search for a materialist epistemology—who hope to demonstrate the significance of embodied rather than purely mental knowledge—to turn in increasing numbers to Melville's writing. Throughout his career Melville strove to supplement "Plato's theme" (Melvillean shorthand for the view that reality is not the realm of sense perception but the realm of Ideas or forms) with an amplified attention to materiality. By "materiality" I mean, with Branka Arsić, the capacity of material life to move and transform mental life—the heightened awareness of "feeling as thinking" captured in the current critical moment by the surge of interest in "affect."[14] Because some materialist epistemologies are crafted in reaction to their rationalist counterparts, however, they can contribute to the dualism they seek to vanquish. Either the salient emphasis on embodied knowledge degenerates into a newly legitimized, science-backed championing of the material world at the cost of the spiritual world or it institutes a familiar balancing act, an attempt to combat dualism by *synthesizing* or *combining* the material and spiritual realms. This option simply will not do. For as some theorists are laboring to make clear—and as Melville demonstrates in his whaling narrative—that which truly confounds a dualistic ontology emerges not as a mingling of matter and spirit but rather, as Arsić writes, "the concreteness of things that includes the spiritual, which moves it."[15]

Moby-Dick, I think, best shows us what this means. In Melville's whaling narrative the third realm (the realm of objects that are from their inception both material and spiritual) comes looming into view. Objects in the third realm are at once incommensurable to and in line with practical experience. Melville's book not only emphasizes everything that gives our mental concepts their distinctive vividness and force (the essential attribute of affect, as Charles Altieri writes)[16] but also provides a satisfying explanation for experiential life's influence on thought and its linguistic expressions.

In sum I cannot agree with Brodhead's seminal claim that "Melville does not have a well-defined philosophy—or rather he has a hundred of them."[17] For the feeling that Melville is proving a case is what gives *Moby-Dick* its radiance. I do not mean that the thinking revealed in *Moby-Dick* is divisible from this book's language, its patterns of irony, its characters' fate, or its titanic plot. The argument that Melville's intellectual position is philosophically defensible in *Moby-Dick* doesn't suggest the presence of an abstract thesis one might cleanly extract from the book, without attending to the mode of representation by which the author draws readers into his complex imagined world. I mean, rather, that Melville's writing "builds up like Euclid," as the critic William Empson writes—speaking of a different work, though one subject to the same treatment. Modern critics seem unable to feel this, Empson points out ("apparently because it is forbidden by their aesthetic principles") even when the author tells them he is doing it.[18] Given how many of Melville's older critics have blasted his desire to "philosophize," in Brodhead's withering expression, and how many of his newer critics see him as a principled opponent of anything in the nature of philosophical "argument," even while his books are declared philosophically rich, it seems time for a serious reconsideration of Melville's philosophical project in *Moby-Dick.*

First, though, we should better understand the case against Melville, particularly since it emerges from the work of his most ardent admirers. The most common charge is that Melville prepared writing bound for publication hurriedly or even injudiciously, with the result that *Moby-Dick* is technically a muddle. From the most conscientious of archive-based scholars, those who help readers make sense of Melville's biography, sources, aesthetic values, and compositional practices, comes proof of the existence of so many textual problems that readers of critical editions of *Moby-Dick* have learned, alongside the editors of these editions, to affirm the novel's greatness despite its actual imperfections. According to our most expert and trusted editors, Harrison Hayford and Hershel Parker, the grossest of these are not limited to unauthorized editorial intrusion or errors of transcription but include "conceptual discrepancies, factual inconsistencies, patched-over flaws in transitions, lapses in technique, and stylistic lurches"—defects serious enough to give credence to those contemporary reviewers of *Moby-Dick* who recognized "qualities of greatness in the book and qualities of genius in the author" but "found serious anomalies in its genre, characters, language, and thought."[19] These editors are adamant that "their examination of the textually imperfect body of *Moby-Dick* has revealed flaws that help to explain Melville's own sense that it was by his standards a hash or a botch" and that Melville's confessions in this regard "have never been taken as literally as he meant them and as editorial scrutiny of the text has now shown they should be understood." To those many modern readers who as "an article of faith" argue that *Moby-Dick*'s formal anomalies actually establish the work's unique form, Hayford and Parker insist that "there is in fact no need to rationalize" all the novel's aberrations "or to attribute them all to Melville's principle, promulgated in *Moby-Dick*, that in some enterprises 'a careful disorderliness is the true method.' "

The readers toward whom such scholars express opposition do not, presumably, think of themselves as rationalizing the novel's peculiarities so much as resituating them in a modernist context. Critics interested in *Moby-Dick* as a work of art are likely to take exception to the tendency among Melville's editors to include in the same category those errors that eventuate from a manuscript's many revisions, insertions and deletions, and Melville's habits of research and composition. These aesthetically minded readers cry foul when scholars identify as one of *Moby-Dick*'s "conceptual discrepancies" Melville's "greater concern for a scene's dramatic qualities than for its local consistency of realistic detail or its consistency with other parts of the manuscript." They contest the claim that there is something wrong or disingenuous about the author's practice of interpolating passages rewritten from other people's experience or plundered from their books. And they find in Melville's later works some hint of the distinction he made between inevitable but nominal technical error and the hard-won concentrate of a writer's preoccupations—when, for example, in *Pierre* the young author knows his proofs to be full of mistakes but, "preoccupied by the thronging and undiluted, pure imaginings of things, he became impatient of such minute, gnat-like torments; he randomly corrected the worst, and let the rest go; jeering with himself at the rich harvest thus furnished to the entomological critics."[20] Where genetic scholars see a confession, readers who think it necessary to distinguish between errata and Melville's manner of composition find in his remark about his botched books a declaration. Were the book any less weird or muddled or maddening, they suggest, or less obviously a patchwork with visible seams, it would not be improved. Just as if it were stripped of its philosophical meanderings or extended excursions into the technical details of whaling, it would simply cease to be what it is: a half-mad masterpiece and an original work of art.

Antagonistic as they are, the rival views of genetic scholars and modern readers are not, I think, unconnected, and what interests me here is the matter over which they bond: the certainty that *Moby-Dick* is by Melville's own critical reflection a "final hash"—that there are elements at odds in Melville's writerly impulses and for that reason elements at odds in the book. Melville's editors and archival-based scholars find his state of internal discord to be a failing or disadvantage, while modern readers take it to constitute or at least characterize his genius, but neither party disputes the botched-book thesis, and both are effectively grounding their impressions in the idea that *Moby-Dick* is in fact *two* books: the story of a whaling voyage, illustrated by the author's personal experience, and an inspired revision of this whaling yarn, philosophically recast. The first book stars Ishmael, the second, Ahab. The first book is a personal, nationalist narrative, the second a metaphysical romance of almost impossibly comprehensive sweep. The first is the kind of book that pays, in other words, the second the kind Melville felt moved to write.

Thus intermingled with the conviction that *Moby-Dick* is a botch is the belief that the book contains two noticeably different representational modes. The famous "two *Moby-Dicks*" theory is said to have begun in 1939 when, on the basis of the slight evidence then available, Leon Howard inferred that Melville undertook a major revision of the novel after August 1850. (On August 7, 1850, Evert Duyckinck had written to his brother that Melville's new manuscript—"a romantic, fanciful, & literal & most enjoyable presentment of the whale fishery"—was "mostly done.") Then in 1947 Charles Olson announced in *Call Me Ishmael* that "Moby-Dick was two books written between February, 1850, and August, 1851. The first book did not contain Ahab. It may not, except incidentally, have contained Moby-Dick." In 1949 Howard P. Vincent theorized a revision begun much later, in the spring of 1851. Howard returned to the subject in his 1951 biography *Herman Melville*, describing in a chapter called "Second Growth" Melville's inspired revision, under the tutelage of Shakespeare and Hawthorne, of his early whaling narrative. Finally in 1954 George R. Stewart argued in "The Two *Moby-Dicks*" that there were two distinct narratives written during two distinct periods, an "Ur-Moby-Dick" that told the Ishmael story, and a later version that superimposed a grander vision on the novel without substantially revising the early chapters. In 1970 Harrison Hayford deflated Stewart's thesis by showing that the early chapters were revised many times in the course of Melville's writing, and in 1975 James Barbour argued that Melville wrote *Moby-Dick* in *three* distinct stages, but the conclusion drawn from what Barbour rightly calls "a history of investigation frequently marked by shrewd and brilliant literary scholarship" was decided. The disparity between the two types of writing in the novel as well as the contrasting moods in which Melville worked on it encourage the conclusion that *Moby-Dick* consists of dissimilar and patched-together narratives and is for *that* reason a botch and a failure, notwithstanding its most excellent and deserving qualities.[21]

Worth noting from this brief history is the way various hypotheses about the manner in which *Moby-Dick* was put together—whether or not it was of seriatim composition, and in what order revision took place—shades unnoticeably into an argument about the disparity between *types* of writing in the novel. The "two *Moby-Dicks*" theory suggests both that there was more than one stage of writing and that there was more than one kind of writing. While scholars have proved the first assumption dubious, the second goes largely unquestioned. Also, although Melville's remark about his botched books was made in direct connection with what he saw as the competing pressures of popularity and literary merit, it is taken to name or be an admission of formal incongruity in the narrative, as if his remark about his rival impulses translates without question or doubt into a confession that his novel includes separate and opposing narrative modes.

I wish to raise that doubt: *has* Melville openly admitted that *Moby-Dick* "was by his standards a hash or a botch," as his editors insist? This question is of particular importance since Melville's remark has been put into service as prophecy. (In the final paragraph of "The Composition of *Moby-Dick*," for example, James Barbour cites Melville's "all my works are botches" remark, giving the line the full force of the final word on the matter, and sums up his own argument like this: "Melville's appraisal for his effort is ironic, but also prophetic, for he realized that his Whale was the result of antithetical forces that he could no longer resolve—the need to secure an audience for his writing, coupled with an intense compulsion to tell the truth. The artistic paradox finally resulted in his long silence. For Melville his greatest effort was a failure.")[22]

Perhaps because Melville himself names the feeling that he will in the end be caught between pleasing his audience and pleasing himself a "presentiment,"[23] his proposition that "all my books are botches" is taken to offer a comprehensive account of a career Melville, writing in 1851, might well have imagined to be just getting started. *We* know his audience will never respond to him in the way he deserved or required, but in the months of aroused ambition in the summer of 1851, does he? Must the "all" of his remark include the book on which he was excitedly at work, as well as the books he had not yet begun, in addition to those whose fates he partially knew? Many scholars take it as self-evident that Melville included among his "botches" the manuscript on which he was then laboring—that *Moby-Dick* is the best or most perfect consequence of Melville's contradictory impulses. Certainly, the application of this remark across all time provides a framework in which each of Melville's books, as well as all his issues and conflicts, can be neatly sorted. But it also turns Melville's description into both an explanation and a formula, and there is something clearly fallacious in the argument that whatever Melville felt about work completed before 1850 must be applied to writing that was by all accounts having a transformative effect on him.

How do we square scholars' assurance that during the year and a half of *Moby-Dick*'s composition Melville undergoes change at something like the cellular level (again, his reading of Shakespeare and Hawthorne are generally cited as the catalysts) with the premise that the work he produces in these months is essentially the same: different in quality but not in kind? Here is the critic James Barbour arguing both that in the final stages of writing Melville and his manuscript were undergoing a conversion and that regardless of this change to the book's form and the author's state of mind, Melville decidedly grouped his new writing with the rest of his creations:

> By the early months of 1851 his good humor has passed: he resents intrusions upon his time and becomes irritable with Duyckinck. He then turns to Hawthorne to share his thoughts with his famous neighbor. His letters begin to reverberate with a fresh vigor and renewed energy. The voice and attitude they reflect are Ahab's, the statements are very much those of Shakespeare and Carlyle. Melville's mounting excitement continues throughout the spring and summer months, tempered only by his critical reflection that what he had produced was a "final hash."

This example should hold our attention for another reason. Barbour notes that in the June 1 letter to Hawthorne, Melville's voice is not, properly speaking, his own: his voice and attitude "are Ahab's," his statements "very much those of Shakespeare and Carlyle." Barbour is no doubt right. But then he is wrong to propose that Melville uses the opportunity this letter affords to "share his thoughts with his famous neighbor," as if Melville's letters were vehicles for introspection, occasions to record what he *really* thinks, with an honesty presumably not possible in his fiction.

Melville's letters do not contain news, or do not simply communicate the result of Melville's observation and experience—the descriptions out of which they are constructed are not empirical descriptions. Empirical descriptions have a settled or decided significance: that is why, as in the descriptions of natural science, the objective is to determine whether they are true or false. In contrast, what we might call Melville's aesthetic descriptions in these letters are used for elucidatory effect: the point is to grasp them rather than check whether or not they are accurate. When a writer attempts to represent something aesthetically, his descriptions do not grow out of a desire to report on what has actually happened to him. They are a result of his being intrigued and wanting to bring his vague impressions and marginalized feelings into distinct consciousness, and to do so with an audience in mind. The descriptions grow out of his attempt to manipulate and arrange and *make sense of* his experience, not give a direct account of it. That is why writing that attempts to represent aesthetically (*darstellen*) is characterized by the force of its illustrations, its synoptic qualities, its sublime connotations. It is a mode of presentation that pictures things vividly—that feels alert and tuned-in.

The descriptions in Melville's letters feel built to last. The impression that they are designed to endure—to feel real or credible or relevant to generations of readers—is underscored by our sense that Melville writes for an audience that may be amused or moved (as conceivably Hawthorne is not) by what he has written. For if Melville is not entirely Melville in these letters, it is also the case that Hawthorne is not Hawthorne; the person to whom Melville addresses these remarkable letters has more in keeping with the Hawthorne he hoped for than the Hawthorne he had. Melville declares his solidarity with Hawthorne "a little too flamboyantly," notes Kenneth Dauber. Though Hawthorne's inspiring influence on Melville is well known, Dauber argues that "it is important for an understanding of both Hawthorne and Melville not to exaggerate such a notion of inspiration. For a certain asymmetry in their dealings—the fact that our sense of the strength of their bond comes almost exclusively from a reading of the documents on Melville's side of the story"—suggests that Melville had to exaggerate their relation or aggressively assert the unity of his spirit with Hawthorne's "precisely because it did not in fact exist."[24] We could also put the matter this way: If Melville sounds like a character, or if the person writing these letters and the person to whom they are addressed are not exactly people historians would recognize, then we ought to read Melville's letters the same way we read his books. As with his fiction, Melville's letters reveal underlying suppositions about what art can do and how people and events can be represented in prose. And just as the writer of fiction describes states of affairs that feel real and are *contrived* to feel so, the ingenuous descriptions Melville assembles in his letters can hardly be understood as either an account of his mind or an exact rendering of his daily life. That is what, for Melville, makes them true, rather than a record of one person's (his) experience.

I have touched on the reason Melville should not be taken literally when he tells Hawthorne that all his books are botches—namely, that Melville's letters are written in that special mode of discourse in which reference isn't fixed and stabilized, or in which a writer's descriptions do not spring directly from his own experience but rather set up a movement between his thought and his life. What I want now to show is that this criterion of imaginative writing or of literature—its banishment of an exact correspondence between a given discourse and the world—is conveyed simply and clearly by Melville in "Hawthorne and His Mosses," the composition in which Melville engineers a view of himself and of his life's work that markedly contrasts with the "botched book" premise.[25]

Hawthorne appears in the title, but as Charles Olson first noted, the subject of Melville's critical review is "Hawthorne, Shakespeare, and Herman Melville."[26] By adopting the Emersonian position that genius recognizes genius, Melville assembles a portrait of the original American writer and makes unmistakable its likeness to himself.[27] Moreover, the picture here is emphatically not of a writer divided of mind and dissatisfied with his powers but of one marveling at his achievements and inventing a criticism that lays them out. This original writer is unrecognized, or recognized for the wrong things; he writes books that can be said to fail; he is a man of the times; the world feels as young to him as when it was created; he is master of "the great Art of Telling the Truth," "though it be covertly, and by snatches"; and, above all, for this is what furnishes the rest, there is a "blackness" in him, the "blackness of darkness beyond."[28]

This last claim is the one I want to look at closely, since it bears directly upon the question of what kind of writing Melville supposed he brought forth. Melville has gone to the trouble of producing his own criticism, the better to read him by, but the "mystical blackness" that figures centrally in his account of a writer's genius or originality has yet to be adequately understood. Olson, for example, locates Melville's blackness in his narratives, in Ahab's drama, his "hot hate for the white whale, and his vengeful pursuit of it," and thus thinks of blackness in dramatic terms, as a force of evil that finds its way into the writing "through the mouths of the dark characters."[29] But the blackness that so fascinates Melville isn't the cunning or wickedness that is lodged in characters or that powers dramatic action. Nor should the "power of blackness" as Melville frames it in this essay be simply understood as deriving from and pushing forward "that Calvinistic sense of Innate Depravity and Original Sin," an atavistic fear "from whose visitations, in some shape or another, no deeply thinking mind is always and wholly free" that Melville identifies as the ancestral force evident in all Hawthorne's writing.[30]

As I understand it, the blackness "*in* Hawthorne" or *in* Shakespeare that Melville describes in "Hawthorne and His Mosses" (the "black conceit" that pervades a writer "through and through") has rather a lot to do with the way a writer makes imagined events convincing. Blackness, as Melville introduces it in this essay, is the precondition for poetic mimesis:

> Now it is that blackness in Hawthorne, of which I have spoken, that so fixes and fascinates me . . . this blackness it is that furnishes the infinite obscure of his background,—that background, against which Shakespeare plays his grandest conceits, the things that have made for Shakespeare his loftiest, but most circumscribed renown, as the profoundest of thinkers. For by philosophers Shakespeare is not adored as the great man of tragedy and comedy.—"Off with his head! So much for Buckingham!" this sort of rant, interlined by another hand, brings down the house,—those mistaken souls, who dream of Richard-the-Third humps, and Macbeth daggers. But it is those deep far-away things in him; those occasional flashings-forth of intuitive Truth in him; those short, quick probings at the very axis of reality:—these are the things that make Shakespeare, Shakespeare.[31]

In Melville's account, *Richard III* or *Macbeth* reveal the "flashings-forth of intuitive Truth" in Shakespeare because these plays demonstrate the poet's expressive working out of an attitude—scheming ambition or a monarch's unscrupulous rise to power. In daily life, this attitude could be named and put to immediate practical service, but as Charles Altieri writes, "poets tend to want their attitudes more complex and more perspicuous than that. They want a sense that the poem realizes something by having its naming process produce a fresh twist on our standard cultural repertoire."[32]

Shakespeare's Richard or Macbeth are in other words not persons but figures, as Auerbach calls them, wholly fictitious characters whose distinctive personalities are fully encompassed by the event that is being related. Hence it isn't simply verisimilitude that gives Shakespeare's characters the appearance of vigorous life and freshness, or changes them from remote sketches of legendary villains—all humps and daggers—into finely drawn, idiosyncratic beings in whom palpable, concrete reality is intensely preserved. In dress, in the inflections of his speech, in the features of his castle's interior, the titular character of *Richard III* might well resemble the Richard who ruled England from 1843 to 1845, but what really leaves a strong impression on readers' senses is Shakespeare's representation or realization of a complex state of mind. In *Richard III* it is ambition itself (and ambition as an attitude that reconciles competing pulls, not all of which are unsavory) that is rendered so clear and palpable it seems to be part of the physical, natural world.

By emphasizing Shakespeare's realism, his "short, quick probings at the very axis of reality," Melville isn't extolling Shakespeare's impression of actual people and the readily perceivable world. Instead, he is admiring the emergence of certain states of affairs in Shakespeare's writing—for example, the ardent desire for rank, fame, or power. The ability to picture the objects *Plato* called real—conceptual objects—is Shakespeare's commendable achievement and, as Melville says, the reason philosophers adore him.

Melville's submission in "Hawthorne and His Mosses" is thus that Shakespeare and other masters of the art of telling the truth are masters of hypotyposis. As a rhetorical term, hypotyposis indicates the ability to present imagined events as if they were practically going on—to present an abstract entity or spiritual event as if it were visible to the eye.[33] The aesthetic goal of hypotyposis is sensible illustration (*subjectio sub adspectum*), likenesses so strikingly represented they seem to be present. However, because the ability to create these likenesses precludes the possibility of a direct correspondence between a writer's modes of expression and sensual reality (since representing something that is both material and spiritual requires *more* than experience alone can provide), the writer who cooks them up must have "blackness" in him. In "Hawthorne and His Mosses," Melville makes the case that only a writer who has blackness in him is able to generate real and evident figures in a work of art. Like Richard and Macbeth, these figures are not copies of persons but rather spiritual matters made manifest, intangible states of affairs artfully arranged to give the impression of independent existence.

Melville's theorizing about blackness in "Mosses" thus calls to mind exactly why imaginative writers must "establish a theater," as Hawthorne writes in his preface to *The Blithedale Romance*, "a little removed from the highway of ordinary travel, where the creatures of his brain may play their phantasmagorical antics, without exposing them to too close a comparison with the actual events of real lives."[34] In his preface, Hawthorne entreats readers to recall the contrived setting fiction requires and in this way establishes a connection, the same one Melville spelled out in "Hawthorne and His Mosses," between his *Blithedale Romance* and the great imaginative works of European literature. However, after noting that his book should be understood as mimetic fiction, Hawthorne explains why it won't be:

> In the old countries, with which fiction has long been conversant, a certain conventional privilege seems to be awarded to the romancer; his work is not put exactly side by side with nature; and he is allowed a license with regard to every-day probability, in view of the improved effects which he is bound to produce thereby. Among ourselves, on the contrary, there is as yet no such Faery Land, so like the real world,

> that, in a suitable remoteness, one cannot well tell the difference, but with an atmosphere of strange enchantment, beheld through which the inhabitants have a propriety of their own. This atmosphere is what the American romancer needs.[35]

As Hawthorne had perceived, granting the usual privilege of fiction writers to American authors was proving difficult for mid-nineteenth-century American readers, who hungered for faithful accounts of actual people and events, not descriptions of people and events contrived against darkness—*creations* or the kinds of being modeled in Genesis. America's taste for believable fantastic fiction (for an imagined "Faery Land, so like the real world that . . . one cannot well tell the difference") was increasingly giving way, before it was even properly established, to a preference for narratives that recounted the writer's genuine thoughts and lived experience.

Because the readers of personal narratives are invited to peer *through* writing to the world it ostensibly depicts, theirs is a critical act devoted above all to finding out how much of a narrative is bona fide, as Melville discovered to his dismay after writing *Typee*. It is then the decidedly "un-American" prize of a reader's gradual struggle to look *at* a writer's chosen words and so perceive their meaning—the slow flowering of insight that attends the study of an author's conceived or imagined world—that Melville champions when he favors literature as Hawthorne writes it: lifelike writing designed to showcase an author's speculative powers.[36]

What Hawthorne and Melville call "romance," accordingly, is mimetic fiction—imagined worlds so like the real one in some respects that it can be hard to tell the difference, were it not for the signs the author gives (the introduction of a narrator, for example) that there is "blackness" in him, a blackness that "furnishes the infinite obscure of his background" or allows him to play out his grandest conceits. A writer who has blackness in him is free to draw on personal experience to color his fiction, as Hawthorne says, or avail himself of his actual reminiscences "in the hope of giving a more life-like tint" to a work of imagination, precisely because the mode in which he writes indicates that what is reflected in his writing aren't things in the world but what Melville calls "the conjectural parts of the mind that produced them." By the same token a writer who does *not* have blackness in him, or whose writing lacks the perceptible limit between art and life, finds himself restricted to the most meager kind of copy or reflection of sensible life. As Hawthorne writes, the "beings of his imagination are compelled to show themselves in the same category as actually living mortals; a necessity that generally renders the paint and pasteboard of their composition but too painfully discernable."

Now, the surest indicator that an author has blackness in him or that his picture of reality is invented is his creation of the figure—the character who, for all his or her individuality, also embodies a rigorous doctrine. Thus Hawthorne's Zenobia, who is scorned for her radiance, or who in her person and her fate reveals the outcome of masculine egotism, never ceases to give off a very distinctive, particular, sensuous charm.[37] Only by encompassing his character's personality in the event that is being related is Hawthorne able to bring his creature of the imagination palpably to life.

In Melville's portrait of poetic genius, accordingly, the original writer or writer worth adoring helps himself to his actual reminiscences, but the books he authors are wholly structured as invented narratives. Melville's explicit insistence in "Hawthorne and His Mosses" is that those writers he calls "masters of the great Art of Telling the Truth" do *not* simply copy what they have seen or felt. They do not, as Gilles Deleuze says, "impose a form (of expression) on the matter of lived experience," since "to write is not to recount one's memories and travels, one's loves and griefs, one's dreams and fantasies."[38] What Deleuze calls that "infantile conception of literature" is in "Mosses" replaced by the view that no matter how much it resembles the tangible world, the world the writer summons is conjured by the writer. Instead of merely reflecting the lives of people he knows or proceedings he has lived through (unavoidably making "the paint and pasteboard of their composition . . . painfully discernable," as Hawthorne—echoing Plato—writes), the writer who wishes to express truths or imitate reality must exercise his occult power of invention, his faculty for creation, his power sublime and supernal, the holy power of language to call forth a world.[39]

Melville's promotion of himself and Hawthorne as poets for a new age, masters of the art of truth telling, should thus have troubled what lives on as the most unquestioned feature of the botched-book thesis: critics' conviction that different modes of representation jostle one another in the pages of *Moby-Dick*, or that Melville's book is *by turns* fanciful and factual. Brodhead, for example, says that "having begun one sort of book," nautical adventure narrative, Melville was "willing to throw that over in the middle and pursue an entirely new direction"—to write sentimental romance; that Melville was bored by the conventions of fiction writing and careless about his novel's form.[40] Some critics have even suggested that Melville throws together fictional and *nonfictional* modes, that out of carelessness, or inadequate preparation for the task he had set for himself, or an exaggerated commitment to conflicting instincts, an unwillingness to be guided by literary tradition or to conform to the conventions of genre, Melville put together a book that is not even properly fictional.[41] Citing what they take to be the heterogeneity of Melville's book, its "ill-compounded mixture of romance and matter-of-fact," as one of Melville's contemporaries writes, such critics conclude that *Moby-Dick* is not a book created out of whole cloth from Melville's generating mind.

As a result, and however clear that an imaginative writer's prolonged feat of mimesis is not merely a reflection of physical things or actual events, it is still a commonly held theory that large sections of *Moby-Dick* offer transcriptions of the physical, temporal world; that parts of the book portray life in a faithful manner, unclouded by the imagination or by literary conventions. And yet what Melville says about blackness wrenches that hypothesis all out of shape, since the author who uses blackness as a background in order to present "more reality, than real life itself can show"[42] is never or under no circumstances reporting on things he's discovered through his senses. He is rather trying to offer a convincing or persuasive picture of objects and events his powers of imagination have called forth. We must therefore conclude that *Moby-Dick* is written in a single register, for a writer who avails himself of blackness writes *only* fiction, and of fiction, *only* romance.

Of course the idea that Melville understood himself to be writing a romance is commonplace, since for certain writers of the American renaissance that was the term associated with fiction that gained its unity not through plot but through a central conceptual focus.[43] For Melville and his near contemporaries, chief among them Poe and Hawthorne, romance represented a "farther realm of fiction," as Richard Chase has noted, a "freer, more daring, more brilliant fiction,"[44] whose great interest did not come from the order of events in a book but rather from the aesthetic purpose to which the telling of those events could be put. For these writers, romance was never "mere" romance; it was above all the form that enabled what Poe in his preface to *Eureka* calls "literature proper." A book of romance could not be considered alongside books of nonfiction or books of fiction that recount their authors' genuine thoughts and lived experience, for the reason that a book of romance was, as Poe observes, "an Art-Product alone." And yet for all that the ambition of such writing was to effect a close correspondence between art and life. It fell to the author of romance to summon what Auerbach calls the "real and evident figure" in a work of art: something *envisaged*, but believable all the same.[45]

In naming his mature fiction "romance," then, Melville undoubtedly signals his intention to uphold what philosopher and literary critic A. D. Nuttall calls the "robust possible relation between fiction and the truth."[46] Today "fiction" is practically synonymous with "falsehood," but fiction's autochthonous connection to the truth was a central preoccupation for Melville, who understood his work to carry out in prose what had traditionally been the province of poetry. The value of this writing lies in its power to interpret the natural world, to express "with magical felicity the physiognomy and movement of the outward world," as Matthew Arnold notes, and at the same time to interpret the moral world, to express "with inspired conviction, the ideas and laws of the inward world of man's moral and spiritual nature."[47] Such writing has at times been known as "higher fiction" or "literature" or "poetry," but to Melville, who wished to import the techniques of Shakespeare into a novel, the way Goethe had, replete with the ordinary novelistic requirements of verisimilitude, it was known as "romance."

Why, then, the universal impression that Melville's *Moby-Dick* isn't *wholly* a romance? Why is Hawthorne the exemplar of this kind of literary narrative, while Melville's most consummate art product is thought to fish regularly in the waters of what one of Hawthorne's reviewers calls, disdainfully, "the realm of fact"?

Perhaps because even as Hawthorne and Melville wrote their great romances, and despite their ready protestations, the writing known as romance was typically understood to be *less* concerned with real life than writing that imposed form on lived experience—fictional narratives that drew on the author's firsthand observations, or personal narratives like Richard Henry Dana Jr.'s *Two Years Before the Mast* and Frederick Douglass's *Narrative of the Life of Frederick Douglass*, which, as Jonathan Arac notes, served as reports of activity on the margins of national life. That Melville's romances seem full of what Hawthorne in *The Marble Faun* calls the "insisted upon" actualities of everyday life is the reason many readers assume that Melville anchored his literary or romantic narratives in an accurate or faithful account of his own experience. This in turn has led to the conviction that the generic basis of *Moby-Dick* is personal narrative—even if, as Arac notes, it is personal narrative "pushed beyond its limits."[48] As Hershel Parker reasons, "it seems most likely that Melville started to write *Moby-Dick* on the pattern of his five earlier books, as a sailor-voyager's firsthand account of his experiences and observations, ashore and aship, amid ways of life strange at first to him and still strange to his stay-at-home readers."[49]

What this insistence on *Moby-Dick*'s genesis in personal narrative reveals is that for the majority of Melville's readers, a romance can be truthful, but only at the *cost* of its connection to the material world. The more frequently concrete reality seems to appear in Melville's writing, the more exactly he proves able to relate temporal events and corporeal substance, the less like a writer of romance he seems.

This view is defensible, but those who hold it have not recalled how, in the great imaginative works of Dante or Shakespeare, the material world has been intensely preserved. Indeed, the truths these writers express hinge on their astute, unflagging attentiveness to earthly existence, to history and politics. Rather than dispense with close observation of how things appear to his senses, a conceptual or imaginative writer is obliged to center his attention to a remarkable degree on material life. The conceptual writer's frank investment in the world as he experiences it is requisite to his effective representation of reality, the realm in which mental life is moved and transformed by material life.

Moby-Dick is thus rightly called "realism" or "romance"—but not a *mixture* of these, since this would be to suggest that the realist and the romancer offer contrasting effects. Pitting the believability of Melville's writing against the author's powers of imagination has confused Melville's standing as a master of the art of telling the truth. For as critics have long enjoyed pointing out, the natural world or experiential life is rendered closely and in comprehensive detail in *Moby-Dick*; at the same time, much of the book is written in a heightened poetic tone, characters don't speak the vernacular natural to them, and the author is liable to "stand about in his scene, talking it over with his hands in his pockets," as William Dean Howells complained of Thackeray, "interrupting the action and spoiling the illusion."[50] This seeming juxtaposition has led many critics to conclude that *Moby-Dick* is a work of fascinating modernity, but not a proper romance, and not an accurate representation of American life.[51]

Thus it hardly matters whether Melville is deemed to be writing romance anchored in personal narrative or personal narrative that bursts the fetters of genre and becomes romance. For the reason that they are mistakenly set in opposition, Melville's powers of vision and of observation are assumed to rival one another. Or as Brodhead argues, in his romantic narratives Melville "enacts a strong imagined design but always eventually gives in to the impulse to look over his shoulder to see how it squares with the texture of actual life; he creates shapely and self-enclosed forms, and then makes room within them for the ragged edges of mangled realities. In *Mardi*'s terms Melville as a novelist wants to be both poet and historian."[52]

Finally, the case against Melville, his reputation as the author of botched books, boils down to the accusation that there are times Melville tries to accurately reflect his experience, and times he tries to transcend experience altogether in order to aim at some abstract, idealized truth. While some critics think this a problem Melville didn't adequately solve, and others think that the book's triumph is premised upon his not solving it, few hesitate to describe the novel as a kind of "mixed medium," a rich confusion of different kinds of fiction, if indeed it qualifies as proper fiction at all as opposed to what the novel's contemporary reviewers itemized as "instructive sketches of the fishery, of sea-life in a whaling vessel, and of the manners and customs of strange nations," with the less-pleasing addition of a "vein of moralizing" and the "piratical running down of creeds and opinions."[53]

This emphasis on *Moby-Dick*'s heterogeneity—the view that it is what Melville's own generation knew as "a singular medley of naval observation, magazine article writing, satiric reflection upon the conventionalism of civilized life, and rhapsody"; "a romance, a tragedy, and a natural history, not without numerous gratuitous suggestions on psychology, ethics, and theology"; "an odd book, professing to be a novel"—has in time only grown, as new readers find better ways to celebrate what they see as the book's composition from dissimilar parts. If some nineteenth-century critics believed that Melville's unclassifiable hodgepodge of literature, essay, political tract, and natural history brought to mind an author not properly in control of his powers, many twentieth- and twenty-first-century critics see Melville's decision to tell his story in a number of ways as characteristic of writing that aims to reproduce something like the expansiveness and range of life itself—and so find in the dual nature of his book the source of its richness and grandeur.[54] In consequence, almost all Melville's current readers have continued to call attention to the strange contrast, in *Moby-Dick*, between what Melville's contemporary George Ripley takes to be the author's "minute, painstaking fidelity" to actual or likely events in his life and the "weird, phantom-like character" of his book's plot.[55] Even though Melville himself gives a strong impression of his sincere and sober yearning to produce one kind of writing, therefore, our prevailing picture of him is of a man undecided, who abruptly and as if by uncontrolled impulse shifts suddenly between analyses of data to wonder about the ultimate coordinates of existence, from painstaking fidelity to recorded fact to an investigation into the nature of the world, and back again.

Interestingly, the most damning, and, it turns out, lasting view of Melville was provided by his friend Evert A. Duyckinck, who articulates first and most memorably the connection between what falls short in Melville's books and what Duyckinck calls their "double character." Duyckinck's pronouncement that Melville's novels of romance are "in one light . . . romantic fictions, in another statements of absolute fact" has stuck like little else in the history of Melville scholarship.[56] The past century and a half of Melville criticism have not overturned this judgment, though critics have taken it in diverging directions. In his review, Duyckinck might as well have called *Moby-Dick* a "botch" and its author the unwitting wrecker of what could have been writing of the highest quality:

> Under the combined influences of personal observation, actual fidelity to truthfulness in description, a taste for reading and sentiment, a fondness for fanciful analogies, near and remote, a rash daring in speculation, reckless at times of taste and propriety, again refined and eloquent, this volume of Moby Dick may be pronounced a most remarkable sea-dish—an intellectual chowder of romance, philosophy, natural history, fine writing, good feeling, bad sayings—but over which in spite of all uncertainties, and in spite of the author himself, predominates his keen perceptive faculties, exhibited in vivid narration.

Publicly, as a man of letters, Duyckinck calls *Moby-Dick* "an intellectual chowder." Privately, and in the admiring but condescending tone he often used to describe the young author he thought of as a protégé, he writes to Joanne Miller, "I am glad that you were favorably impressed with Moby Dick—I fear that you will not close the volume with the same satisfaction—I feel out of all patience with Melville for almost willfully spoiling his book."[57]

Thus we have it: the case against Melville. The author's "spoiled" book or book professing to be a novel is part authentic account of his actual experience, part metaphysical romance; on the one hand marked by its direct stand on issues of local or national importance, on the other by a distance from current events sometimes associated with the dreaming poet. Half voiced in the good-humored, casually chatty narration beloved of popular readers, half delivered in the elliptical, ambiguous narration wherein a reader cannot always be sure what is meant. And behind this miscreation is Melville, springing back and forth repeatedly and heedlessly between these two incompatible modes of representing, pausing only long enough to lament his fate.

And yet . . . and yet. Our strongest evidence that the book is as Duyckinck says a mixture of romantic fiction and statements of absolute fact is only that we *feel* it to be so. Parts of the book appear to come out of an analytic or empiricist tradition, particularly those parts heavy, we now know, with interpolated passages Melville has gathered from natural histories. Parts of it—the intense and tragic parts, or as Duyckinck writes, "the romance of Captain Ahab, Queequeg, Tashtego, Pip & Co., who are more or less spiritual personages talking and acting differently from the general business run of the conversation on the decks of whalers"—have the "romantic spiritual cast of the German drama."[58] Readers have long believed they could tell the difference between these parts. Also that they could be sure there *was* a difference or that what had been generated was a kind of mixed medium because Melville himself admitted to it when he confessed that all his books were botches.

I hope to have at least troubled the assumption that Melville felt himself to be making a confession in that remark, or that he believed himself to be writing in two different representational modes. There is more evidence in his writing (as well as in his letters, if that is where we wish to look for it) that suggests otherwise. Indications on the surface of these texts confirm that Melville did not think he was moving back and forth between realism and romance—which, when done rightly, were for him identical. If there is overwhelming evidence for the "double character" of Melville's work in Melville criticism, there is not very much in his *Moby-Dick*, which rather astonishingly subsumes all the verisimilitude required of depictions of material and temporal life into a larger order, the form of the romance.

What happens, then, if we take as an initiating premise the idea that Melville's whaling narrative *has no* double character or is not, as Duyckinck and so many others have worried, part observation and part invention—that on the contrary the book is through and through a romance, what Melville, describing *Mardi*, calls "a *real* romance," a book that "is no Typee or Omoo" but "made of different stuff altogether"?[59] There is much to be gained by not concluding that Melville starts his most energetically conceived romance like a personal narrative and then decides to alter the frame in which he works—that he writes down his experiences, then feels compelled to embellish them; that he writes two books, a going-to-sea story and a daring metaphysical adventure.[60] We are then free to argue instead that Melville turns *from the beginning* to what Elizabeth S. Foster names a "remarkably varied but by no means random cluster" of writers in order to help manufacture what Robert Milder calls "a home-grown version of German Encyclopaedic Romance."[61] Inspired no more by Dana than by Goethe (whose large, liberal view of human life seemed in Melville's day novel, and salutary, and educative), Melville never does attempt to construct the kind of book that springs from observation—*especially* when that is what his book seems most to do.

Melville's meticulous descriptions of whaling life have led many readers of *Moby-Dick* to see two books rolled into one—to see, in short, a literary narrative perched precariously atop accounts of the author's firsthand observations. But in this we have been mistaken. Better to say, as Auerbach says of Dante, that Melville transports his readers into a strange world so seemingly palpable and concrete "that it seems real while life itself becomes a fragmentary dream." Not that the empirical world has vanished in the fiction. Rather, "it has grown doubly plain and tangible. But the light is different and the eyes must grow accustomed to it; they must acquire a new and sharper vision which passes over no detail as unimportant, commonplace, or fragmentary; whatever appears in that place is definitive and immutable, demanding the fullest and most careful attention."[62]

Melville, like Shakespeare and Hawthorne, has blackness in him. We ought to be secure in the impression that Melville's *Moby-Dick* is a romance (a book that preserves the everlasting distinction between the world the writer depicts and the world he inhabits) because only then are we able to see *Moby-Dick* as a work of realism: an invented narrative vested with the capacity to put real things—made up of matter and spirit both—before our eyes.

Melville's ambition in his whaling narrative is to imitate real life: to put together *postulated* objects in such a way as to make them visible. That is why the language of *Moby-Dick* is the language of living record, not of extravagant and unrestrained fantasy. The meticulous details that constitute *Moby-Dick*'s bulk are essential to the book's overall aim—to present "the configured truth," as Auerbach identifies mimesis, the conjuring art, and, as Auerbach reasons, the first demand that the configured truth makes on one who sets out to communicate it is the ability to take note of concrete reality.[63] To our discussion of the configured truth in *Moby-Dick* we are now free to proceed.

Chapter 2

✦

Melville's Reconstructed Realism

> The Universe is true for all of us and different for each one of us.
>
> —Proust

Melville's aesthetic problem in *Moby-Dick*, Hershel Parker has argued, "was how to reconcile a realistic account of whaling processes with a poetic treatment of the subject"—how to work a faithful depiction of whaling (such as the one Richard Henry Dana Jr. envisaged when he advised Melville to write a book based on his experiences) into literary form.[1] However, the trouble with this explanation is that it subtly continues the tradition of opposing "things visible" to "things imaginative"—of understanding our world and ourselves in terms of the conflict between the phenomenal world, what the Greeks called nature, or *physis*, and the noumenal world, *nomos*, all that responds to or is the creation of the human mind. In addition to being the source of a good deal of intellectual anguish, this division of the world into two realms (and the related claim that everything nonmaterial must be subjective, private, internal to the mind, and, therefore, devoid of objective, communal, cognitive value) has grievous repercussions on the way we conceive of language. Typically language is regarded in one of two ways: as a device for describing the nature of empirical reality, in which case meaning is created externally to language, or as a symbolic system wherein meaning is determined internally through the relation of words to one another, in which case the natural world is not a source of meaning in language.

Neither account serves Melville. My suggestion in this book is thus that in Melville we find a thinker antagonistic to the practice in Western philosophy of contrasting the natural world to the workings of mind, and in *Moby-Dick* a powerful alternative to it, one that advances an altogether different view of both literature and language. I show how the mimesis of a Melvillean scene (or, to employ a term that has become uncertain and confusing, *Moby-Dick*'s realism) follows from Melville's conclusion that the material world and conceptual life are *not* at odds, and thus that in his writing he needn't theatrically reconcile objects of sense and creations of the understanding.[2] For Melville the important thing is not to separate imaginative life from reality but rather to safeguard the imaginative writer's flair for devising clarifying pictures of the world in which we find ourselves. By this account, no matter how faithful it is to his own experience Melville's fiction never simply reports on daily life. It is better understood as an instrument for helping readers participate self-reflexively in our shared world, by these means making the world a more vital place for habitation.[3]

For that reason it is helpful to emphasize another way of grasping Melville's aesthetic problem in *Moby-Dick*—the same problem Melville lays out in his chief contribution to literary criticism, "Hawthorne and His Mosses." For the subject of Melville's essay isn't (as Parker's digest would suggest) the difficulty of turning a redescription of everyday life into elevated art. Melville's subject is rather the representation of reality in writing—what transpires when, through *sheerly verbal means*, imaginative writers contrive to help readers catch glimpses of earthly life. Instead of undermining the whole terminology of representation, the relation of writing to anything outside itself, Melville's essay defends and helps justify what Auerbach calls "the configured truth" and Melville calls "the great Art of Telling the Truth." The writer's capacity or incapacity for mimesis is the central concern of Melville's essay.

Rather than describe an existing world in language, Melville thinks writers who represent reality ultimately renovate their readers' outlook and mood. But because this dispositional shift demands a reader's full engagement with the fictional world, the portrayal of the fictional world must be convincing. The careful selecting of details is a sure means by which an imaginative writer produces a world that solicits a reader's corresponding imaginative activity—and these *details* must not be imagined but in keeping with the world the writer inhabits. In his chief work of literary criticism Melville shows how an author's creative or imaginative powers are kindled by his struggle for historical concreteness, by, as Auerbach says, the possibility of configuring man "not as a remote legendary hero, not as an abstract or anecdotal representative of an ethical type, but man as we know him in his living historical reality, the concrete individual in his unity and wholeness."[4] As Melville emphasizes, however, the writer's obligation isn't to individual historical people but to the creation of what Auerbach calls the "real and evident figure" in a work of art, the "figure full of reality" or what Melville names an "original character," one whose eternal attitude shows the concordance of personal traits with the providential course of the world.[5]

In "Hawthorne and His Mosses," the matter under investigation is how an American might write the way Shakespeare did (with "that decided originality that merits great praise" and with the literary genius's "patience, or palate, for the spiritual truth") without quitting the country, as Melville says, or without lavishing his insights on an alien land. For "believe it or not," Melville writes, "England, after all, is, in many things alien to us." To Melville, the "great mistake" seems to be that even "those Americans who look forward to the coming of a great literary genius among us . . . somehow fancy he will come in the costume of Queen Elizabeth's day." Getting in the way of Americans' trust that "Shakespeares are this day being born on the banks of the Ohio" is the certainty that the writer who shares Shakespeare's genius will share his Elizabethan outlook and attire—that he will "be a writer of dramas founded upon old English history, or the tales of Boccaccio." [6]

Thus to the problem of finding an American genius Melville poses a ready solution. It lies in the discovery that "great geniuses are part of the times," as Melville writes, "they themselves are the times; and possess a correspondent coloring." By the time Melville fires off his essay in August 1850 he is convinced that the great writer his countrymen await will be fully a part of teeming, contemporary daily life, as was William Shakespeare in his own lifetime.[7] As in Shakespeare's plays, the writer's description of imaginary events and situations will manifest what is unique to the world in which the writer actually lives, his particular time and identifiable place. Melville's answer to the question of how an American might rival Shakespeare, in other words, is that he must trumpet rather than suppress the sensory concreteness, the unique physical presence, of his imagined beings. The great writer will demonstrate convincing knowledge of the notable events and particular characteristics of his age because his writing's realistic imperatives (and consequently his ability to give characters who are entirely fictitious what Hawthorne calls "a propriety of their own") is what allows him to play out his "grandest conceits," as Melville writes in "Mosses"—the sublime visions that give the writer his renown.

Naturalistic observation is accordingly indispensable to an author when what he is writing is unmistakably *romance*, or when the world his writing generates isn't a direct imitation of the world in which he lives but is instead a kind of parallel world in which objects and events can be seen clearly. That is, a master of the art of telling the truth can dream up imagined worlds so like our own that one cannot well tell the difference precisely because he never loses his hold on the definite particular. As readers of Melville's whaling narrative are reminded, the desire for mimesis prevents the writer from simply letting his imagination roam, gathering up random fragments or snippets that titillate his fancy, as did the painter Guido Reni in his picture of Perseus rescuing Andromeda from the whale. ("Where did Guido get the model of such a strange creature as that?" Ishmael wonders when he takes note of the "very picturesque but purely fabulous" creatures touted as whales in Guido's painting.) An author wishing to represent reality—to portray, as Ishmael says, "something like the true form of the whale as he actually appears to the eye of the whaleman when in his own absolute body the whale is moored alongside the whale-ship so that he can be fairly stepped upon there"—cannot simply adopt the sort of license that prevailed in what Ishmael calls the "inventive but unscrupulous times" in which pictures of whales were based on artists' mistaken, erroneous, or wildly embellished impressions.

Though Parker names "formidable" the question of how an ordinary inhabitant of Melville's time and place might ascend to Shakespearean greatness, and describes it as an aesthetic and cultural problem Melville "must have been brooding about," by May or June of 1850 Melville had a clear sense of how to achieve that goal. In a letter to the English publisher Richard Bentley of June 27, Melville makes the second known reference to what became *Moby-Dick* when he characterizes his new manuscript as "a romance of adventure, founded upon certain wild legends in the Southern Sperm Whale Fisheries, and illustrated by the author's own personal experience, of two years & more, as a harpooner."[8]

The vital point here is that Melville's story is *founded on* "wild legends" or is at base imaginative, and that it is *illustrated by* experience—that the author uses his sensory knowledge and gift for realistic detail to color the story or give it what Hawthorne in his preface to *The Blithedale Romance* calls a "life-like tint." The arresting feature of Melville's description to Bentley isn't therefore that "Melville strained the Truth by claiming such service as a harpooner," as Parker writes, but that in his summary of what kind of book he had written, Melville offers an elucidating hint regarding his determination "to give the truth of the thing," as he tells Dana, in his poetic treatment of whaling.

In Melvillean terms, the relation between fiction and the truth is borne out when a conceptual object (for example, what Ishmael calls "the true form of the whale") is portrayed in a way that is convincing, or that doesn't clash with any actual experience of those natural objects that bear the same name (in Ishmael's phrase, "the whale as he actually appears to the eye of the whaleman").

An inspiring instance of such writing is the book of Job, which "apart from all theories about it," as Carlyle argues, is "one of the grandest things ever written with pen."[9] For Carlyle, Job's great merit as a work of literature has to do with its anonymous author's "true eyesight and vision for all things; material things no less than spiritual." Regarding Job's depiction of a horse ("Hast thou clothed his neck with *thunder?*" "he *laughs* at the shaking of the spear!"), Carlyle writes, "Such living likenesses were never since drawn." The phrase "living likenesses" is a useful one for the way it emphasizes that real life is what is *captured* in the picture, not what engenders it. A horse truly drawn is an imitation of the concept "horse," not an imitation of a living horse. What is being successfully imitated in the book of Job is what Carlyle calls the "poetic beauty" of the horse, its "inexhaustible significance." Yet without what Carlyle names "the seeing eye, the mildly understanding heart" in evidence in the poem, the concept "horse" could not be made manifest. The Jobian horse would be indistinct; what is most particular and discernible about it would not be fully preserved. The book of Job's most striking feature is consequently its author's refusal to dissociate the inexhaustible significance of objects, what Plato called their "beauty," from their intelligible, tangible manifestations.

A "living likeness" is what is achieved when a cultural hypothesis like "horse"—an abstract entity postulated to ground and illuminate the relations of qualitative identity and resemblance between particular, tangible objects—is so vividly and palpably rendered that it seems visible to the eye. Talking about living likenesses is another way of describing hypotyposis, a rhetorician's way of naming what happens when a conceptual entity is so strikingly portrayed it seems to be present.[10] Living likenesses as Carlyle identifies them are spiritual matters made manifest—intangible states of affairs artfully arranged to give the impression of independent existence. In a book that is "*true* in every way," as Carlyle says of Job, what the writer summons is a conceptual object, a linguistic construct or a being that has no existence in nature prior to its constitution in language. But this conceptual object is what the writer is then able to scrupulously furnish with a believable outward aspect, a set of features not unlike those that decorate natural objects as they actually appear to those who have encountered them.

Writers who purport to imitate real life must be able to discriminate between conceptual objects and natural objects, it thus stands to reason, since even when a natural object instantiates a conceptual object (as when the visible, palpable creature a whaler hunts would seem to represent, by a concrete instance, the conceptual object "whale"), we must admit that it is not *the same* as the conceptual object. Even so, and this is what fascinates the author of *Moby-Dick*, what gives the conceptual object "whale" dimension in a written work, what allows the writer's representation of what is ultimately abstract to feel substantial and convincing, is his ability to apprehend natural objects in respect to how they appear momentarily and simultaneously to his senses.

In order to depict "the true form of the whale as he actually appears to the eye of the whaleman," that is to say, Melville has to employ that "sensuous knowledge," as Alexander Baumgarten calls it in *Aesthetica* (1750), that governs the consideration of the particular in a work of art. The goal of sensuous knowledge (*cognitio sensitiva*), or what we now call aesthetic knowledge, is "consideration of the particular," as Martin Seel reports. "To know the particular in its particularity is the real accomplishment of *cognitio sensitiva*, which is something no science will be able to achieve."[11] Aesthetic knowledge is employed not in order to analyze complex phenomena in their composition "but to make them present in their intuitive density." When something is apprehended aesthetically, it "is not determined *as something*; "rather, it is apprehended in the repleteness of its features."[12]

Now, in *Moby-Dick* the whale is apprehended aesthetically. However, and for the reason that Melville's whale is, God knows, fully determined *as* a whale, it is also depicted truthfully; that is, what is depicted is not a natural object but a conceptual object. Rather than say Melville makes the whale "present in its intuitive density," then, we should say that in his whaling narrative Melville creates a living likeness of the conceptual object "whale"—in short, that he makes visible this *true thing*, an instance of what Plato called the "more precious things" (*timiotera*), beings from the conceptual realm. For Melville, however, this feat demands the inclusion of aesthetic knowledge, that sensuous comprehension lingering with individual things at the moment of their appearing. Like the author of Job, Melville refuses to dissociate the inexhaustible significance of the whale from its intelligible manifestations.[13] From his book thus emerges "visible truth," as Melville names it in a letter to Hawthorne of 1851: the visible rendering of conceptual matter.[14] Melville's ability to generate moments of visible truth is why *Moby-Dick* is rightly compared to the book of Job; like the biblical original, it records the sentient dimension of the noumenal world.

When Melville gives the cultural hypothesis or conceptual object "whale" a sense of particularity, in *Moby-Dick*—when he outfits the eternal, absolute (or, better, ubiquitous) whale with those features he's drawn from discrete, corporeal whales, those natural objects that are not immortal or imperishable but unique, distinctive, and destructible—he helps readers apprehend an object that can really only be seen intuitively.[15] He clothes conceptual matter in a perceptible guise. For Melville, appreciably, the descriptive features or characteristics that can be put into operation in his depiction of the generality "whale" are never determinative; they do not fix, settle, or define what the whale is, but they do impart to representation all the luster of desire, as Barthes says, or turn what is otherwise only an abstraction into a palpable, unmistakable entity.

In light of these deliberations, I'd like to reframe the problem Melville tackles in *Moby-Dick*—the problem to which the whole of the novel is in some sense a response. For what troubles Melville isn't the choice of his imaginative or his perceptive powers, since to be a master of "the great Art of Telling the Truth" requires maximum commitment to both ways of apprehending reality, as each type of consideration beholds the given in an essentially different manner.

No. As I see it, the more serious concern for Melville is how to defend the integrity of language as a means for communicating truth. Language needs defending in this manner because words are unquestionably human inventions, while what our words *signify*, the situations outside in the world our words pick out—"the living whale in his full majesty and significance," when the word is "whale"—cannot be attributed to human inventiveness.

In *Moby-Dick* Melville defends language as a means for communicating truths. That is, he defends the relation of identity between words and what they signify. For Melville, not doing so—failing to show that a relation *does hold* between language as a semantic order and "what the world is like"—allies him with one or the other of two equally contemptible views. Either he will be guilty of Platonism, which, as Melville introduces the term, indicates a debased, vulgar form of spiritualism that can neither apprehend nor give an account of the phenomenal world, *or* he will be guilty of an essentially amoral aestheticism, which, as Plato first decreed, allows the poet to convincingly represent people, things, and events while feeling indifferent to moral development and the achievement of a just society.

Put this way, the necessary reconciliation in *Moby-Dick* isn't between "a realistic account of whaling processes" and "a poetic treatment of the subject." Rather, it is between "literature" and "philosophy," a conflict that in Plato's presentation is "already ancient even at the moment of philosophy's inception," as Stephen Mulhall writes.[16]

Calling the interface between literature and philosophy contentious is indeed now part of a long tradition, one that shows no signs of diminishing. Rightly so, for what reference to this ancient quarrel should bring to mind is the state of affairs in which literature without philosophy's intervention or challenge presents a threat of corruption to the soul of the poet as well as to that of his or her readers. (The poet's creative and descriptive capacities are exercised without obligation to rightness and wrongness, as Plato forcefully argued, if the poet feels no duty to achieve self-knowledge and live the good life, the duty to which philosophy is distinctively devoted. What worried Plato—and has this not come to pass?—is the poet's ability to construct convincing representations of historical individuals whose knowledge and understanding the poet himself does not properly grasp; also that poets are often more attracted to the representation of interesting, vivid evil than of banal and boring good.) It is equally true that philosophy without literature's insistence on frankly attending to what there is to be seen, in all its variety and complexity, blocks the possibility of modes of thinking philosopher Stephen Mulhall, citing Stephen Clark, calls "genuinely responsive to 'the heart's affections and the plain evidence of sense.' "[17] As the student of literature sees it, philosophy is severely hampered by its disregard for what *can* be discovered through the appropriate use of the senses, a disregard that manifests as the philosopher's refusal to examine the details of any particular case. Thus when literature returns the favor, or gives to philosophy what philosophy gave poetry in the way of a new impulse and a new aim, what is highlighted is philosophy's aridity when it writes off or regards as unpromising the category of experience to which concepts of being-so (*Sosein*) do not speak at all.

For Mulhall, accordingly, as for Stanley Cavell, the ancient quarrel is more of "a dialogue, in which philosophy and literature participate as each other's other—as autonomous but internally related. One might say: their distinctness is constituted by the very distance that not only allows but requires that they address one another," since for each properly acknowledging the other requires "both to confront the challenge of reconceiving their self-images, and so their defining aspirations."[18] The distinction between philosophy and literature is thus not meant to be leveled, as Cavell has written; better to understand the philosophical and the literary as modes that occur simultaneously, with the writer or critic working "to deepen their differences, even to bring them to crisis."[19]

Moby-Dick makes vivid this stimulating interdisciplinary encounter. For it is possible to think of Melville's book as, at bottom, an investigation into the nature of concepts and not an investigation of phenomena or the objects of perception. Melville's writing in *Moby-Dick* is thus distinctively philosophical. What is more, the book shares the aim of classical metaphysics: to make explicit what is not primarily so. Insofar as *Moby-Dick* is Melville's attempt to illuminate the human condition by making explicit what is only implicit in that condition, it may be said to characterize the deeply challenging goal toward which philosophy (certainly the kind Plato writes) aspires.

However, it is also the case that *Moby-Dick* mounts a sustained attack on what Stephen Mulhall calls "philosophy's aversion to the concrete reality of the putative objects of its attention."[20] Philosophy's distaste for or even antipathy toward worldly things and events is what Melville denounces when he refuses to strip his material, corporeal whale of its distinctive personality and turn it into an allegory. We might say that Melville's high regard for the concrete reality of putative objects determines his style—or that the mode of attention exhibited in *Moby-Dick* matches exactly the mode Plato deplored in the poets. For the poet, "no word is too crass or too plain," as Auerbach says of Dante; "he summons all the senses to help him, the most common, everyday experience has its place if it helps to give his thought concreteness."[21] As Auerbach argues, the poet is compelled to take note of concrete reality, to which he always subordinates his extraordinary technical resources.

The outcome of Melville's determination in his whaling narrative to open philosophy's assumptions to question (having already shown himself willing to consider philosophy's censure of the poets by writing romance, or working in the literary genre most transformed by philosophy) is thus what I'm calling Melvillean mimesis—Melville's strategy of registering something true by dint of attending to, rather than discounting, the appearance of things. For why should the mode of attention generally associated with poets, a yearning to focus on the details of what goes on, not actively contribute to philosophy's struggle to do conceptual justice to the world? Why should Melville's determination to apprehend an object in the repleteness of its features frustrate rather than reinforce the robust possible relation between fiction and the truth? Because Melville believes it possible to identify failures of thinking, particularly moral thinking (because Melville, like Plato, was a moralist in the grand architectonic sense of believing that it is possible to educate people, if they are philosophically inclined), we must take his matching resolve to write in the mode of attention traditionally associated with poets as proof of his conclusion that it is impossible to identify such failures of thinking *without* embodying certain kinds of affective response to things, and inviting readers to share those responses, as well as to critically evaluate them.[22]

Of course the reverse is true as well. Just because a Melvillean scene gives expression to a particular style of affectionate interest in and inspired engagement with sensible reality, we should not assume that as a writer Melville is fully satisfied by attending to the world of material objects, or that he has relinquished the hope of representing in language what scholastic realists of the Middle Ages called real objects and classical realists called the world of Ideas or forms—the generalized concepts we postulate to bring experience to coherence. To use Melville's commitment to sensuous knowledge in order to neatly ally him with a modern aesthetic sensibility (to deny him his belief in an order of reality that is not directly answerable to empirical investigation) is to have misjudged Melville's undertaking in *Moby-Dick*. In his whaling narrative Melville's duty is to bring forth "visible truth," a term he glosses as "the apprehension of the absolute condition of present things as they strike the eye of the man who fears them not, though they do their worst to him."[23] The way Melville links "absolute" with "present" in this sentence, "visible" with "truth," would seem to reflect his intuition that literature (literature worth emulating, at least, like the book of Job) awards readers with the embodiment, the concrete expression, of abstract objects or concepts. These "living likenesses" or poetic images, like the Jobian horse, are examples of truth made manifest by a writer's choice expressions. A poetic image conveys what Althusser identifies as a "lived" relation to the real.[24]

In consequence, and while there is much that Melville shares with thinkers associated with aesthetics, there is a view he does *not* share: that reality is essentially particular, that only particular objects really exist, and that the generalities to which we refer and on which our understanding of the world depends ("whale," for example) belong simply to the way that the mind deals with these particulars. My point is that many thinkers associated with aesthetics are part of an antirealist tradition—and Melville, I am arguing, is not.

The conclusion that Melville is well suited to represent aesthetics, understood not merely as art criticism but as part of a "general inquiry into how we come to know the world from the evidence of our senses," has attracted much careful critical notice, but I think we introduce some confusion when we think of him this way.[25] For as Martin Seel reports in *Aesthetics of Appearing*, the "modest message" of aesthetics is that the encounter with the particular has meaning in itself. The desired result of aesthetic knowledge "is not the universal (which is grasped by classification and generalization) but consideration of the particular."[26] To know the particular in its particularity is the real accomplishment of aesthetic knowledge, argues Seel, who furthermore proposes that apprehending objects in respect to how they appear momentarily and simultaneously to the senses "represents a genuine way for human beings to encounter the world." Doubtless aesthetic knowledge has required such defending ever since philosophers tried to lay down requirements on the nature of moral thought. And yet rather than be unassuming or moderate in the estimation of human abilities, the branch of epistemology associated with sensuous knowledge—aesthetics in its current incarnation—supposes that our confrontation with what Adorno and Horkheimer call the uniqueness of the world is what makes possible the seeming occurrence of objects. I take the author of *Moby-Dick* to be making quite a strong objection to this view.

Thus the claim I'm putting forward is rather different. It is that Melville's *Moby-Dick* shows evident connections to the work of Plato and other theorists rightly associated with classical realism—thinkers, that is to say, for whom concept formation *as such* represents, in some substantial sense, a grasp of "what the world is like," but according to whom concepts are curious precisely because there isn't anything in the sensible world to which they correspond.

Identifying Melville with classical realism is useful because, for Melville as for the classical realist, (a) there is nothing in the natural or sensible world to which our words or concepts correspond (no extant being standing over against the concept "whale") and (b) this certainty does not force the conclusion that concepts are essentially illusory or arbitrary.

In fact, the notion that concepts are not in their own right part of our understanding of "what the world is like"—that language has no objective basis or that what the word "whale" names isn't real—is precisely the notion Melville candidly rejects.

Melville's stubbornness on this count derives, as I hope to make clear, from his having determined that our concepts are embedded in human activity—that our concepts are situated in complex ways within the instinctive (unconscious, involuntary) dimension of our lives. For Melville the conceptual world is not separated from the body and from experience but is interdependent with them (or as Wittgenstein will come to say, concepts of language and the activities of life are *internally* related to one another, which means that they are intelligible only in relation to one another.)[27] Before we can see the significance of this conclusion, though, it is helpful to understand why, in some respects, the logic on display in Melville's writing comes out of a realist tradition, and what this fidelity to realism foments in his whaling narrative.

The dispute between the realists and their opponents has a long history. But as the philosopher H. O. Mounce writes, in its essentials it adheres to the debate in classical philosophy between the Sophists and Skeptics, who both "argued that the measure of things is in the human will as it expresses itself through the individual, social consensus or the conventions of language," and the Pythagoreans, Plato, and Aristotle, who "denied that order is imposed on the world by the human mind," and who maintained, rather, that "the mind can make sense of the world only because it partakes of an order which exists independently of it."[28] Effectively the same dispute can be found running throughout the philosophy of the Middle Ages and modern philosophy, the philosophy since Descartes, but with, as Mounce notes, this significant difference: "In classical philosophy and for much of the Middle Ages the anti-realist view was a minority one. In modern philosophy it is the view of the majority."[29] Needless to say, theorizing in the twentieth and twenty-first centuries is practically defined by the view that objective order is a delusion—that as Plato's Protagoras insists, "man is the measure of all things."[30]

There is one obvious difficulty in locating Melville on the antirealist side of this debate, though that is where he's typically located. It is that actually *being* an antirealist profoundly impairs a writer's ability to help his or her readers enlarge their moral imaginations. So, the vast majority of Melville's critics find him to be a writer notably invested in looking at the implications of cultural biases—for example, those having to do with race—in order to arrive at more reliable or less-discriminatory accounts of experience and of the world. But Melville's desire to seek a greater fairness or greater truth than what the hegemonic perspectives allow him to scrape together goes hand in hand with his realism. For if he were an antirealist, or were to deny that the mind can make sense of the world only because it partakes of an order that exists independently of it, he would deny, too, the condition for the existence of objective standards. Deny the existence of objective standards, and he loses the foundation upon which his effort to overcome socially produced distortions rests.[31] In contrast to the moral relativist, who does not accept any universalizable grounds for deciding among different beliefs, Melville offers a specifically *realist* response to the question of whether there are moral values or beliefs that have objective validity and are in theory universalizable.[32]

Still, moral realism is easy to give good reason for when what is at issue is the wrongness or injustice of slavery, say. Harder to accept, though quite as necessary, is that Melville sided with the classical realists in thinking that language must have an objective basis. Plato's belief in the integrity of language as a means for communicating truth brought him into conflict with the Sophists, who saw language as a flexible set of conventions contrived only for the purpose of achieving material and personal advantage. The Sophists' view was reinforced by the two theories to which Plato was implacably opposed: relativism and skepticism. However, for Plato—who, like Parmenides and Heraclitus before him, was preoccupied with the very possibility of language and meaning—language must have an objective basis if it is to be the means by which an unjust society learns to examine and repair itself.[33] In other words, philosophers who profess realism maintain that since the word "whale" is true of something, that which "whale" means is true.[34] Melville, I am saying, is this kind of philosopher.

It has become necessary to emphasize and even exaggerate this aspect of Melville's thinking because so many readers of *Moby-Dick* are certain of Melville's antirealism. These readers are confident that, for Melville, man is the measure of all things. They think Melville holds that there is no objective basis for our words or concepts. They believe this perhaps because they take Ahab's failed pursuit to demonstrate the dangers of believing otherwise. Thinking that the word "whale" cannot have an objective basis is preferable to thinking it must have one because the latter belief would seem to give rise to what Martin Seel calls "epistemic fixation," that questing, unremitting resolve Ahab is thought to embody and that emerges as a determination "to dispel the mysteries by reducing them to knowledge or to pull down heaven in the attempt," as Henry Pochman writes, a preoccupation with the inscrutability of the universe that ultimately only enrages or torments.[35]

To the readers for whom Ahab's sad story represents the dangers of philosophical realism (or for whom realism is a kind of folly), the idea that language has an objective basis only advances the skeptical thought that has haunted man since Descartes introduced it: as Bernard Harrison reports, "the thought that neither in contemplating our mental representations of reality, nor in amassing the sensory evidence for those representations, do we ever encounter anything extramental: anything but our own mental states."[36] Realism is thought to promote skepticism because the realist is taken to put trust in a connection *he is unable to explain* between some element of language and some aspect of reality. When this connection can't be convincingly drawn, the realist collapses in the acutest grief—and perhaps tries to take whomever he can down with him.

All the same, this formulation suggests another possibility, which is that the difficulty of finding a connection between discourse and what it concerns is the difficulty a certain kind of realist takes himself to have resolved. This more flattering view of the realist is the one I take up here. In this book I argue that the relation between language and "what the world is like" is what Melville understands himself to have spelled out in his whaling narrative.

There is, however, another obstacle to talking about Melville as a realist. It is that in its philosophical context, realism was for a long time understood to mean the view that the true realities are not the particular, concrete objects of sense perception but "universals," "real generals," or other ways of naming objective concepts—those concepts that (as Plato argued) are the means by which we classify the world. But as Ian Watt reports in *The Rise of the Novel* (and Stephen Mulhall elegantly summarizes), "What happens in the modern period in philosophy, in the defining work of Locke and Descartes, is that this inheritance is rejected. Distinctively modern realism begins from the position that abstract universals are of dubious validity, that truth can be discovered by the individual through the appropriate use of her senses, and that the methods to be employed in the pursuit of truth should be at once critical, antitraditional, and innovating."[37]

Simply using the term "realism" gives rise to confusion, then. Accordingly in my identification of Melville with philosophical realism I mean specifically the tradition of classical realism, not modern realism. It is distorting to associate *Moby-Dick* with modern realism because Melville's thinking in this book does not proceed from the position that "abstract universals are of dubious validity." That characteristically modern notion is not his. Indeed, Melville is captivated by the world of form objects (or more precisely, the *formal element* of all our concepts) for the same reason Plato is—because he's struggling to understand how an unwavering notion like "whale" can at the same time have various subdivisions and many diverse instantiations. Anyone intrigued by concept possession, anyone who comes quickly to understand that the meaning of our words or concepts can't be settled by pointing to anything in the observable world (anyone who is a student of Plato's, in other words, or who learns from Plato's so-called theory of forms that we understand a concept fully only when we grasp an unpredictable variety of examples and instances) has evident connections to the tradition of classical realism.[38]

In *Moby-Dick*, I argue, Melville ultimately sides with those logicians who think language has an objective basis. It is just as clear, however, that for Melville the ability to classify the world (to decide, for example, what are and what are not instances of a whale) is *not* analogous to knowing or deciding the essential features of the thing in question. Melville in this way nimbly leaps over the trap in which so many thinkers following Plato (or following Aristotle) have been ensnared. The picture that holds many philosophers captive sounds something like this: believing that language has an objective basis means believing that it is possible to determine something's intrinsic nature or indispensible features—but that kind of thing is impossible to determine given the empirical dissimilarity of things classed under the same name. To thinkers who equate "what a whale is" with the whale's essential nature, hypothesizing the objective existence of the concept "whale" or thinking language has an objective basis does indeed lead to a preoccupation with the inscrutability of the universe that only enrages or torments.

Yet as Melville shows in *Moby-Dick*, it is quite possible to adopt Plato's genuinely profound conclusion that we know our concepts have objective existence because they are what enable us to function rationally (or as H. O. Mounce writes, "we know the forms are real not because we can prove it but because they are the condition for our proving anything at all")[39] *without* carrying out a complete analysis of any concept or trying to determine once and for all what something is. As Wittgenstein argues, what matters about conceptual life (and the sign language that gives rise to it) is our capacity to put details and states together in ways that do not depend on knowledge claims. Speakers of language routinely evoke a state of affairs, like a whale, without being able to adequately describe in empirical terms what a whale is.[40]

This point of logic has become confused doubtless because modern realism has overshadowed or obscured the view of language and meaning Plato and the classical realists were working through. The difference between modern and classical realism should be clear, though, since only for *modern* realists is it customary to call the features of a thing that enable us to recognize it the "criteria" for the proper use of the word that we use to refer to the thing in question. That is, only in realism after Descartes and Locke is there an entailment relation between something's essential features and "what it is."

As Melville would have us remember, identifying a whale by its features is a *special kind* of activity; it is the activity of answering the question, Is this a whale? when we are standing around talking about the (usually dead) specimens in front of us. The impression we get from this activity is that we know how to use the word "whale"—that we can follow rules for the proper use of this word—by observing empirical similarities only.

Easily forgotten is the fact that "we have to use our words at times and for purposes other than to identify a thing when we are confronted by it," as the philosopher Julius Kovesi writes. "Comets and revolutions do not appear or occur as often as we have occasion to talk about them."[41]

This is the point Plato and the classical realists were making. As Kovesi understands Plato to argue, "The features do not provide us with the rules for the use of a word and so it is misleading to think they are the criteria for the proper use of a word. For the rules we have to look elsewhere."[42]

The aspect of the concept "whale" that enables us to follow rules for the proper use of this word is what Kovesi calls the concept's "formal element" and Plato calls its *eidos*, or form. Holding that our concepts have formal elements that transcend (that is, are not answerable to) empirical observations does not on its own solve the difficulty of finding a connection between discourse and what it concerns—the difficulty I take Melville, in his own inimitable style, to have addressed himself to. But it does clear the way for understanding how language can have an objective basis, as Plato argued, since objectivity is tied not to anything's essential features but to the rules for the uses of words.

I liken Melville's realism to Plato's because I want to make clear Melville's quarrel with modern realism, or realism after Locke. For in his own account of the relation between discourse and what it concerns, Melville staunchly opposes the central claim of Lockean or empirical realism—namely, that what we say has a bearing on reality only if its content is "conformable," as Locke says, to "some real being."[43] For realists after Locke, the meaning of the word "whale"—"what a whale is"—can be explained simply by indicating (or as Bertrand Russell would have said, by becoming *acquainted* with) its sensory correlate.[44] For a modern or empirical realist, the word "whale" can be understood only through acquaintance with the extralinguistic entity to which it corresponds.

In *Moby-Dick*, Melville shows that he is not a realist of Locke's type—someone for whom our words would lapse into meaninglessness if the possibility of associating them with objects of acquaintance were to be denied us.[45] In his whaling narrative Melville constructs a scathing critique of the belief that, as Russell self-assuredly puts it, "all our knowledge, both knowledge of things and knowledge of truths, rests upon acquaintance as its foundation."[46] As readers of *Moby-Dick* discover, it is misguided and quite simply inaccurate to believe what philosophers sufficiently Lockean in their assumptions have traditionally believed: that in order to guarantee the applicability to reality of the thoughts formulated in terms of the words in our language we should say that the meaning of a word or name arises from the natural object or class of objects that bears the name—that the meaning of a name, like the name "whale," can be explained by pointing to the *bearer* of the name.

Melville's realism is thus closer to the realism of C. S. Peirce. Peirce was one of the few philosophers in the nineteenth century who made an explicit defense of classical and medieval realism (that is, realism prior to the defining work of Locke and Descartes).[47] Like Plato, Peirce hypothesized the existence of abstract universals, what he called "real generals," because he, too, could see that thinking language mirrors nature or the world of natural objects makes people eminently foolish in their attempts to construct an account of meaning in language. Like Plato, Peirce took issue with the convention of saying that the meaning of a word is its bearer. As the great American logician recognized, trying to explicate the meaning of a word or name by indicating the bearer of that name gives the philosopher a headache—as Wittgenstein will go on to describe the effect of looking in just the wrong place for an answer to the question of how language is related to the world—since it obliges the philosopher to try to bring out *the* relationship between a name and a thing, and this he cannot do.[48]

Evidently, Peirce saw the point of the classical realists' most valuable observation: that there is no way to establish the meaning of a sign by attending to the contents of the sensible world. It follows, therefore, that a sign doesn't need a connection with the sensible world to be capable of signifying. Intriguingly, this two-part lesson is formulated precisely by the catchphrase that runs throughout Wittgenstein's *Tractatus* (and its accompanying *Notebooks 1914–1916*) and constitutes that book's recurrent theme: "Logic must take care of itself."[49] What this memorable phrase suggests is that the generalities on which our understanding of the world depends (signs, like "whale," that are irreducible to any finite set of instances) do not get their meaning from natural objects or objects in the physical world. *Not any one whale in existence, nor indeed all the whales in existence, supply the word "whale" with its meaning.* Thus for Wittgenstein, as for Peirce, anyone hoping to explain the relation between language as a semantic order and "what the world is like" (or in Melville's illustrative example, between the word "whale" and "the living whale in his full majesty and significance") is going about it in the wrong way if he or she is counting on a direct referential relationship between the signs of our language and empirically accessible features of the sensible world.[50]

What Peirce and Wittgenstein could see is that the relation between a sign and the situation it picks out is not what Hume called a natural relation, one that is established by empirical inquiry. It is rather an internal or logical relation.[51] In accordance with philosophers from Plato to Derrida, they dismiss as inadequate the argument that a word has no meaning if nothing corresponds to it; instead they show how meaning is a matter of the relation of linguistic sign to linguistic sign.[52] Or as they make clear, all questions of meaning must be settled internally to language. For Peirce and Wittgenstein, the important point is that sense can be found in the sentences of our language even when language "*goes on holiday*," as Wittgenstein writes, or where language suggests a body and there is none.[53]

As these logicians argue, it cannot be the case that we establish the meaning of signs by attending to the contents of the sensible world. (For if the meaning of the word "whale" really was established by an empirical inquiry, or by matching linguistic expressions to features of sensible reality, what would happen if whales were fished to extinction? Any sentence that contains the word "whale" would contain a word that had no meaning and the sentence would be nonsense. But it is clear that such sentences *make sense*, whether or not whales are in existence.[54] Or as we might also ask, Would Ahab's pained sob—"Aye, Starbuck; aye, my hearties all round; it was Moby Dick that dismasted me; Moby Dick that brought me to this dead stump I stand on now"—be any less intelligible if the captain had in fact hunted Moby Dick to his death?) Rightly grasping the certainty that "logic must take care of itself" helps to illuminate *Moby-Dick*'s recurrent theme: that it is not possible to explain the meaning of a word by correlating it with any constituent or aspect of the natural world; that the meaning of the word "whale" cannot be traced back to the *bearer* of that name, irrespective of whether the bearer is thought of as a particular natural object or as a vast assemblage of natural objects sharing a common quality.

My suggestion so far has been that Melville's writing in *Moby-Dick* shows evident connections to classical realism, or to the tradition that gives our concepts (and their linguistic expressions) objective existence. Rightly understanding Melville's realism is, as I see it, prerequisite to grasping the central or engrossing difficulty in *Moby-Dick*, the difficulty of finding a connection between written or spoken signs, like the word "whale," and a situation outside in the world—the unbounded, unconditional object Melville identifies as "the living whale in his full majesty and significance." ("What *is* it?" Wittgenstein asks. "Naming appears as a *queer* connection of a word with an object," in consequence tempting many philosophers to "fancy naming to be some remarkable act of mind.")[55]

However, understanding Melville's realism involves appreciating that his realism is not entangled from the start with empiricist assumptions. *All realism after Locke* is entangled in this way, which is perhaps why Melville would have us throw the "thunderheads" Locke and Kant overboard. What this humorous symbolic gesture arguably puts forward is that, for Melville, realism after the empiricists have meddled with it is worthless or meaningless, a kind of junk. To be sure, like Locke and Kant Melville is repelled by idealism, or by the attempt to make reality dependent on the activity of mind. But unlike these empirical realists (each of whom is a "scientist-philosopher," as David Charles McCarty calls Hume, "a full partner in the great firm of empirical science"), Melville does not forget that "logic must take care of itself."[56] The empirical realists with whom Melville finds fault have failed to recall Plato's injunction not to confuse logical knowledge, or the kind of knowledge speakers of language possess, with empirical knowledge, or the kind of knowledge epistemology since Descartes has occupied itself with establishing the grounds and conditions of, the kind of knowledge rightly associated with the propositions of science.[57]

It is because the empirical realists have overlooked or disregarded this precept of logic that their work eventually promotes a skeptical attitude. For having failed to distinguish between the logical and empirical realms, and thus not understanding that a sign doesn't need a direct connection with the natural world to be capable of signifying, the empirical realist throws himself into trying to bring out *the* relation between signs and things signified.[58] The post-Lockean or empirical realist's disappointment is thus inevitable, for (as Melville is able to show in his whaling narrative) the kind of relationship between language and the world that does in fact exist cannot, without the risk of serious misunderstanding, be imagined as a link between a linguistic expression and an extralinguistic entity.

In *Moby-Dick* Melville mounts an eloquent, sustained, uncompromising objection to the view that knowing the meaning of a word is a function of becoming acquainted with the extralinguistic entity it picks out. Now, to some readers Melville's dazzling evisceration of the correspondence theory of meaning appears to lend support to the notion that it is impossible to give an effective account of the relationship between words and "what the world is like." But I think this misconstrues entirely Melville's project in *Moby-Dick*. For as Melville shows in this work, questions about the bearing of language on reality cease to be puzzling the moment we recall that the relationship between discourse and what it concerns is not natural but logical.

The remarkable thing about a word or sign, as Plato was the first to point out, is not that it gathers together things with *empirical similarities*; rather, it is that it brings a variety of things together as examples of the *same thing*.[59] For philosophers who learn from Plato a way of thinking about our sign language, the crucial point to remember is that it is a word's formal element that enables us to decide what will or will not amount to the same thing. That is, the formal element of the word or sign "whale" is what provides us with the rules for the use of this word, and quite simply the formal element cannot be deduced from nor can it be defined in terms of the empirical similarities between various instances of whales.

What Melville seems to have accepted in *Moby-Dick* is precisely the logical insight Plato prepared his readers to accept: that the formal element of the sign "whale" (what enables us to follow the rules for the proper use of this word) cannot be determined on the basis of the analysis of material objects bearing that name. Or to put it another way, what Melville shows in his whaling narrative is that in addition to the many and diverse ways of instantiating the given concept "whale" (concrete instances impossible to give the complete enumeration of), there is a *role* the word "whale" plays in our lives, and this role must be understood if the concept is to be understood.

In *Moby-Dick* Melville reminds his readers how language actually works, which, as Bernard Harrison reasons, is not by turning its resources of representation outward upon the natural world but by turning them inward upon the vast web of culturally relevant practices that (as Wittgenstein insists) underpin both the meanings of words and the assumptions of their human users.[60] In *Moby-Dick*'s "Cetology" chapter, in particular, Melville's readers find a concentrated account of concept formation and concept use—of what it is to be in a position to *understand* the signs in our language, or how it is we can employ words at times and for purposes other than to identify a thing when we are confronted by it. To "Cetology" we now turn.

Chapter 3

✦

Gospel Cetology

> Words are like a film on deep water.
>
> —Wittgenstein, *Notebooks 1914–1916*

In this chapter I aim to make sense of *Moby-Dick*'s startling conclusion—by which I mean not the demise of the *Pequod* and its crew but the resolution to the philosophical puzzle that gives Melville's book its momentum. What connects the word "whale" to the situation outside in the world it picks out? What is the relation of our words to those aspects of reality irreducible to mental representations?

Melville, after all, is convinced that there *is* a solution to this puzzle, one that does not entail accepting the deeply problematic view that the words in our language have bearing on reality only when they enjoy what William James calls "cash value in experiential terms"—when they can be shown to designate some aspect of the extramental, extralinguistic world. As it happens, Melville rejects in all its forms the doctrine that a proper name or general term has bearing on reality only when it corresponds to some entity whose existence owes nothing to language. This is not to say that for Melville reality is merely a projection, as readers who think him hospitable to skepticism have often argued—a widely held assumption that has resulted in *Moby-Dick*'s misdirected reputation for being existentially bleak. On the contrary, Melville's great accomplishment is to have convinced his readers that even though there is nothing in the natural world to which the word or concept "whale" directly corresponds, there is something more than just made up or chimerical about this concept—that this concept is sufficiently deserving of the label "real" to drive out the worry that it is the mere projection of a human mind.

The author of *Moby-Dick* is, of course, aware that when we speak of the entities referred to or designated by the word "whale," we speak not of things but of *things-in-language*, figments of discourse. And to make this concession, as Bernard Harrison writes, is to raise the specter of "the Prison House of Language," as philosophers since Locke have conceived it: "For it makes it appear that the main obstacle to the achievement of a language capable of representing accurately how things stand in Reality is the creative fertility of the mind in the elaboration of concepts. And that in turn raises the possibility that that very fertility might shut the mind off from Reality, blinding it, to employ a graphic phrase of Berkeley's, with a 'false imaginary glare.'"[1]

As Melville's whaling narrative invites us to recall, language speakers are subject to a special kind of worry, belonging to the category of skeptical doubt.[2] The worry is that since we think and speak in language, and language is a creation of the human mind, the concepts fabricated within language—the things our words name—are, likewise, creations of mind. As philosophers gripped by such doubt might wonder, "what assurance have we that, when we speak, we speak of the furniture of the universe, of Reality itself, rather than merely of the homely, and home-made, furniture of our own minds?" How are we not condemned to converse solely with the conceptual fictions fabricated entirely within language?[3] In *Moby-Dick*, Melville frames the worry this way: How does the *thing signified* by the sign "whale" ("the living whale in his full majesty and significance") not as a matter of course evade the grasp of language speakers?

My suggestion is that Melville's rejoinder to this age-old anxiety is surprisingly heartening. For the problem disappears, as he demonstrates, when we finally stop acting as if the things our words name are bits of extramental reality, creatures of the purely physical universe, and yet hold out against the suspicion that our words name merely mental entities. In *Moby-Dick*, Melville dispels the illusions systematically developed by Locke and Kant. That is, he shows how our ability to form the concept "whale" is *not* a consequence of using this word to label some recurring feature of experience (as Locke contended), *not* a result of the human mind imposing its order on supposedly incoherent materials (as Kant claimed). Indeed, with his whaling narrative Melville attacks the entire multifaceted philosophical tradition enthralled by the belief that forming a concept (bestowing meaning upon a general name in a language) is an activity of mind.

Melville's vital discovery is that the conceptual object the word "whale" names is neither an object of our senses nor is it an inhabitant of the subjective, private, "inner world" philosophers since Descartes have associated with the world of ideas. For Melville, the admission that concepts are fabricated within language comes as a great relief because it forces the conclusion that the meaning of a word doesn't issue from the mind, as it were, but from the role the word plays in language—a role established by the needs and relevant interests of people engaged in specific practices. Without the need for the word or concept "whale" in a way of life, Melville's whaling narrative makes clear, we would not start forming the concept or using the word, and the word would not acquire meaning.[4] Melville's discovery that concept formation is a *public process*, that we form and use concepts according to interpersonal rules (otherwise people could not use this word in the same way; the word could not become part of our language), supports his conclusion that concepts can be objective, as Plato first suggested. Melville's drawn-out hint in *Moby-Dick* that the concept "whale" is objective and indeed that objectivity is a general feature of concepts offers a powerful reorientation, a lesson of great magnitude, because showing how concepts are *not* formed in the theater of the individual mind is a way of restoring to the human mind its power and dignity—of rescuing it from the corner to which much post-Cartesian philosophy has relegated it, as Henri Bergson writes, "like a schoolboy in disgrace."[5]

For many philosophers, the thought that concepts can be objective seems far-fetched. And yet, as Melville understood, the crucial point about concepts is that they are what enable us to function rationally.[6] They must therefore be true outside a subject's individual biases, interpretations, feelings, and imaginings. To put it another way, the author of *Moby-Dick* does not hold with the view that our concepts are merely mental representations, from which follows the disabling conviction that the conceptual fertility of the mind continuously threatens to bar us from an adequate knowledge of "what the world is like." The revelation in Melville's whaling narrative is that even though there is no extant being standing over against the word or concept "whale," nor any possibility of explaining this word's meaning by correlating it with any constituent or aspect of the natural world, it is incorrect to think that our possession of the concept—what it is to be in a position to *understand* the word "whale"—depends on the operations of mind.

What we might call Melville's philosophical achievement in *Moby-Dick* is thus related to the way he works out in concert what concepts are and in what ways concepts are embedded in human activity: how our concepts are situated in complex ways in the instinctive—unconscious, involuntary—dimension of our lives. For as the philosopher Hugh Knott writes, "our concepts are placed centrally in our lives. They are not in this sense a tool which we may pick up or leave as we wish: our possession of them is constitutive of our lives, and *their* constitution too is a function of the way they are embedded in our lives."[7] Melville's preoccupation with concept *possession*, with how our concepts are *seated* in our lives, in this way takes us far beyond the opposing theories (generally represented by Locke and Kant) that presently dominate investigation into the nature of human knowledge. Melville knows what he is doing, that is to say, when he throws the "thunderheads" overboard—when he summarily dispenses with both empiricist and rationalist attempts to establish contact between thought and the world.[8] The marked consequence of Melville's decisive break with these contesting accounts is that he clears the decks for a more practicable reason for trusting that concept possession *as such* dependably reveals our knowledge and understanding of "what the world is like." In *Moby-Dick*, Melville shows how our concepts, in addition to being creatures of the fertility of the mind, are tools for handling reality.

Such a view of Melville's philosophical acuity is not prevalent, but this chapter aims to encourage it. To that end my strategy will be to enlist the descriptive vocabulary of an investigative tradition equally determined to work out the relation between a word or sign ("whale," in Melville's illustrative example) and a situation outside in the world (the living whale in his full majesty and significance). I mean the tradition associated with Wittgenstein's work in logic, as understood by some of Wittgenstein's most ingenious readers.[9] In what follows I consider Wittgenstein's provocative intervention in what he calls the "study of sign-language" in the hope of throwing more light on Melville's own theory of concept formation—of what it is to be in a position to *understand* a sign when it is said or written.[10] Enlisting Wittgenstein's wariness about the empiricist tradition in English-speaking philosophy (his sense that some philosophers were looking in just the wrong place for answers to the question of how language is related to reality) should, at the very least, help us to read *Moby-Dick*'s notorious "Cetology" chapter with more pleasure and profit.

Wittgenstein changed the course of philosophy when he showed in the *Tractatus* and its accompanying notebooks that sentences or propositions have sense despite the fact that the words that make them up do not correspond to extralinguistic entities. Like Plato and C. S. Peirce, Wittgenstein saw the futility of trying to match linguistic expressions to some category of extralinguistic objects. For as he came to understand, the relation of identity between signs and things signified—what makes it possible to "read off" a situation from a sign, without making a mistake—attests to an *internal* or *logical* relationship between written or spoken signs and the situations they pick out. We say that signs and things signified are internally or logically related to each other because they are intelligible only in relation to one another. For Wittgenstein, that is to say, the relation between a sign and the situation outside in the world it heralds cannot be what Hume called a "natural" relation, a conventional association between some element of language and some aspect of extralinguistic reality, because if it *were* a natural relation, it would have to be—absurdly, as Wittgenstein sees it—established by empirical inquiry. In consequence, Wittgenstein argued that a sentence must be a logical portrayal of its meaning, and thus that philosophers trying to completely analyze sentences—to conceive of the link between linguistic expressions and the extralinguistic entities they supposedly designate—had been hunting chimeras.[11]

Wittgenstein's discovery is trailblazing because its essential thrust is that what allows a well-formed sentence to make sense isn't determined by the relation between the words or signs that figure in the sentence and the nature of the objects they pick out. It is determined by the relation, internal to the sentence, between *signs* and *things signified*. For Wittgenstein the "thing signified" by a sign isn't the sign's referent (the natural object it indicates) but the sign's sense, what is expressed by the sign.

On this point Wittgenstein departs radically from his teacher, Bertrand Russell. Russell thought that knowing whether a sentence had sense depended on knowing its truth conditions, and since the truth condition of a sentence is the condition of the world under which the sentence is true, stipulating truth conditions ultimately requires an appeal to the nature of things. For Russell, determining the sense of any sentence in which a word or sign figures requires a complete analysis of the word; that is, it depends on finding a connection between a word like "whale" and what philosophers after Hume called natural facts. In Wittgenstein's theory of logical portrayal, in contrast, grasping the whale's nature is inessential to grasping the thought expressed by a sentence employing this word. That is because the meaning of the word "whale" is *not* conferred through what Hume called a natural relation. The meaning of the word, if by that we indicate not its referent but its sense, what the word expresses, is not determined by the nature of the object that bears the word as its name.

As Wittgenstein explains in his notebooks, the difficulty of his theory of logical portrayal was always the difficulty of accounting for the relationship between a sentential sign and the situation that can be read off from it. As he notes, "The difficulty of my theory of logical portrayal was that of finding a connection between the signs on paper and a situation outside in the world. I always said that truth is a relation between the proposition and the situation, but could never pick out such a relation."[12] But accounting for this relationship is precisely what Wittgenstein achieves in his so-called picture theory of language when he insists that there is a logical relation between the written or spoken signs that make up a proposition and the situations (*Sachverhalte*, the Tractarian term commonly translated as "states of affairs") the signs pick out.[13] When Wittgenstein says that there is a logical relation between signs and things signified, he is saying that knowing the meaning of a sign as it figures in a sentence has *nothing to do with* knowing the nature of the sign's referent and *everything to do with* knowing the role the sign plays in our vast and continually ramifying language.

What Wittgenstein in effect argues with his theory of logical portrayal is that philosophers' problems disappear when they stop enshrining the correspondence theory of meaning, or stop acting as if the meanings of words must in some way be determined by the nature of things. For Wittgenstein, what we know as the "meaning" of a word is quite simply not the result of associating the word with some natural fact. (Nor is it contrived privately, as it were, in the theater of the mind.) As Wittgenstein makes clear, there is something illegitimate about the way philosophers talk about the "meaning" of a word, as if meaning were a function of matching names to natural entities. This is a funny way of talking, since as Wittgenstein points out in *Philosophical Investigations*, "For a *large* number of cases—though not for all—in which we employ the word "meaning" it can be defined thus: the meaning of a word is its use in the language."[14]

Now, the certainty that the meaning of the word "whale" is its *use* in the language is what Melville's "Cetology" chapter demonstrates. The whole of the chapter is committed to advocating a version of the belief that "meaning is use," introducing a precept dear to Wittgenstein but at present, unfortunately, "one of the more threadbare and overworked philosophical clichés of the twentieth century."[15] "Cetology" offers what is therefore a much-needed illustration of precisely what is to be understood by the slogan "meaning is use."

For Wittgenstein, "meaning is use" is intended to spell out the certainty that meaning is not determined by the nature of things. (Or as a philosopher might say, it is meant to make clear that linguistic competence is nonepistemic in character.)[16] In Harrison's reading of Wittgenstein, the claim "meaning is use" is the claim that meaning is a function "not of the bare association of elements of language with elements of reality essentially fitted to become their referents, but rather of the roles assigned to words in the conduct of socially devised and maintained practices."[17] This is the *Sprachspiel*, or "language game," Wittgenstein tried to make understandable. Wittgenstein emphasized the human action into which language is woven because he came to understand that the way meaning is bestowed on a word isn't by associating the word with some bit of the natural world but by specifying a role for the word in the conduct of some practice.

In coming to this conclusion, Wittgenstein jettisons the founding principle of the empiricist tradition. As Locke argues in *Essay Concerning Human Understanding* (1689), when any man uses a term he must "have in his mind a determined idea which he makes it the sign of."[18] As Locke writes, we can expect nothing but "obscurity and confusion" from a person who uses a proper name or general term in language ("Moby-Dick," "whale") unless it can be shown to be what Locke called a "determined idea," a way of thinking demonstrably in touch with empirical reality.[19] For Locke and for philosophers sufficiently Lockean in their assumptions, such as Bertrand Russell, to be in a position to understand a proper name or general term in language is to possess the ability to identify items or characteristics of the sort to which the name or term applies. The problem with this view is that it forges an intimate link between the meanings of words and the nature of things.

The baselessness of the presumed connection between the meanings of words and the nature of things is the subject of Melville's "Cetology" chapter. In "Cetology," being in a position to understand the meaning of the word "whale" does *not* involve knowing the nature of this sign's referent. The theory of meaning put forward in "Cetology" relies heavily on the notion of practice.

Most readers of "Cetology" can agree that Melville's chapter does battle with reductionism. Reductionism is the idea that advances in the understanding of complex phenomena always involve showing the latter to be constructions out of simple elements, themselves self-evident for the reason that they can be established on empirical grounds.[20] Reductionism, now very deeply rooted in the practice of both science and philosophy, was seeded by Descartes's notion that if we are to "perfectly understand a problem we must abstract it from every superfluous conception, reduce it to its simplest terms and, by means of an enumeration, divide it up into the smallest possible parts" and propagated by Locke's theory that if complex ideas aren't to be dismissed as phantoms of the mind they must be analyzable into "simple ideas" originating in experience.[21]

Misgiving about the method fostered by Descartes and Locke is introduced in "Cetology" when Ishmael describes the pointlessness of attempting a clear classification of the leviathan founded upon the whale's observable features—even those that seem designed to afford the basis for a regular system of cetology, such as the whale's baleen, hump, back fin, or teeth. The problem, as Ishmael reports, is that the baleen, hump, fin, and teeth "are things whose particularities are indiscriminately dispersed among all sorts of whales, without any regard to what may be the nature of their structure in other more essential particulars." (The naturalist's difficulties increase, as Ishmael points out, if he attempts a classification of the leviathan founded upon the whale's internal, anatomical parts. For "if you descend into the bowels of the various leviathans, why there you will not find distinctions a fiftieth part as available to the systematizer as those external ones already enumerated.") For Ishmael, the only avenue open to the would-be systematizer is "to take hold of the whales bodily, in their entire liberal volume, and boldly sort them that way." This bibliographical system, as Ishmael calls it, is "the only system that can possibly succeed, for it alone is practicable." Ishmael accordingly lays out his unfinished cetological system, from the humpbacked whale to the mealymouthed porpoise.

The unstated purpose of Ishmael's report is to overthrow the whole philosophical aesthetic according to which the breakdown of an object into distinct and separable elementary parts renders it interpretable. But in "Cetology" Melville also goes further, laying out in full the dispute between what David Charles McCarty calls *semantical atomists*, philosophers whose account of meaning in language is governed by their faith in the analyzability of complex objects, and *semantical wholists*, who shun the comforts both of semantical atomism and of the scientifically based worldview.[22] For a semantical atomist, the content of a sign (like "whale") is fixed exclusively by a vertical linkage between some element of language and some bit of the world. The semantical atomist assumes that there is a direct referential relationship between words and things.[23] As I argue, semantical atomists are anathema to Melville because their basic assumption is that "the world's structure tells us how to speak," as McCarty writes—that it is possible to explain and justify the inner character of language by pointing to the way the world is.[24]

In "Cetology" Melville's inspired repudiation of reductionism and the semantical atomism to which it gave rise commences when Ishmael's "science of cetology" can't get off the ground without a generalizing definition of the word "whale"—or as Ishmael says, without defining the whale "by his obvious externals, so as conspicuously to label him for all time to come." As the chapter makes plain, Ishmael's definition of a whale ("*a whale is a spouting fish with a horizontal tail*") is not the outcome of his systemized exhibition of the whale but the guiding principle that makes such exhibition possible. For how else would Ishmael know to include a porpoise in his list of whales? Ishmael's statement of the meaning of the word "whale"—his abbreviated account of precisely that nature of the whale in its "more essential particulars" that can't be hit upon by classifying a whale's baleen, hump, fin, or teeth—cannot be the result of his "systematization of cetology" because his definition itself is what allows that kind of arranging to get under way. In other words, Ishmael's generalizing definition of "what a whale is" does not derive from his efforts to examine methodically and in detail the constitution or structure of individual whales. Instead, his definition is "the result of expanded meditation."

"Cetology" is thus a recitation of Plato's argument that when speakers of language understand the meaning of a word, they understand something that is not discoverable through empirical investigation. "Cetology" calls attention to Plato's reminder of what the speakers of language must *already* know in order to start classifying any object.

"Cetology," I argue, lays emphasis on two interrelated logical claims: first, that there may be *no empirically similar characteristics* between many creatures rightly called whales; and second, that we cannot see why creatures with *different characteristics* amount to the *same thing* ("whale") unless we understand why they do, for unless we understand why they do, we cannot follow a rule in finding further examples.[25] Disclosing why a sperm whale, a narwhal, a killer whale, and a porpoise are all examples of "whale" is what Ishmael's generalizing definition that "*a whale is a spouting fish with a horizontal tail*" accomplishes.

Ishmael's attempt to classify the whale shows why we must have a definition of the word "whale" *before* we start sorting whales into groups and families. However, it also makes clear how certainty about the meanings of words *comes before* the construction of definitions. As Plato first pointed out, the generalizing definition of any object is an instance of knowing incomplete for the reason that it is parasitic upon always understanding more than the definition can provide on its own.[26] As readers of *Moby-Dick* are well aware, "whale" means more than "being a spouting fish with a horizontal tail." The whale-boat captain, the perfumer, and the biblical scholar would all rightly object that what "whale" *really* means is a certain sort of observable shape, or that "the observable shape is the *fact*," as Julius Kovesi writes, "and the rest is added theory.[27]

What, then, is the generalizing definition of any object parasitic *upon*? To solve the riddle of how we *start forming a notion*, which must be in place before we start constructing generalizing definitions, scientists and many philosophers have argued—just as Plato worried they would—that the meaning of a word can be explained by pointing to its *bearer*.

When the constitution of meaning in language is explained this way, as if the content of a concept is modeled on the template of "some real being from which it is taken," as Locke argued, or as if sentences make sense because they are composed of "constituents with which we are acquainted," as Bertrand Russell maintained,[28] the supposition is that the meaning of a word or name *just is* something in the phenomenal world that bears the name.[29] In "Cetology" this deeply intuitive thought (that knowing what the whale is means knowing that bit of the world to which the name "whale" refers—knowing, in short, the essential nature of a whale, as discoverable through empirical investigation) is represented by "those lights of zoology and anatomy," as Ishmael calls nineteenth-century naturalists: "the great Cuvier, and John Hunter, and Lesson."

And yet under scrutiny the view that the word or name "whale" means the object cetologists divide into groups and families doesn't hold up either. The reason (again, as Plato argued) is that we cannot define what a whale is in terms of its material elements. Deducing what a whale is from its material elements is impossible because the whale's material elements, all the many and diverse ways in which something can be a whale, cannot be enumerated in a final list. That is why, in "Cetology," the claim put forward by the nineteenth-century naturalists—essentially, that we can discover from the *material elements* of the object "whale" its *formal element*, "what a whale is," or the basis upon which we decide what is and what is not a whale—is mocked and ridiculed by Ishmael and his friends in the whaling industry. In fact, as the whalers point out, the meaning of the word "whale" is *not* determined by the connection between this word and some bit of the world this word names. In the argument waggishly put forward by the whalers, meaning is use.

In the argument that meaning is use, meaning is not something passively "read off" from the face of natural reality.[30] The meaning of a sign is not fixed by the bare fact of its standing in a denotational relation to some bit of the world.[31] Meaning is rather a product of our system of signs, for it is the logical role of the sign in the whole structure of explanatory narrative that determines the sign's meaning. It follows that the sign's logical role isn't determined apart from the situations in which the speakers of language find themselves but *is generated out of* those situations; linguistic practice is intimately woven into social practice, ways of engaging with the world as it presents itself to creatures with the physical constitution and perceptual powers of human beings.[32]

In "Cetology," the idea that meaning is use (that language is intertwined with social practice, and thus that meaning in language is more connected to our constitution as living, active persons than can be understood from the naturalists' oversimplified point of view) gets under way when Ishmael reports having submitted Linnaeus's definition of a whale to former messmates Simeon Macey and Charley Coffin of Nantucket, who are united in the opinion that the naturalist's reasoning is "altogether insufficient," even "humbug."

In the first edition of *Systema Naturae*, published in 1735, Swedish botanist, zoologist, and physician Carl Linnaeus had classified whales as fishes. But in the tenth and most important edition, published in 1758 (considered the starting point of zoological nomenclature) as well as the much-enhanced twelfth edition, of 1776, the last under Linnaeus's authorship, whales were moved into the mammal class. As Ishmael reports, "the grounds upon which Linnaeus would fain have banished the whales from the waters, he states as follows: 'On account of their warm bilocular heart, their lungs, their movable eyelids, their hollow ears, *penem intrantem feminam mammis lactantem*,' and finally, '*ex lege naturae jure meritoque*.' "[33]

It is with Linnaeus's classification of the whale as a mammal that Ishmael and his friends take issue. For as they in effect argue, if the generalizing definition of a whale (the way to "define the whale . . . so as to conspicuously label him for all time to come") is going to avoid being false talk or basically gibberish, it should not be forgotten that there is a vast web of socially created and maintained *practices* in connection with which the word "whale" acquires meaning. Words acquire meaning when they serve the purposes of language speakers engaged in procedures and activities of one sort or another—established human practices (measurement, for example) that generate the systems of meaning in terms of which we live. The practices in which the meanings of our words are enmeshed are themselves carried on in a matrix of natural conditions and circumstances.[34] And as the whalers emphasize, the predominant condition or circumstance underwriting the various practices that all together make up the whale fishery is being at sea, as Ishmael says in *Moby-Dick*'s opening pages, or later and more darkly, being "launched upon the deep." In

"Cetology," Ishmael and his fellow whalers represent people who use the word "whale" with the most riding on it, and what they wonder is why a whale should be associated with dry land when everyone knows that a whale is, as Milton writes, "Hugest of living creatures, in the deep . . . and at his gills / Draws in, and at his breath spouts out a sea."

This bone of contention triggers the whalers' impatient irritation with Linnaeus's whole methodology, since it invites the question of *why* the naturalist wants to make the word "whale" into a name for a natural object when it is evidently *not* a name for a natural object. For the very fact that the material elements of a whale are unspecified or vary widely suggests that the concept "whale" has a formal element. As the whalers point out, the concept's *formal* element is what enables someone to decide what will or will not amount to a whale. This vital observation is what the naturalists seem oblivious to. The formal element of the concept "whale" is what allows anyone to answer the question of why a large variety of creatures may be called "whales" and other creatures may not. Not that the formal element of the concept "whale" is something over and above its material elements; there is no extra quality, *being-a-whale*, that may be present in one object but not in another.[35] Nevertheless we rely on the concept's formal element when we say what a whale is and the concept's formal element should be understood in terms of the role the word "whale" plays in language.

Consequently, in their dispute with Linnaeus the whalers call upon the same logical principle Wittgenstein will work to explain: that linguistic knowledge (what is *grasped* by someone who *understands* the word or concept "whale") isn't a matter of knowing something in the empirical world but a matter of knowing how to operate with signs.[36]

As I understand it, the misguidedness of the whole line of inquiry represented by the naturalists with whom Ishmael and the whalers take issue—the attempt to say how a word or name is directly related to the natural object that bears the name—is what the "Cetology" chapter is designed to reveal. For as Melville's readers are free to discover, "the fundamental thing settled" in "Cetology" (when, "waiving all argument," Ishmael takes "the good old fashioned ground that the whale is a fish") isn't the whale's identifying nature; it is the hopelessness of trying to define linguistic expressions the way naturalists do. Defining the word "whale" the way naturalists do is "humbug" because they assume that the empirical similarities between whales are what give the word "whale" its meaning. But as Ishmael insists, it is *not* the recognition of empirical similarities between different instances of whales that enable us to follow rules in the use of this term (that is, to know a whale when we see one, or to be able to find new examples of a whale.) The whales on Ishmael's "ground-plan of Cetology" are, of course, similar to each other: but as the chapter makes clear, even Ishmael and his friends in the industry did not arrive at their notion of a whale by having discovered similarities between species.

As the whalers' amusing hostility to nineteenth-century naturalists brings to light, being able to answer questions like "Is this a whale?" is an important activity to those whom Ishmael tauntingly calls "the best and latest authorities," the "lights of zoology and anatomy." But we thwart our own understanding when we project this pastime onto the rest of mankind as if this were our main activity in using words. As Julius Kovesi explains, people use language as part of *all sorts* of activities, and not just when we are arguing over the inventory of the universe.[37] Being able to answer questions like "Is this such and such?" does not in any case help to answer the question of how we start forming a notion. For as Kovesi writes, "Of course we do not start forming a new notion by first inventing a new word . . . and *then* trying to think how we could use the word or what rules we could give for the proper use of that word. We start forming a new notion by a process which is the reverse of this."[38] For Kovesi, "It is our wants and needs, aspirations and ideals, interests, likes and dislikes that provide the very material for the formation of our notions."[39] This is what "Cetology" emphasizes. Linnaeus's willingness to banish the whales from the waters invites the whalers' special derision because in addition to getting the whole process of forming a notion backward, it separates the meaning of the word "whale" from the environment in which whaling practices necessarily take place and thus shows no consideration for the actual, material (and treacherous, and slippery) activity of whaling.

What we find in the "Cetology" chapter is an account of meaning, of what it is to be able to understand a concept when it is said or written, wholly at odds with the idea that meaning is empirically determined. The belief that the meaning of the word or sign "whale" is empirically determined is in "Cetology" so ludicrous as to be amusing. Or as the whalers point out, what the naturalists' justificatory project laughably leaves out are the wellsprings of language, the "deep water," as Wittgenstein writes, over which words glide.[40]

By my count, "Cetology" is therefore one of the earliest—and most entertaining—assessments of what Bernard Harrison, following Wittgenstein, describes as "philosophers' persistent, not to say ingrained, habit of looking in just the wrong place for an answer to the question of how language is related to reality: at the supposedly unique relationship between words and things, rather than at the multifarious relationships between words, practices, and the world."[41]

As Wittgenstein was instrumental in showing (but many philosophers still have a hard time believing), the relationship between words and the world "cannot," as Harrison writes, "without the risk of serious misunderstanding, be described as any kind of 'linkage' connecting 'items' drawn respectively from two 'realms,' on the one hand, that of language, and, on the other, that of the extralinguistic."[42] Such a view "is crucially incomplete . . . because it leaves out of account practices." It neglects, therefore, precisely what must be taken *into* account when we are trying to understand the formation of a concept.[43]

What actually relates words and the world, as Patricia Hanna and Bernard Harrison argue in *Word and World: Practice and the Foundations of Language*, "is better conceived as a two-level process of engagement, or embedding: at the first level the engagement, or embedding, of linguistic expressions in practices; at the second level the engagement, or embedding, of practices in the matrix of natural conditions and circumstances, in and with respect to which they are carried on."[44] What Hanna and Harrison in effect argue is that "the content of a thought cannot be viewed in isolation from the language in which it is expressed, and that language *per se* cannot be viewed in isolation from the substratum of practices through which its expressions gain whatever meaning they possess; and that in consequence we have no means of representing ourselves, as beings capable of knowledge, in abstraction from practical life: the life we enjoy as physical, embodied beings, manipulators of an equally physical world."[45]

Harrison and Hanna's two-stage model represents a significant innovation to anyone worrying about how considerations outside language affect the constitution of meaning in language. For it posits that the meaning of a linguistic expression can't be divorced from the wide array of socially devised and maintained practices in which the speakers of language are engaged, and that a practice "just *is* a mode of engaging with the contents of reality, as they present themselves to creatures with the physical constitution and perceptual powers of human beings."[46] For a word to be enmeshed in a practice, therefore, Harrison writes, "is for it to acquire a use with respect to a system of procedures, responses, and results of one sort or another, which is always *already* 'connected to the world,' and that would not otherwise be of the slightest value or interest to those who make use of it."[47] Accordingly, if a name has a use in connection with which it has a meaning, it has an application to sensible reality. There is no *further* question of whether a name is or is not reflective of reality. "Its business with Reality was already concluded when it entered the language. It was concluded in, and by, its acquiring a use in connection with some practice that speakers find or have found, perhaps only temporarily, to be useful."[48] As Harrison writes,

> Language gives its expressions meaning by sowing them across the face of a vast web of socially created, possessed, and maintained practices . . . The vast majority of the practices in question—measurement, for instance, or counting, or differentially comparing colors, or sorting animal or plant populations into species—have nothing particularly "linguistic" about them. They are not, at least on the face of it, games played with words; rather, they are techniques of mensuration, or mathematics, or color-theory, or biological science. Nevertheless, they remain procedures in whose conduct *words play a role*, are *given* a role, and it is only because such roles exist for words, are bestowed by words, that we become beings who speak, beings with something to say about the world, rather than silent manipulators of the world.[49]

It is for this reason, as Harrison explains, that Wittgenstein's choice of the term "language game" was an unfortunate one, "one which sits ill with the entire tenor of the arguments in which it is employed, and tends to distort the reception of those arguments." For "the apparent implication of the term is that a language-game is *a game played with words*." For Wittgenstein, however, language games are not word games. As Kovesi writes, "they are activities in which language is a part."[50]

The point that requires emphasis, after all, is that it is the *logical role* of the sign, the role bestowed on a word relative to the practices in which the word is enmeshed, that fixes the tenor of any relation that strikes us as word-to-world.[51] The immense advantage of understanding why what we call the "meanings" of words are really *the roles that we bestow on words relative to practices* (or that the meaning of a name isn't determined by the *bearer* of that name) is that it settles the question of how and to what extent the spontaneities of language are constrained by sensible or material life *without* arguing, the way many contemporary philosophers of language have, that if language isn't to be a hermetic game at least some of our words must be equipped with extralinguistic reference. There is a problem with this latter conclusion, as Hanna and Harrison, following Wittgenstein, have taken pains to show, because it requires that we forge an intimate link between meaning and the epistemic—that we argue once again that if the objects we speak about are real (real in the sense of having the power to escape and to frustrate any representation we may make of them; real in the sense of being outside the "inner world" of the mind), then the nature of these objects must somehow or other enter into the determination of meaning.

As Alan Tapper and T. Brian Mooney note, many philosophers have accepted three key points from Wittgenstein: that our words or concepts are public, not private; that their meaning is in some way a matter of how they are used; and that their usage involves some form of rule following.[52] And yet because it is evidently possible to accept these points and still find far-fetched the claim that concepts can be objectively articulated, or that concept possession as such dependably reveals our knowledge and understanding of "what the world is like," I have used Melville's account of concept formation to throw light on an aspect of Wittgenstein's logic that is yet to find a proper audience. Because for Wittgenstein, the idea that objectivity is a feature of our concepts is *not* far-fetched. For Wittgenstein, concepts are not constituents of extramental reality—but neither are they mental entities in the usual sense.

To read Wittgenstein's work in logic is to find an account of meaning radically unlike the traditional account entrenched for many centuries in Western philosophy. As Harrison reports, "According to that traditional account, . . . to bestow meaning on a noun is, simply, to associate it conventionally with some item or aspect of the real world."[53] Put this way, though, the relationship between words and the world comes to seem strange and uncanny, as Wittgenstein says, making us feel "as if we had to *penetrate* phenomena" or leading to the notion that naming is "some remarkable act of mind."[54] According to Wittgenstein's new account of meaning, however, it is socially instituted and maintained practice that lets the speakers of language know what any given term means. The account of meaning provided by Wittgenstein and referenced by the phrases "meaning is use" and the more unfortunate "language game" does not, in other words, leave the whole business of meaning strangely disconnected from the world of our experience or the life we enjoy as physical, embodied beings. Quite the opposite, actually, and that is what Melville's "Cetology" chapter reveals.

What the chapter brings clearly into view is the cavernous understory of language, as Wittgenstein and his most sensitive readers conceive it: the vast fabric of socially devised and maintained practices that underpin the meanings of words.[55] For as Wittgenstein reasons, "the game with these words, their employment in the linguistic intercourse that is carried on by their means, is more involved—the role of these words in our language other—than we are tempted to think."[56]

"Cetology" bears this out. What the naturalists have failed to account for, in their definition of the concept "whale," is what Wittgenstein calls the "logical space" a concept occupies, which must also be understood if the concept is to be understood.[57] The difficulties we experience when reflecting on the meaning of a word, like the word "whale," have a great deal to do with how words are embedded in our lives. The reason the meaning of the word "whale" can't be grasped simply by pointing to some feature of the natural world, or by learning how to distinguish one object verbally from another, is because the concepts we command sit in a system of concepts as a whole—a conceptual armory from which they cannot be extricated. The more deeply a concept is lodged in layers of concepts, the understanding of which we take for granted, the less the system and structure that give a concept meaning can be given a satisfactory treatment in purely descriptive terms.

On this point Hugh Knott (aiming, like Wittgenstein and Melville, to understand what it is to *have* concepts) is pleasingly clear:

> If I am learning to compare the lengths of objects by measuring with a ruler and am learning how to describe the lengths of objects, and so on, I am learning the concept *length*. But we may also express this by saying that I know, or am getting to understand, what length *is*. It is informative to express the point in this way because it reminds us that to have a concept is not merely to operate with a sign or to have command over a technique; rather, the concept pervades our intelligent relations to the world. My understanding of the concept shows not only in the methods I use to measure and compare, but is distributed throughout my ways of speaking, throughout the *sense* I make of things by means of language. It is not difficult to imagine the breakdown of a person's grasp of the concept *length* and the loss of understanding and general intellectual collapse in the person's life that would manifest it. It would not be adequate in these circumstances to say that the person had merely lost the use of a word. Neither could it be accounted for as the loss of knowledge of any fact that might be referred to in the application of the concept. No, she no longer understands *what length is*, and in an important sense she is losing her grip on reality, on 'what the world is like.'

> Likewise, if a child is getting hold of the concept *cause*, this cannot be shown merely by an ability to make simple judgments of the relation of one event to another. Rather, it is something that has to work its way into the whole of her thinking and is manifested in the myriad ways in which she is able to make connections between things that are said and things that are done. If, on the other hand, the child failed to become fluent in all these connections, again it would not be adequate to say that this was simply a failure to grasp how to use a word (indeed, she might fail to grasp the use of the word even if her grasp of the concept showed in other things that she said). Here again we would have the right to say that there was a failure at the conceptual level to grasp the nature of the reality in which she lived. Beyond the reportage of facts, a person shows she has a grip on reality *in being able to talk sense.*[58]

The enormous benefit to this account is the discovery that something's being a conceptual object—or as we have learned to say now, a linguistic construct ("whale," for example) *makes it no less real.* For as Melville would have us discover, our concepts are not arbitrary, not notions we can take up or abandon at will. As an investigation into the way concepts are seated in our lives reveals, concept possession *as such* dependably reveals our knowledge and understanding of "what the world is like."

There can be no question, then, of dismissing the word or concept "whale" as meaningless on the ground that it fails to stand in some putatively required relationship to empirical reality.[59] As a handful of philosophers working in and extending the Wittgensteinian tradition have helped us see, words acquire meaning by our involving them in specific ways in some of the many practices by which human beings attempt to achieve control over their environment. The meanings of our words are thus neither arbitrary inventions of the human mind nor mutely proffered to us by Nature herself in sensory experience. The meaning of a word is a human artifact, but it is an artifact not of "the mind" but of practical life.

In "Cetology" Melville brings this point home. As he would have us remember, what we know as the meaning of the word "whale" is not something read off from the face of nature (as Ishmael swears the whale "has no face") but something elaborated over long centuries by collective human effort.[60] Of course, in Melville's extraordinary book only one figure has the temerity to insist upon this certainty—Melville's much-maligned Captain Ahab. When we understand Ahab in terms of Auerbach's notion of *figura*, as a character whose imagined principle of unity manifests some larger feature of a common if not universal human condition (as opposed to thinking with Starbuck that the captain is simply a madman who has chosen to pursue an absurd campaign of vengeance against a brute beast, without regard to the cost to his men, his ship, and his backers), we are well positioned to understand the Melvillean lesson: that we can ultimately make sense of the world only through our entanglement or immersion in practical and social life.

The formal lesson of "Cetology," then, is that when we speak of the entity referred to or designated by the expression "whale," we speak of a *linguistic construct*, a figment of discourse. When Starbuck declares that he will have no man in his boat "who is not afraid of a whale," the state of affairs identified by the word "whale" in Starbuck's expression is not a corporeal thing with the power to injure or be injured but a *thing-in-language*, an object postulated to bring coherence to experience. The whale in Starbuck's expression is not a natural object but what Harrison calls a "nomothetic object"—a creature "not of *physis* but of *nomos*." The whale has no existence in nature because it has no existence prior to the institution of the systems of convention that call it into being.[61]

But has Melville, in insisting that the entities designated by our expressions are figments of discourse, embraced the conclusion that our minds never pass beyond the circuit of their own linguistically forged conceptions? Is Melville arguing that the generation of meaning in language just reels arbitrarily onward, or is a function purely of the shifting relations of linguistic signs among themselves, uninfluenced in any way by considerations arising outside language? Is the author of *Moby-Dick* arguing that language (or thought enmeshed in language) cuts us off from truth and certainty? Absolutely not. For as I hope to have made plain, letting go of the idea that the bearing of reality on language must take the form of a direct associative link between a linguistic expression and an extralinguistic entity in fact sets in motion our genuine understanding of the relation between words and "what the world is like."[62]

When Wittgenstein posits a relation of identity between words and existing states of affairs (or as he also says, between *signs* and *things signified*), he strikes out genuinely new paths of thought. But Wittgenstein's central argument, fully developed only in the twentieth century in the work of Maurice Merleau-Ponty, Stanley Cavell, Bernard Harrison, and others, can already be encountered in embryo in *Moby-Dick*. The question around which *Moby-Dick* revolves—a question as central to recent philosophy as to that of the mid-nineteenth century—is whether the human mind can credit itself with access to reality. I've argued that in his whaling narrative Melville shows why, and by what means, it can.

Melville saw the thought of his age stranded between two options. On the one hand, an empiricism derived from Locke teaches us that sensory experience shows us things as they really are. On the other hand, an idealism derived from Kant teaches us that since the system of concepts in terms of which experience structures the world is provided by the mind itself, things in themselves—the Kantian *noumena*—are in principle inaccessible to human knowledge. In my view, Melville rejected both these options in favor of a third. According to this third option, the connection between language and reality is forged neither on the level of sensory experience nor on that of the intellect but rather in relation to our fumbling attempts to manipulate the world in practical ways. So, to begin with, the reasons for the recurrent use of a word or concept must be publically testable and acceptable by anyone. In other words, it is our concrete wants and needs that provide the material for the formation of our concepts. As Harrison writes, a bit of curved steel wire with a barb is a fishhook "not because that word is the one arbitrarily attached to a certain abstract intellectual pattern to which the object corresponds, nor because the word is arbitrarily attached to a collection of qualities that happen to recur from time to time in sensory experience, but rather because fish can, as a matter of practical fact, be caught with such a device."[63] It is also the case, however, that what we find, when we try to give an account of the meaning of the term "fishhook," is that a concept always employs *other* concepts on which it is logically dependent. The use of the expression "fishhook" is not isolated from the way we use other expressions, like "fish." The use of the expression "fishhook" forms part of a whole network of related trains of thought; this, too, is a hallmark of a concept.[64]

Intriguingly, the embeddedness of language in a vast number of socially engineered practices and the extent to which any single concept is inextricable from a system of concepts are what supports Ahab's claim to Starbuck that he, the captain, is one with his crew both in terms of the practical concerns of whaling and *in the systems of significance that emerge from them*. Ahab's repeated remonstrance to his first mate is that it is *Starbuck*, and not Ahab, who is out of sync with the whalers: "The crew, man, the crew! Are they not one and all with Ahab, in this matter of the whale? See Stubb! he laughs! See yonder Chilian! he snorts to think of it. Stand up amid the general hurricane, thy one tost sapling cannot, Starbuck! And what is it? Reckon it. 'Tis but to help strike a fin; no wonderous feat for Starbuck. What is it more? From this one poor hunt, then, the best lance out of all Nantucket, surely he will not hang back, when every foremost hand has clutched a whetstone?"[65] As Ahab frames it, the genesis of meaning is communal. In other words, it is Ahab and not Starbuck who lends moral force to Melville's story because in distinct contrast to Starbuck (for whom the whale has no meaning, or for whom the world exists for men to make of it what they will), Ahab is certain that the concept "whale" does have objectively articulated meaning. However, Ahab shows how meaning is accessible to human beings only at the cost of two kinds of immersion, each involving a certain surrender of individual control: immersion in the world through practical involvement with it and immersion in the communities in which the practices in question must be pursued.

In such an account, the world becomes one in which we are fully at home, but also one in which we are never fully cognitively in control—hence one to which responses of awe and wonder of the kind that pervade *Moby-Dick* are both natural and reasonable.

Chapter 4

The Third Realm

> It is in language that an expectation and its fulfillment make contact.
>
> —Wittgenstein, *Philosophical Investigations*

In *Moby-Dick*, in a cleaving stroke, Melville confirms that the concept "whale" has bearing on reality despite the absence of an antecedent referent to fix its meaning. To put it another way, Melville upholds the view that the concept "whale" is the kind of "non-sensible something" without which "everyone would remain shut up in his inner world," as Frege writes, that the thing signified by the sign "whale" belongs to what Frege calls the third realm, the realm of what is not sensible, and not imagined.[1]

Melville's accurate and at the same time deeply intuitive outlook is made possible by his having arrived at twin certainties. First, that the connection between the word or sign "whale" and the situation outside in the world it signifies is as Plato first argued a *logical* connection; in short, that this single concept can have many diverse applications because knowing the meaning of the word "whale" doesn't depend on knowing something in nature but on knowing how to use this word. This supposition is in line with the belief that it is the formal element of the concept "whale" that enables us to understand this notion. And second, that knowing the meaning of the word "whale" (knowing how to follow rules for the proper use of this word) isn't the kind of knowledge anyone could acquire all by himself.

We can be sure that the way the word "whale" becomes part of our language is a *public* process because learning rules for the use of a word involves understanding and knowing how to communicate expectations for the use of a word, expectations kindled by the activities in which the word is employed. These activities must be accessible in common to numerous individuals, though (as Melville shows in "Cetology") they are typically the activities of specific societies and grow out of the problems specific societies face. In *Moby-Dick* the name Melville gives to a person suitably acquainted with the activities of whaling is "whaleman." (See for example the passage, in chapter 57, "Of Whales in Paint; in Teeth; in Wood; in Sheet-Iron; in Stone," in which Ishmael describes "mountainous countries where the traveler is continually girded by amphitheatrical heights; here and there from some lucky point of view you will catch passing glimpses of the profiles of whales defined along the undulating ridges. But you must be a thorough whaleman, to see these sights.") As Ishmael repeatedly cautions, becoming a whaleman is prerequisite to knowing the meaning of the word "whale" for the reason that a whaleman is attuned not to the whale's identity, which remains undecidable in its own terms, but to the actions, duties, and rituals—the comforts and horrors—of the whaling life. The gift of Melville's whaling narrative is that it turns every reader into someone with a thorough appreciative understanding of the whale. Our view is not simply of the "barnacled hulls" of the leviathan but of its "unshored, harborless immensities."

When Melville pairs these two vital insights in *Moby-Dick*—when he puts the lesson that words do not get their meaning from natural objects together with the lesson that words serve our purposes—he provides evidence in support of the view that the formal element of the concept "whale" is intelligible only in relation to material life. He shows how evaluative judgments *are* tied to factual considerations—just not in the way we imagined. He shows how the concepts of language and the history of human experience are inseparable. In *Moby-Dick*, Melville in effect lays out a solution to the problem that has vexed philosophy since its inception—the problem of how we grasp thought.

As Frege observes, *that* we grasp thought is firmly established by the fact that humans can carry out conversations and conduct inquiries, but the question of *how* we grasp thought "is perhaps the most mysterious of all."[2] The question of how we grasp thought is exactly what Wittgenstein addresses when he attempts to shed light on the connection between "the signs on paper" and "a situation outside in the world."[3] Explaining the connection between a sentential sign and the situation that can be read off from it (or as Wittgenstein also says, coming to understand what the logical identity of sign and thing signified really consists in) is tantamount to answering the question of how we grasp thought, an unsolved mystery Wittgenstein considered a shortened form of "the whole philosophical problem."[4]

In *Moby-Dick* Melville takes up this mystery and, like Wittgenstein, arrives at a singular solution. It is a truly startling solution because its central thesis is that the veridicality of our words (that is, what makes the word "whale" *coincident with reality* and not just a way of naming empirical similarities) can be accounted for when we realize that the sense of a word—not the natural object to which the word refers but the conceptual object it signifies—is something "whose nature is no longer mental in the proper sense," as Frege writes in the essay "Logic."[5] As Melville's whaling narrative makes evident, the concept "whale" (what is grasped by everyone who is sufficiently familiar with the language of which the word is a part) is not sensible *and not mental*—that is, a species of idea and thereby subjective.[6] The thing signified by the word "whale" isn't a thing—but neither is it an idea.

Thus, according to Frege, "A third realm must be recognized." For as he explains, "Anything belonging to the third realm has it in common with ideas that it cannot be perceived by the senses, but has it in common with things that it does not need an owner so as to belong to the contents of his consciousness."[7] By this measure *thought itself* is not mental in the proper sense, as Frege duly points out.[8] Melville reaches practically the same conclusion when he determines that the thing signified by the sentential sign "whale" isn't apprehendable by the senses and isn't engineered in the "inner world" of the mind.

As Melville shows, what competent speakers grasp as the sense of this word—the *linguistic* meaning of the word "whale," the thing signified by the sign—has it in common with ideas that it can't be perceived with the senses and has it in common with things that it doesn't belong to the essentially subjective world of sense impressions, feelings, moods, and other creations of the imagination.

We might also say that the thing signified by the sentential sign "whale" (a nonsensible something correctly regarded as a thought but *not* as a species of idea) has a *formal element* and it has a *material element*. The formal element of this concept can be explained in terms of the role the word "whale" plays in language. But the concept has a material element too, and its material element is perhaps even harder to explain. Think of all the many and diverse ways in which something can be a whale; a whale can be white or vengeful or dead or poorly depicted or made from plastic or whatever. The "whatever" is important, as Alan Tapper and T. Brian Mooney write, because "new ways of instantiating any given concept are always possible."[9]

Now, precisely for the reason that our concepts are open textured or that new ways of instantiating a concept are always possible (evidenced, as Julius Kovesi writes, by the fact that we "cannot give a complete enumeration of the conditions that must be fulfilled for the proper use of a term . . . nor can it be stated how many of these conditions must be present and how many may be absent"), there can be no entailment relation between any actual example of a whale and what we say a whale is. What a whale is cannot be *deduced* from, nor can it be *defined in terms of* any concrete instance of a whale, and that is the root of Melville's quarrel with the naturalists.[10]

As a result, "what a whale is" must be determined by its formal element. As Melville is able to demonstrate in the "Cetology" chapter, it is the formal element of the concept "whale" that decides what a whale is and makes it possible to distinguish what is from what is not a whale. Or as Ishmael and his fellow whalers impart, it is the formal element of the concept "whale" that makes our knowledge of whales inextricable from life at sea.

In consequence, and unexpectedly, we must conclude that it is the *formal element* of our concepts that connects the signs in language to practical life, the life we enjoy as physical, embodied beings, manipulators of an equally physical world. This is the argument Melville brings to the fore in *Moby-Dick*. In the case of the whale, the concept's formal element is what grounds it in the physical world since, as Melville's whaling narrative illustrates, the concept's formal element (the role the word "whale" plays in language) comes into being not in the private theater of the individual mind but in the innumerable public theaters of the marketplace, the forecastle, the tryworks, the pulpit—that is, in the countless theaters of operation that "continually form and reform themselves," as Bernard Harrison writes, "in the course of the detailed working-out of inter-personal relationship and social-life."[11]

The internal or logical relation between a concept of language and socially devised practice explains why, for Melville, familiarity with the theaters of operation out of which the meaning of the word "whale" is generated is so indispensible—why Melville works so hard to provide the basis for his readers' proper comprehension of activities such as pitchpoling, baling the case, trying out, and slicing blubber. Understanding of the systematized practices of mid-nineteenth-century whaling isn't supplementary to the imagined action of Melville's novel (what is typically understood as Ahab's quest to destroy Moby-Dick but what I have framed as Ahab's refusal to choose between the phenomenal and noumenal realms) but essential to it. Scholars convinced of the importance of Melville's scrupulous attention to the practices of the whaling industry, no matter how seemingly inconsequential to the action of his story, argue that the book's ostensibly tedious chapters "examine the whale in such a way as to relate the whale and whaling to virtually every field of human endeavor."[12] But an even more practicable way of understanding Melville's detailed inclusion of the systematized practices of whaling is to say that such chapters demonstrate the interdependence of a concept and what Wittgenstein calls a "form of life." The majority of *Moby-Dick*'s chapters are dedicated to showing how the *life* of a whaleman and the word or sign "whale" become intelligible only in relation to each other, and thus why the problems naturalists have knowing "what a whale is" arise out of a failure to see that relation clearly.

Thus for anyone wishing to understand how we grasp thought or grasp a concept like "whale," a very important point to observe is that the formation of concepts must be a public process.[13] This point needs emphasizing because a surprisingly large number of philosophers talk as if "each of us spoke a private language and yet paradoxically lived in society," as Julius Kovesi writes. And yet, as Kovesi notes, "terms used in our language are not formed by a single person who then trims them to suit others, nor are they a selection from private vocabularies made to suit, or be accepted by, others. Nor is it the case that we try to persuade others to accept our privately formed notions."[14] The formation of a concept must be a public process because the rubrics that govern the meaning of our words are the same rubrics that govern the rules for their proper use. That is what Melville emphasizes in "Cetology" when he has Ishmael and his friends in the whale fishery raise such a hue and cry over Linnaeus's attempt to banish the whales from the waters or (as the whalers see it) dissociate the meaning of the word "whale" from the actual, rather specific practices in connection with which our notion of a whale has been formed. I say "our" notion because, as the whalers rightly observe, the formal element of the concept "whale" issues from the operation of interpersonal rules established on the basis of considerations that concern the relevant needs and interests not of "Simeon Macey and Charlie Coffin, of Nantucket" but of *anyone* caught up, in one way or another, in the various procedures and operations the term "whale" was invented to serve.[15]

Precisely because the meaning of the word "whale" is a function of the way this word engages with or is involved in a variety of socially derived and maintained practices, there is a public or "objective" dimension to this concept. What emphasis on the shared or communal aspect of concept formation underscores is that our concepts do not, as Julius Kovesi writes, "reflect the needs, wants, aspirations or ideals of any one person or a group of individuals, but those of anyone." This is so "not because we happen to be such nice people that we formulate our notions from the point of view of anyone, but because our language is public."[16]

To concede that language is public is to grant that the meaning of a word issues from the operation of interpersonal rules established on the basis of considerations that concern the relevant needs and interests, not of one person, but of anyone caught up in the various procedures and operations the word was invented to serve. It is to admit that what makes it possible for us to communicate by means of language isn't the aid of exact, agreed-upon definition but the way the meanings of our words, left indeterminate in everyday usage, are decided by the roles those words play in connection with the practices speakers of language have found (perhaps only for a time) to be of practical, heuristic use.[17]

Hence the significance of Ahab's discovery, in chapter 36, "The Quarter-Deck," that the white whale haunting him—the same white whale "that some call Moby Dick"—is known to those hands and feet of his enterprise, his harpooners. At Ahab's mention of the creature's wrinkled brow and crooked jaw, Tashtego, Daggoo, and Queequeg each started as if "separately touched by some specific recollection":

> "Captain Ahab," said Tashtego, "that white whale must be the same that some call Moby Dick."
>
> "Moby Dick?" shouted Ahab. "Do ye know the white whale then, Tash?"
>
> "Does he fan-tail a little curious, sir, before he goes down?" said the Gay-Header deliberately.
>
> "And has he a curious spout, too," said Daggoo, "very bushy, even for a parmacetty, and mighty quick, Captain Ahab?"
>
> "And he have one, two, tree—oh! good many iron in him hide, too, Captain," cried Queequeg disjointedly, "all twiske-tee be-twisk, like him—him" faltering hard for a word, and screwing his hand round and round as though uncorking a bottle—"like him—him—"
>
> "Corkscrew?" cried Ahab, "aye, Queequeg, the harpoons lie all twisted and wrenched in him; aye, Daggoo, his spout is a big one, like a whole shock of wheat, and white as a pile of our Nantucket wool after the great annual sheep-shearing; aye, Tashtego, and he fan-tails like a split job in a squall. Death and devils! Men, it is Moby Dick ye have seen—Moby Dick—Moby Dick!"

In this passage the concept "Moby Dick" isn't reduced to an essential collection of traits; each harpooner's specific recollection, after all, is *different*. Rather, the lesson we can take from the passage is that concepts, even a highly specialized concept like "Moby Dick," have to retain an indeterminacy of meaning if they are going to remain dynamic—that is, if the concept is going to go on satisfying the needs of those whose language is suited for a range of purposes, many of them unforeseen. At the same time, the meaning of a word is constituted by or sedimented out of long usage in many contexts. A word acquires meaning in relation to the role given it by people who are themselves inhabitants of the material world and as such are engaged in certain practices, socially devised modes of engaging with material reality—measuring, for instance, or counting, or differentially comparing colors. In other words, neither Ahab nor anyone else can give the word "Moby Dick" any private, arbitrary meaning he pleases. In everyday language what we know as the meaning of a word is both indeterminate and objectively articulated.

That the meaning of a word is both indeterminate and objectively articulated is what Plato means to emphasize when he suggests that the solution to many problems in philosophy lies in the art of proper divisions—that when we attempt to divide a conceptual object, or as Plato says a *form object*, into a number of different categories, we have failed to understand how concepts work.

That is the accusation Plato's Socrates levels at the rhetorician Lysias—of whom Phaedrus is a disciple—in Plato's *Phaedrus*. As Socrates argues, Lysias's and the other rhetoricians' way of talking about "love" (or about any other nebulous concept) isn't to be trusted because the rhetoricians' way of talking doesn't follow two important principles. The first principle is what Socrates identifies as "the comprehension of scattered particulars in one idea."[18] So, rather than understand how *one concept* can have *many diverse applications*, Lysias feels himself shrewd (and scores points as a public speaker, as Socrates sagely points out) by saying that "love is this" or "love is that" when it suits him. The second principle is what Socrates identifies as "that of division into species according to the natural formation, where the joint is, not breaking any part as a bad carver might." The suggestion in the *Phaedrus* is that we speak less falsely when, speaking of a concept like "love," we adhere to the concept's objective articulation and do not "hack off parts like a clumsy butcher."[19] One of Plato's central insights is that our concepts are complex, interconnected structures, and that these structures are not based on arbitrary choice or personal whim. Accordingly, concepts—which are necessarily open textured or left undetermined—nevertheless have a state or quality of being true outside a subject's individual biases, interpretations, feelings, and imaginings.

In the "Cetology" chapter it is ironically the naturalists and not the whalers who hack off parts of the concept "whale" in their attempt to say what a whale is. The whalers' urge to consider the *whole* story of the whale is a good one, that is to say, one that is in keeping with Plato's instruction. For as "Cetology" helps us to understand, what Plato identifies as a concept's objectivity isn't the starting point of transcendent truth but the end point of countless, ordinary conceptual distinctions made (and remade, as times and conventions change) by the speakers of language. We say the concept "whale" is *objectively* articulated because the theater in which this notion is formed is never the private theater of the mind but the public theater of a specific social order—that is, not society-as-a-whole but the particular society in which particular problems of mutual coexistence have arisen. In other words, the concept "whale" becomes "universal" only by spreading from its particularist roots.[20] What confronts us in this notion is, as Bernard Harrison writes, "an endlessly shifting dance of conceptual creation founded in the development and subsequent modification of reasoned patterns of practical mutual accommodation."[21]

In "Cetology," and in the many short chapters that cumulatively contribute to our thorough appreciative understanding of the whale, Melville is obliquely introducing and also laying to rest the problem of the One and the Many: the problem of how *one concept* can have *many diverse applications*—or as we may also put it, how a concept like "whale," whose meaning must be left indeterminate in everyday usage, can also be True. Melville returns again and again to this problem in his whaling narrative not because it prostrates him but because he believes himself to have effectively dealt with it. His reasoning sounds something like this. Heralding or indicating what in "The Battering-Ram" Melville calls "a mass of tremendous life" (the particulars of any state of affairs, actual examples of a given case) is a form object or linguistic construct. We say the word "whale" is a *sign* of the many instantiations of this concept because, as Melville notes, a mass of tremendous life can only be "adequately estimated as piled wood is—by the cord." This is also to say that our specifically human way of measuring life, the sense of a word, is *not* an idea. The sense a word expresses is an artifact not of "the mind" but of practical life. Or as Melville's whaling narrative illustrates, in every generalizing concept lurks the practical details of some state of affairs: general concepts like "whale" do not discount or leave out the minutely particular.

Naturally, a fiction writer's business is not with argument. Melville hasn't the duty to spell out for his readers the account of meaning in language I have been assembling here—what it is to possess a concept; why concepts *are* in the public domain; how concept possession *as such* dependably reveals our knowledge and understanding of "what the world is like." All the same, perhaps because imaginative writing requires an intellectual and spiritual atmosphere to which philosophical argument contributes, and (as Hawthorne and Melville complained) American mid-nineteenth-century authors operated largely in the absence of such an atmosphere, Melville felt compelled to manufacture his own kind of philosophical investigation—not systematically in lengthy prefaces or literary manifestos but widely dispersed throughout his fiction, poetry, journals, reviews, and marginalia.[22] All Melville's imaginative writing is shot through with that critical mode of discourse that signifies a powerful mediating force between author and text, text and world. In *Moby-Dick*, this critical intervention sometimes takes the form of dissuading readers from seeking answers to questions that are *themselves* confused and disorienting. (For as some critics have shown, many of the problems in philosophy arise out of a mistaken impression about the kinds of questions we should be asking.)[23] Melville's whaling narrative vigorously if not explicitly shows how we are asking the wrong kinds of questions and by these means repositions its readers, affording us the best chance to think through on our own the conceptual tangles that bedevil us.

One question that routinely holds us captive is this one: What is the relationship between a word or name or sign in our language and its extralinguistic counterpart? As *Moby-Dick* reveals, attempting to answer this question either turns us into naturalists, struggling in vain to connect words to things out in the world that we access with our senses, or it turns us into puzzled and puzzling metaphysicians, philosophers who make naming look like some remarkable act of mind.

In *Moby-Dick* Melville supplies evidence for why we should simply stop asking the question about the relationship between words and extralinguistic entities, since its presumptive picture—that language reflects a world structure, or that there is a logically primeval landscape that later gets reported in language—is grossly distorted.[24] In marked contrast, the presumption informing *Moby-Dick* is that there is nothing statable to which our words must conform. In *Moby-Dick*, the abstract structure of the world is formed within language and not the other way around.[25] This view is curative because it offers a way out of what has come to seem like an unsolvable problem, what Melville slyly names "the Problem of the Universe" but what is more generally speaking the whole thorny question of how we grasp thought—the urgency of which, after all, stems from the requirement to bridge the ontological chasm between *nonspatiotemporal thoughts* (objectively articulated concepts like "whale") and the *spatiotemporally bound mortals* (perishable, transient fellows fettered to their mortal frames "like an oyster to its shell") who think them.[26]

The Melvillean solution is to see that the linguistic meaning or thought expressed by a sentential sign belongs to the third realm and therefore that *there isn't any ontological chasm* between a thinker and the thought he thinks; to see, in short, that although we have grown accustomed to calling the things signified by the signs in our language "ideas" and thus of associating them with the idiosyncratic privacy of impressions, the things signified by signs are not ideas. True, they cannot be perceived by the senses, but neither do they belong to the contents of any one person's consciousness. Better to say that the things signified by the signs in our language are the special kinds of things Frege recognized the possibility of when he formulated his notion of a third realm.

So, in Starbuck's proviso, "I'll have no man in my boat who is not afraid of a whale," the word "whale" is a sign, and the *thing signified* by this word or impossible not to recognize in this word—the alleged "thing" with which the word "whale" shares a relation of identity—isn't, as poor Starbuck thinks, the sign's physical form, all the many and diverse instances of whales that Starbuck attempts to kill for his living. Rather, the thing signified by the sign is the sign's linguistic meaning, *another* kind of sign, as Plato first intuited, since it isn't found in nature. (Anyhow the thing signified by the word "whale," what Melville calls "the living whale in his full majesty and significance," isn't what killed hundreds of men known to Starbuck—what doomed Starbuck's own father, as Starbuck laments, what tore the limbs of his brother.)[27] On the other hand, despite the fact that the thing signified by the sign "whale" is not a thing but another kind of sign (the word's *linguistic* meaning, what we know without being told how to read off from the sign), the thing signified is in no sense the product of an "inner world," the world of sense impressions or creations of the imagination. In this special sense Starbuck's assumption that the whale is more like a thing than an idea is quite correct. As *Moby-Dick* helps us to see, the thing signified by the sign "whale" is determined by the logical role this word plays in language. That is to say, the thing signified by the sign "whale" is not private but public; it is ordered by the needs and interests of *anyone* caught up in the various procedures and operations the term "whale" was invented to serve.

Handily for Melville's readers, the radical view around which *Moby-Dick* is organized—the view that the thing signified by a sign in a subject-predicate sentence is neither a thing in nature nor an idea—does have a defender among the ranks of professional philosophers, for it is the view Wittgenstein puts forward in his *Tractatus Logico-Philosophicus*. That the things signified by the signs in language are the chief occupants of the third realm is, as I see it, the provocative claim that coincides with and galvanizes Wittgenstein's decision not to conduct his work in philosophy as his predecessors had—that is, as David Charles McCarty writes, by acting as if "the world was something we comprehended by building up to it, following from below an order which we took to lie entirely in it."[28]

For McCarty, to read the *Tractatus* is not to read a mild revision of Russell's atomism; it is to read the destruction of atomism root and branch. As McCarty notes in his long essay "The Philosophy of Logical Wholism," the *Tractatus* is "from the very first" a rejection of semantical atomism, just as Wittgenstein's work in logic "was anything but acquiescence in what had gone on in logic before":

> Since Parmenides, the study of ontology has been a study in world lists or world inventories . . . The first step is to run through all the sorts of things in the world. The world becomes a stockroom whose contents we debate. You say, "Perhaps there are only elementary particles" and I might reply, "No, everything is pure spirit or neutral monad." This is the comfortingly familiar approach to philosophy.
>
> In ontology, it would be wholly alien to start the other way altogether—from the world as undifferentiated whole. This would defeat our ontological expectation for world overview by world list. This is why Wittgenstein's first sentence
>
> Die Welt ist alles was der Fall ist.
>
> ought to shock. Neither Russell nor Frege would have taken the *whole world* as philosophical starting point.[29]

The first sentence or proposition of the *Tractatus* (usually translated as "The world is all that is the case") takes the whole world as philosophical starting point in order to put a stop to philosophers' tendency to think of the world as constructed or built up out of discrete units and thus interpretable through analysis into distinct, separable, and independent parts.

When Wittgenstein says that the world is *alles was der Fall ist*, "he is giving notice," as McCarty writes, for though the English translation of Wittgenstein's phrase is "all that is the case," Wittgenstein's construction of the sentence is meant to rule out the possibility that we can continue to think of the world as the collection of *all things*.[30] As McCarty notes, "*der Fall*" is not just any old thing that goes on during the course of the day. Isolated events, easily reported, will not do as an answer to the question, *Was war der Fall?* Answering this question requires, rather, "a confluence of influences, a pattern of considerations which the speaker assembles in order to explain or to make sense of a complex issue, say, the course of a treaty negotiation or the passage of legislation." As McCarty reasons, the difference is one of exposition, or lies in the style of the telling. World as *alles was der Fall ist* is in McCarty's more deft rendering "world as structured not in itself but in the arrangement of the story." McCarty's contention is therefore that "one can see the error of atomism from the very first sentence of the *Tractatus*."[31]

Wittgenstein's yearning to produce an alternative for what was going on in logic is further demonstrated by the "comments," as he calls them, that follow proposition 1, "The world is all that is the case." At the first of these, comment 1.1, Wittgenstein writes, "The world is the totality of facts, not of things." Having declared in a footnote that the decimal numbers assigned to his individual propositions—there are seven in the *Tractatus*—"indicate the logical importance of the propositions, the emphasis laid upon them in my exposition," Wittgenstein's clarification of what is accordingly his most important proposition, his first proposition about the way the world is structured, ought to be given matching importance. For in his comments Wittgenstein clearly rejects the notion of the world as a stockroom whose contents we debate. Instead he characterizes the world as that which is divided into "facts." "The world divides into facts," writes Wittgenstein in his fifth comment. What Tractarian "facts" are at this point remains unclear, but in Wittgenstein's fourth comment, comment 1.13, he usefully glosses them as "facts in logical space," an edifying phrase that prepares readers for the difficulty of proposition 2, "*Was der Fall ist, die Tatsache, ist das Bestehen von Sachverhalten* (usually, "What is the case—the fact—is the existence of states of affairs"), and the set of explanatory remarks that follow that proposition.

Since the totality of what Wittgenstein calls "facts in logical space" are the world, as he writes, it is only to be expected that in the comments that follow proposition 2 Wittgenstein labors to establish what a Tractarian "fact" is. No doubt this labor does not in every case produce its desired or intended result. My suggestion, though, is that Wittgenstein's great effort to characterize the "facts in logical space" that all together constitute the world (comments 2.01–2.225) in the end encourages the conclusion that

Tractarian facts are the not sensible and not merely subjective inhabitants of Frege's third realm. Tractarian "facts in logical space" are the *things signified* by sentential signs, concepts, like the concept "whale," whose formal element relieves the need to look for empirical similarities between various instances of the same thing in order to explain *why* they are instances of the same thing, and whose formal element (the role the word "whale" plays in language) comes into being not in the private theater of the individual mind but in the numberless public theaters that form and re-form themselves in the course of everyday social life—in short, around people living or disposed to live in companionship with others in a community, rather than in isolation.

And yet the conclusion that Tractarian facts (*Tatsachen*) are not entirely material and not merely subjective—that they are *not things* and *not ideas*—is not possible if Tractarian "objects" (*Gegenstände*) as Wittgenstein identifies them in comments 2.01–2.225 are simply translated as "things." Great confusion has come from rendering Tractarian "objects" into "things." Pears and McGuinness turn Tractarian objects into things when they translate Wittgenstein's first comment on proposition 2—"*Der Sachverhalt ist eine Verbindung von Gegenständen* (*Sachen*, *Dingen*)"—this way: "A state of affairs is a combination of objects (things)." In the Pears and McGuinness translation, Wittgenstein's short inventory annotating the word "objects," his parenthetical "*Sachen, Dingen,*" is replaced by the single word "things" (*Dingen*). Lost, then, is Wittgenstein's astonishing claim that the "combination of objects" that constitutes an extant state of affairs (*Sachverhalt*) is a combination of natural objects (*Dingen*) and nonnatural objects (*Sachen*). This is an indefensible loss because Wittgenstein's claim is that "*Was der Fall ist*"—the Tractarian fact—unites *material* and *nonmaterial* parts. A Tractarian fact has in other words a material element and it has a formal element. Thus, though Wittgenstein writes at 2.011 that "it is essential to a thing that it can be a constituent part of a state of affairs," it is perhaps more to the point that *no matter how many things go into their constitution*, facts, existing states of affairs, belong to the logical realm, the realm of what is not sensible and not merely subjective. This insight has weight, since showing how facts in logical space or the things signified by the signs in our subject-predicate sentences can have material elements and still be creatures of *nomos* is what makes it possible to construct an account of meaning in language without forgetting that signs and things signified enjoy a logical and not a natural connection.[32]

Wittgenstein was handicapped by the established terminology in expressing his view, but the truly remarkable argument Wittgenstein makes in the opening pages of the *Tractatus* is that a natural object (an object it *is* possible to encounter by way of the senses—a "thing," as Wittgenstein says) can form part of a fact in logical space (the kind of objectively existing, nonsensible object Plato called "real") *without altering the character* of the fact or without changing what is necessarily logical-philosophical matter into empirical matter.

To see Tractarian facts in this light—to see them as third-realm objects—is to see that Wittgenstein's logical investigation is nothing like the investigations of his predecessors. As McCarty writes, Wittgenstein's investigation is "not one of surveying individual verdicts conveyed in or by formulae of particular logical systems. It is not one of specific formal rules. It is a gauging of the potential in all signs and their symbols, the potential for the battery of signs to become a logical medium of thought. It is a search after the origin of life, of what gives life to the sign."[33]

In *Moby-Dick*, the whale is a fact. Melville achieves the aim for which Dante invoked the help of the Muses—"*si che dal fatto il dir non sia diverso*" (so that speech is not different from fact)—when he illuminates or makes perceptible "what is," or what belongs to the logical realm, what Frege calls the third realm, which is the realm of that which is neither purely material nor merely subjective.[34] As *Moby-Dick*'s readers come to understand, the fact or existing state of affairs Melville identifies as "the living whale in his full majesty and significance" isn't a thing but a thing-in-language, a figment of discourse whose formal element grounds it in the physical world. The whale is a fact, *was der Fall ist*, that combination of the natural and the conceptual (as Wittgenstein argues) that emerges to make intellection possible and without which everyone would remain shut up in his inner world. What Melville makes visible in his whaling narrative is the nonsensible but objectively real thing signified by the sign "whale."

For Melville, the whale is one of the "facts" into which the world divides. But then so is every other blessed thing signified in language. As Melville would have us recall, all the things we have names for (the line, the monkey-rope, the tryworks, the Pacific, the quadrant, the chief mate, the life buoy, cutting in, stowing down, and so forth) are not "things" but *things-in-language*, things given an immense depth because they are not put together in the material or empirical realm but in the logical realm. Things configured in the logical space of language (within the horizons of sense, in a network of relations) have added dimension because, as signs, they can be used to decipher the continuous aspects of reality. Things-in-language have great energy and life because that is the nature of signs. What we know as the "meaning" of a word or sign has it in common with ideas that it can't be wholly perceived by the senses, and has it in common with things that it doesn't belong to the essentially private realm of personal fancy. What a word or sign means satisfies the requirement for being real because it is not subjective. Or, since the word "whale" is true of something, what "whale" means is true. Quite simply, signs are real.[35]

In *Moby-Dick* Melville opens readers to the vital experience of sense, to the way a situation, structured not in itself but in the pattern of its telling, comes to have meaning for us. *Moby-Dick*, like the *Tractatus*, is a gauging of the potential in all signs. It is a search for the origin of life—which to human speakers of language really means a search for what gives life to the sign.

As I have tried to show, such an undertaking requires and is precipitated by a view of language and of the structure of the logical world wholly unlike the view promulgated by the philosophers and scientists of Melville's day. For from the empiricist tradition in English-speaking philosophy came the idea of language not as a means to register and test but as an instrument for accurately representing the sensible world—a world defined by the fact that it is, precisely, extralinguistic: in existence before and despite our ways of conceiving it. That is why, to theorists hailing from the empiricist tradition, the requirement for accurate and meaningful discourse is that, as Locke writes, "when any man uses a term he may have in his mind a determined idea which he makes it the sign of."[36] As Locke reasons in *Essay Concerning Human Understanding* (1689), we can expect nothing but "obscurity and confusion" from a person who uses the term "whale," for instance, unless it can be shown to be what Locke called a "determined idea," a way of thinking demonstrably in touch with empirical reality.[37] For empiricist philosophers, to understand a general name in language is to possess the ability to identify items or characteristics of the sort to which the name applies. The consequence of this way of thinking is that it ties knowledge of "what is" to knowledge of something's essential nature.

And yet the notion summarily dispensed with in *Moby-Dick* is that without fully grasping the essential nature of the whale, the writer of a whaling narrative can have no idea of what he is talking about. As to what the nature of the whale might be, Melville suggests, the writer of a whaling narrative need possess only the vaguest and sketchiest ideas; actually, if it comes right down to it, he needs to know nothing at all.[38]

Accordingly, the whole idea that words designate or stand for things that are altogether external to language or in no way constituted by it (an idea that has a very long history in philosophy, in both the thought that preceded Melville's time and the thought that followed it) is rejected and lampooned in *Moby-Dick*. The work of the present volume has been to show how Melville engineers in his readers an immunity or resistance to philosophical doctrine *then as now* utterly convincing to the vast majority of critics and theorists. For in his whaling narrative Melville cunningly and deliberately abandons the notion that meaning in language is determined by the connection between words and the nature of things. Rather, what we know as the "meaning" of a word is (as "Cetology" makes clear) something elaborated over long centuries by collective human effort.[39]

This view—that the meaning of a word issues from the operation of interpersonal rules established on the basis of considerations that concern the relevant needs and interests not just of a single individual but of *anyone* caught up in the procedures and operations the word was invented to serve—is the position staked out by Ahab, the fiercest of Melville's "original characters," as he calls them, characters in whom there is discernible something prevailingly "of the age."[40]

In *The Confidence Man*, Melville distinguishes between characters in which there is "but something personal," something "confined to itself," and *original* characters. An original character, Melville writes, "is like a revolving Drummond light, raying away from itself all around it—everything is lit by it, everything starts up to it (mark how it is with Hamlet), so that, in certain minds, there follows upon the adequate conception of such a character, an effect, in its way, akin to that which in Genesis attends upon the beginning of things." Pip, Starbuck, Queequeg, Bulkington—each comes palpably to life in *Moby-Dick*, however briefly he appears, because, for all their evident personality, these characters exceed the personal (as Melville insists, they are *not* imitations of living people) and embody besides the "event" that is being related. When a character's crucial traits or personality is governed and limited by what can only be intellected, by the event that is being related, the result is, as Auerbach reasoned, "the real and evident figure" in a work of art.[41]

But how much more this holds true for Ahab. What a figure is Ahab, standing before us "with a crucifixion in his face"; his wasted, branded, dismasted body broadcasting "all the nameless regal overbearing dignity of some mighty woe." Ahab's "whole grim aspect" is his own—he's a scarred, one-legged old Manxman with preternatural powers of discernment—but Ahab's crucial traits are brought out or given dimension through his embodiment of the very definite event that is being related: the agony of finding himself caught between two worlds, the finite and the infinite, and feeling himself split apart.

What might it mean, then, that Ahab refuses to be so riven? That, perfectly aware of the forced choice he must make between things visible, "conceits of the eye," and things imaginative, "conceits of the fancy"—between things and ideas—Ahab persists in saying he hasn't a choice, that "choice" as such is unavailable to him?

My suggestion is that Ahab's pursuit (which the mate Starbuck can see only as Ahab's strenuous effort to "wreak his vengeance on a dumb brute") throws light on an issue of central importance to Melville's age: the issue of whether, and by what means, the human mind can credit itself with access to *what is*, the domain with which no one person's experience can be coextensive, as Melville writes, but to which experience is the only guide.

Accordingly, when Ahab finally says what's on his mind—when in "The Quarter-Deck" he reveals what Ishmael calls his "intense bigotry of purpose"—what he discloses isn't just some private torment but one of the great sources of philosophical bewilderment. "Blasphemous" is what Starbuck calls Ahab's determination "to be enraged with a dumb thing," and perhaps for that reason Ahab has become associated with notions of monstrous impiety. But in fact all Ahab's soliloquies and even his offhand remarks about the whale intelligibly recount the problem that since ancient times has occupied our noblest minds: what Ahab confronts head-on in his quarrel with the whale is the seeming discontinuity between the whale's abiding, unassailable significance (evidenced by his indisputable grasp of the concept "whale") and the limitations of his person, the certainty that his actual dealings are with the objects of his senses, those fleshy, fatty creatures he may or may not get his hands on.

To be sure, Ahab refuses to go along with the vision of the world that speaks itself through Starbuck. For Starbuck, the world is built up out of discrete, material things, "dumb" things whose names somehow signal their natures. Ahab responds to Starbuck's conviction that material objects are cognitive starting points (that the world tells us how to speak) by insisting that the things we name are *not* "things." As Ahab well understands, there is nothing in the natural world to which the word or name "whale" corresponds. The whale is not a perceivable object in the world, nor is meaning achieved when we attach names to perceivable objects. That subtle latticework of pernicious fallacies is what Ahab tears into when he notifies Starbuck that "all visible objects, man, are but as pasteboard masks." That the ground floor of Starbuck's explanatory structure can't bear any weight is what Ahab calls attention to when he tells his first mate to look again at "the little lower layer."

Ahab then advances a halting step further, deliberately pushing his argument in the opposite direction. By insisting that "in each event—in the living act, the undoubted deed—some unknown but still reasoning thing puts forth the moldings of its features from behind the unreasoning mask," Ahab argues that in any *given* situation his hold on reality feels sure; in everyday life it does not feel like he is living in two worlds, the material world of ships and oceans, wood and stone, and an inner world of conscious states or creations of his imagination, a world of sense impressions, of feelings and moods, directly knowable only to him.

Rather than go on trying to explain to Starbuck the difference between the things man can apprehend through his senses (the totality of which is the world, according to Starbuck) and the things signified by the signs in our language (the totality of which is the world, according to Ahab), Ahab determines to show how, to *speakers of language* (that is, to the children of Adam, with whom Ahab, "staggering beneath the piled centuries since Paradise," is identified), the things signified by words seem so autonomous or so much like material things they feel within striking range. With Ahab's almost painfully concrete image—"If man will strike, strike through the mask!" "How can the prisoner reach outside except by thrusting through the wall?"—Ahab sets about proving the case: that to have the use of words is to have all the world before us; that the world our words open on to is as palpable and concrete as it is ethereal and dreamlike.

To put it another way, Ahab refuses to concede that there are two sorts of whales, those we conceptualize and those we encounter; for Ahab there is only what Melville calls "the true form of the whale as he actually appears to the eye of the whaleman when in his own absolute body the whale is moored alongside the whale-ship so that he can be fairly stepped upon there."

Of course, in Ahab's ruthlessly efficient speech the captain also makes known his intention to hunt Moby Dick, but what powers this pursuit isn't a hysterical refusal of the view, now commonplace, that truth and certainty are unavailable to individuals imprisoned, perforce, in the material world. It is rather a frantic, feverish grab at a feature of the situation theorists skeptical about the whole possibility of truth have failed to observe. For while we cannot but agree that the whale is not a perceivable object in the world, the conclusion we take from this needn't be that the whale is not the object of our reason (as Hume would have us believe) but that the whale is not the object of our senses.[42] In an important sense, in the world there *are* no whales. But as Melville's whaling narrative underscores, our language is not about that world in which there are no whales. The object lesson in *Moby-Dick* is not that whales don't really exist but that *our language does not mirror the natural world.* Whatever might be the advantages of a language that mirrors the natural world, our language is not such a language: as Julius Kovesi writes, "in our language, to be able to understand the significance or the meaning of a term, we have to be able to follow a rule in using this term, not to be able to perceive an entity of which our term is a name."

To the worry that in chasing the whale he is chasing an apparition—a figment of the imagination, a collection of "outblown rumors," "morbid hints," and "half-formed foetal suggestions," gathering volume from "transit over the widest watery spaces"—Ahab thus offers a stout reply: thinking that the living whale in his full majesty eludes him is the real fantasy, since the meaning of the word "whale" hasn't emerged out of some kind of ratiocination. On the contrary, the meaning of the word is constituted by, or sedimented out of, long usage in many contexts.[43]

That the meaning of the word "whale" is an artifact of *practical life* is the lesson Ahab's pursuit will eventually emphasize. Through Ahab, Melville calls attention to the material composition of those "facts"—as Wittgenstein calls them—into which the world divides. Sureness about the potentialities for meaning in everyday life is what Melville energetically defends, in other words, when he sends the pursuer Ahab out to his foreseeable demise.

For of course the idea that a *whale* should, of all things, require pursuit wasn't determined at random, or simply because Melville had spent some time on a whaling ship. Since the book of Job, the whale has figured as the epitome of third-realm objects—the realm of facts, or the realm of objects that are objectively real but not part of the natural world. In Job, God uses the whale to remind Job that he has no thorough understanding of this realm. Job has forgotten about the limitations of human knowledge and, as God says, "uttered that which he knew not" (42:4). Provoked by those who "darkeneth counsel by words without knowledge" (38:2), God speaks to Job out of the whirlwind, reviewing the grandeur and multifariousness of the created world in the form of questions addressed to Job. Job is asked about the earth's foundation, if indeed he has "understanding," if he "knows" (38:4). Here God calls attention to the *basis* of man's material and intellectual life, the basis of everything empirical—that is,

God. Or as Job is forced to remember, just because he is able to perceive sensible objects and call things by name doesn't mean he knows anything about the absolute: "Will you catch the leviathan with a fishhook?" God asks contemptuously. "Will merchants bid for his carcass and parcel him out in shops?"

These questions about the leviathan form the most stinging part of God's rebuke: that having confused the empirical realm with the logical realm, man has lost sight of the distinction between things and the meaning of things. As Job has failed to recall, it is the logical realm (God's realm) and not the empirical realm that man is operating in when he uses the signs of his language.

God's admonishment of Job is thus designed to accentuate the contrast between epistemic knowledge and intuitive knowledge. Epistemic knowledge of the whale is what man makes use of when he enumerates the whale's properties, assembles the criteria for distinguishing between whale species, packages the whale as a commodity, and develops other methods of hacking off parts of the whale like a clumsy butcher, as Plato says.[44] Intuitive knowledge of the whale, on the other hand, is what is demonstrated when the sentences in language make meaningful use of the word "whale." Intuitive knowledge of the whale isn't knowledge of *what* the whale is but *that* it is.

The book of Job in this way maintains the hierarchical distinction between *things* and *facts*—between what can be apprehended and what is. A fact, God reminds his servant Job, is what is the case. According to this story, when man grasps a fact, what he has hold of is his knowledge of a thing, *together with knowledge of its cause*, God.[45] When God ridicules Job for thinking the leviathan is something he could catch or peddle, therefore, what is being ridiculed is Job's naïveté on this count—his propensity for treating facts as if they were things.

In other words it is his belatedness, his absence at the laying of foundations, that God hammers into Job. "Where wast thou when I laid the foundations of the earth?" (38:4) God demands. "Whereupon are the foundations thereof fastened? Or who laid the corner stone thereof? (38:7); "Or who shut up the sea with doors, when it break forth, as if it had issued from out of the womb?" (38:9). Man was not present for the world's beginning, God tells Job, so does not understand its underpinning. That is why he is relegated to the shadowy, insubstantial world his limited powers afford him.

For Ahab, however, man gives up too much if he accepts or even welcomes the news (if he does not fall to weeping, or to laughter, or to reviling) that God has wrested from him his connection to the absolute. To Ahab, the unprotesting acceptance that he has no grasp of reality is appalling, intolerable—and completely unnecessary, given that in the *living* act, the undoubted deed, "some unknown but still reasoning thing puts forth the moldings of its features from behind the unreasoning mask." Thus we find Ahab "chasing with curses a Job's whale round the world." Job's whale is an agent of God or a "king over the children of pride" because God uses it to make Job see things as God's creations—to see them as existing beyond man's purview. And yet, Ahab protests, the story in which man is an interloper in the real world (the realm of third-world objects or the realm of what is not exactly sensible and not merely subjective) ignores a vital detail—namely, the workings of language.

If Job is Adam after the expulsion, Ahab is Job after divine communication makes him recognize his place in an inscrutable universe. Ahab is sufficiently alive to the possibility that God's actions, executed in "terrible majesty" (32–37), are beyond human understanding—as are God's creatures. He concedes his inability to know in an unlimited sense what the whale is—concedes that "knowing" the whale means knowing it as a set of reciprocal and overdetermined influences, impossible to get behind. But in Ahab this concession, once made, prompts an about-face. For if it is true that there is nothing in the world to which a concept *corresponds* (if, as Ken Dauber writes, the meaning of any word "is not the history of the education of the subject" who uses the word but "the word as object itself, meaning beyond man's experience of it. It is meaning requiring no subject to make it mean")[46] then by the same token we do not, as linguistic creatures, confront the world, as it were, from behind a system of mental representations that might turn out to represent falsely.[47]

As an unreconciled, unyielding Job, Ahab's especially sharp reply to God's angry rebuke is that the meaning of a word *isn't something he holds in mind.* Knowing the meaning of the word "whale" (knowing that some objects are whales and others not, without needing to look for empirical similarities between various instances of whales in order to say why they are whales) quite simply does not entail his cognitive grasp of the object known by the name "whale." He does not need to know the nature or essence of a whale in order to know its meaning. For ever since meaning was forged in the context of an ethical relation (ever since God made language a device not simply for representing but for *constituting* reality), knowing a word's meaning is in effect the same as knowing how to follow rules for its proper use.

Isn't that what Job was taught? Because it isn't a thing in nature, the true form of the whale can't be caught; and because it isn't a creation of mind, the true form of the whale can't be thought; but *because of the way language works*, the true form of whale is something about which human beings ordinarily talk. And in this version of creation God hasn't put reality out of human reach. That is because when God (who Ahab *defyingly* worships) gave man the power to fashion names for the creatures He had already created—when God brought the creatures to man "to see what he would call them" (Gen. 2:19)—He also introduced a way to resolve the seeming opposition between appearance and reality.

The contradiction underwriting Ahab's life is that his everyday dealings are with things—points, merely, in an unrepresentable process—which explains why a whale fished from the ocean is nothing like a living whale in his full majesty and significance. However, when he employs the word "whale" in meaningful ways, he does not name any individual or natural object, an object fixed or limited in length, size, duration, or quantity, but a seemingly everlasting, indefinite object, a fact in logical space. Thus it is, oddly, that the things God made—things in flux—aren't the things man discovers through his senses but the things that, in ordinary language, he names.

And while this insight might just torture the naturalist, it awakens in Ahab the hope that his way of naming things makes the third realm—the realm rightly called *real*—his own. Ahab was listening, we might say, when God told Job that his words aren't tied to things at all, or that man can speak meaningfully only for the reason that his words don't name things at a point in time but things in logical space, things *sub specie aeternitatis*. Few men would have heard in God's instruction what Ahab hears, and fewer still would think of it as assurance, but for Ahab the Jobian lesson is that the words he uses don't find their significance in relation to his own tiny and restricted catalogue of experiences but in relation to the vast, unabridged record of human experience. What Ahab hears is that when man was given language he was given a world of true things for the reason that his ordinary use of words magnifies his individual perspective, boosts it to encompass the entire time the chronicled world has gone on and will continue to go on, adapts his point of view to a duration in which the whale, for example, while being what it is and not some other thing, can continuously evolve. If, as God commands, the word "whale" doesn't name the whale's being but its *meaning*—if there is no object anterior to the word "whale," nothing to which it refers, no antecedent referent to fix its meaning—then as Ahab insists there is perpetual creation built into man's use of this word. The words or names that make up ordinary language *are* the things God is the creator of.

As Peirce, Wittgenstein, and a handful of other hardworking philosophers have made clear, the "meaning" of any object is fully incorporated into the character of its real sign.[48] At great length but in rich, amplified detail, Melville also shows why what any object *is* emerges from the meaning of the word we have for it and not from its intrinsic nature—of which the less said the better.[49]

Rather than divorce language from the rigors of practical life, this view ties language to life. The very strong connection between the meaning of a word and the need for a word in a way of life is what Melville demonstrates in *Moby-Dick*. As I've argued, one important function of the narrative is to bring before his readers' consciousness the vast fabric of human practices that serve to constitute the meaning of any word. That the meaning of any word is grounded in social practice and thus that our concepts are necessarily *outside* the "inner world" of the mind is I think what Melville underscores when he has Ahab pursue the white whale in the company of his motley crew. For it is no accident that Melville has a diverse assembly (like the deputation Anacharsis Clootz led into the French National Assembly in 1790 to symbolize all mankind's support of the French Revolution) accompany "Old Ahab in the *Pequod* to lay the world's grievances before that bar from which many of them never came back."[50] Melville's point is not that people from different nations and races have something in common, or that at all the ends of the earth there exists something like a "common continent of men." His point, rather, is that each of these "Isolatoes," as he calls them, each individual "living on a separate continent of his own," is in shared enterprise "federated along one keel." As the novel makes obvious, it takes collaborative human effort to devise and maintain whaling practices—and it is such practices (lowering boats, breaking out the hold, finding longitude, skylarking, having a gam) that the word "whale" was invented to serve.

In Melville's account of the nature of meaning, the meaning of the word "whale" cannot be regarded as either an inhabitant of the natural world or as an inhabitant of the private, interior theater of the mind as Descartes conceived it.[51] Meaning goes to ground in practice, which is to say that meaning is not essentially private but essentially public.

Melville thus leaves behind the problem of Cartesian dualism. Of course reading his whaling narrative this way also makes his book wholly unlike the one in which a protagonist for whom readers feel a strong aversion goes about wrecking his life and the lives of others. For as I see it, Melville doesn't aspire to write the kind of story in which mortal man is punished for his wrested independence—for wanting, and finding himself in, a world in which he has immediate jurisdiction. Having rather decided the question of sovereignty in man's favor, or finding his independent, self-governing mode to be the right one, Melville opens an older inquiry into what *supports* or *sustains* this felt independence.[52] How does man's natural sovereignty survive "the powers of heaven, hell, and earth"? What makes his brooding doubts about his own powers not sound and requisite but unwarranted and morbid? These are the questions Melville sets out to address in *Moby-Dick*.

Chapter 5

✦

God's Servant

> For the good reader the experience of *Moby-Dick* is a participation in the act of creation. Find a key word or metaphor, start to pick it as you would a wild flower, and you will find yourself ripping up the whole forest floor.
>
> —Walter Bezanson

That we *can* grasp the facts into which the world divides is what Melville's "whole story of the white whale, more especially the catastrophe," ultimately affirms. An affect laden concept like "whale," a fact in logical space, can be grasped precisely because it is not a thing and not an idea; it is a notion that has specific meaning even though, in order to judge something to be a whale, no specific group of properties or qualities have to be present.[1] As Melville's whaling narrative demonstrates, the meaning of the word "whale" grows out of socially devised and maintained practices and in this sense issues from the material world—but there is no entailment relation between a whale's features or characteristics and "what a whale is." In other words, the way our concepts map reality is performative and not representative. Concepts do not name, copy, or trace preexisting features of the world.[2] As the things signified by the signs in our language, a concept is neither substantial nor in possession of an essential nature; what we mean by the "nature" of any given concept is really just the power of a word or sign to express logical representation. Despite being sedimented out of practical life, the thing signified by the sign "whale" is an essentially *symbolic* arrangement and thus the very kind of thing our language has over time evolved to capture.

There is accordingly a materialist bent to Melvillean logic—reason to situate Melville's view of concepts within the current radical rethinking of experience, our growing recognition that reflection, thinking itself, grows out of our attachments to the physical world. However, *Moby-Dick* deliberately complicates a theory many materialists hold dear—namely, that "a concept emerges as a result of the cancellation of the real difference among singular cases under its jurisdiction," as Branka Arsić writes; that because concepts represent the merging of singular cases into an imagined entity ("which, by the same token, is a cancellation of real connections, transgressions, and mobility in a contrived stability"), concepts can be rightly understood as "representations of the illicit and irrational longings of the mind."[3] As I understand him, Melville does not see concepts in this light; he does not think concepts unaccountable to corporeal life.

In a curious way, then, Melville's writing in *Moby-Dick* is in keeping with the American transcendentalists' aspiration, as Arsić shrewdly identifies it, "to move words in the vicinity of things—to make them literal or to even turn them into what they mean."[4] Yet Melville outmaneuvers the materialist critics when he shows how the hope of "recalling actual bodies" when we use general names need not remain a regulative wish.[5] Melville recovers the presence of bodies in names when he shows how our words already have in them special devotions to particular interests. In Melville's whaling narrative *words themselves* are understood as profound enactments of the inseparable relationship between abstract concepts and particular things.

This view supports the conclusion that in the literature of the nineteenth century, and more particularly in the work of a few American writers haunted simultaneously by the implications of the American wilderness, the quest for spiritual truth, and the search for new literary forms (as F. O. Matthiessen shows in *American Renaissance*), Melville helms the boldest and most determined search for a materialist epistemology—for the use of embodied rather than purely mental knowledge to "assure us that we do know the existence of the world," as Stanley Cavell writes, "or that what we understand as knowledge is *of* the world.[6] Like Emerson's *Essays* and Thoreau's *Walden*, Melville's *Moby-Dick* transcends the philosophical dualism that governed the thinking of the age. And like the other great American transcendentalists, "writing out of a sense of the intimacy of words with the world, or of intimacy lost," as Cavell says, Melville addresses himself to what Cavell calls the "urgent methodological issue" of the time—"that of accounting for the fact that we are the victims of the very words of which we are at the same time the masters; victims and masters of the fact of words."[7] The degree to which our words, whose meanings we do not govern, are nevertheless suited to our purposes is what Cavell invites us to consider when he argues that we are at the same time victims of and masters over our words. As Cavell concludes, part of the American transcendentalists' uniqueness, their significant contribution to philosophical thinking, has to do with their recognition that "we have a choice over our words, but not over their meaning."[8] This insight is in accordance with what I take to be the central lesson of *Moby-Dick*, namely, that our use of words does not automatically put us out of touch with reality. In *Moby-Dick* Melville shows how the imagined distance or incompatibility between words and the world (what to nineteenth century thinkers was beginning to feel like the burgeoning distance between the life of words and the lives of the people who brandish them) is not the real story—that while we are in danger of thinking our lives pass remotely from our symbols, this is an apprehension a peculiar kind of philosophizing has wrongly introduced.

By this account, Melville's book is centrally occupied with what Cavell calls the "rescue of language," the return of our words to us, and our return to them.[9] (For so long as our lives and our language betray one another, Cavell writes, "we can grant to neither of them their full range and autonomy.")[10] To put it another way, *Moby-Dick* gives grounds for, and makes righteous, declarations about our sign language that do not depict its recurrent failure—for example Thoreau's declaration in *Walden* that "the universe constantly and obediently answers to our conceptions; whether we travel fast or slow, the track is laid for us."[11] Such declarations operate out of a sense of redemption and achievement. Thanks to Cavell, the redemptive aspect of the transcendentalists' recovery project has been made clear. The achievement, however, is only revealed when (or if) we finally come to understand how language speakers "experience the meaning of a word," as Wittgenstein says, and thus discover that there is nothing intrinsically deceptive in the feeling that a word "can seem to carry a particular meaning in itself."[12]

In *Moby-Dick* we can find an extended study of what it is to experience the meaning of the word "whale." I wish now to show why, by this measure, *Moby-Dick* is a record not of loss but of recovery—above all, the recovery of particular objects in the names we have for them. I've argued that Melville's narrative recaptures the whale as a *fact*, a concept or notion that is totally meaningful in language but whose meaning isn't determined by the empirical experience (or by the imagination, the mental resourcefulness) of language speakers. Facts are instances of what Stanley Cavell calls "the wording of the world"—that is, what happens when words *do* honor the dissimilarity between the singular cases under their jurisdictions. As Cavell explains, "a fact has two surfaces because a fact is not merely an event in the world but the assertion of an event."[13] Or as

Wittgenstein explains, facts exist in logical space but they are nourished or sustained by worldly goings on. For these philosophers, "facts" are those words that, when we think or speak them, seem to carry particular meanings in themselves. Because it seems completely filled with its meaning, "whale" is such a word—even though, as Wittgenstein declares, If God looked into our minds while we were thinking or pronouncing this word he would not have been able to see there *what* we were speaking of.[14]

In this chapter I explore how Wittgenstein's investigations of what it is to experience the meaning of a word can deepen our understanding of Melville's attempt, in *Moby-Dick*, to show why we have become unnecessarily anxious about our ability to find meaning in a word or to trust a word's power to manifest sense. The association of Melville's project with Wittgenstein's is useful because both thinkers undoubtedly dispense with the idea that private impressions or sense-data serve as the foundations of knowledge or meaning. Even so, each is committed to defending the possibility of meaning in language, each holds that meaning lies in use, and each attempts to forestall a global misunderstanding of that seminal idea.[15] What is more, both Melville and Wittgenstein show why a philosophy devoted to searching for the underlying ground of our capacity to mean does not begin by offering a complete enumeration of the conditions that must be fulfilled for the proper use of a term but by recalling that "to imagine a language is to imagine a form of life."[16] In addition to denying the existence of a direct referential relationship between words and things, Wittgenstein's well known phrase hints at what, exactly, we are making reference to when we talk about the "meaning" of a word—what Wittgenstein astutely characterizes as the feeling, typical to human beings, that a word "has taken up its meaning into itself, that it is an actual likeness of its meaning."[17]

I turn now to one of Wittgenstein's attempts to prevent misunderstanding of the idea that meaning lies in use—the striking moment in part 2 of the *Investigations* when Wittgenstein wonders why, in connection with the game of experiencing a word (for example, that "You can say the word "March" to yourself and mean it at one time as an imperative and another as the name of a month") we may also speak of "the meaning" of a word. For as he notes, the game of "I meant *this*" is quite different from the activity Wittgenstein identifies as "I thought of. . . . as I said it."[18] It is the latter activity Wittgenstein tackles in the *Investigations* when he considers what it is to "experience the meaning of a word" or wonders how a word—even "a word uttered in isolation and without purpose"—can seem "completely filled with its meaning."[19]

At first this line of inquiry seems out of keeping with Wittgenstein's general approach. For after noting that "when I pronounce this word while reading with expression it is completely filled with its meaning," Wittgenstein asks, "How can this be, if meaning is the use of the word?" His answer: "Well, what I said was intended figuratively. Not that I chose the figure: it forced itself on me.—But the figurative employment of the word can't get into conflict with the original one."[20]

This is a suggestive passage for readers of *Moby-Dick*, I think, because showing how the figurative employment of the word "whale" doesn't and indeed *can't* get into conflict with the original employment of this word is one of this book's preoccupations. As readers of *Moby-Dick* discover, Melville's figurative employment of the word "whale" doesn't dodge but precisely accounts for the very particular, unmistakably concrete objects with which language speakers have (over time) had dealings.

This contemplation of the literal and figurative use of words is not unique to Melville but a vital part of the American transcendentalists' fresh orientation toward our life with language—their way of working out, again, where we are in relation to our signs. In the chapter of *Walden* called "Reading," for example, Thoreau announces the difference between literal and figurative language when he distinguishes between the language of commerce or of social dealings between people, the more-concrete-than-abstract, "almost brutish" language that originates in our empirical experience and which Thoreau calls "mother tongue," and "the maturity and experience of that," the "language of literature" or the "language we must be born again in order to speak"—what Thoreau calls "father tongue," the language "carved out of the breath of life itself."[21] For Thoreau, "father tongue" is not a new lexicon but the "maturity" of the literal use of words. However, in loyalty to our mother tongue (which as Cavell notes "is part of our condition") the words we use figuratively must also make literal or historical sense.[22]

Wittgenstein makes the same point in the *Philosophical Investigations* when he talks about the "primary" and "secondary" sense of a word. And like Thoreau, Wittgenstein argues that "it is only if the word has a primary sense for you that you use it in the secondary one." Wittgenstein can be very funny on this subject:

> "Given two ideas 'fat' and 'lean', would you be rather inclined to say that Wednesday was fat and Tuesday lean, or *vice versa*? (I incline decisively towards the former.) Now have "fat" and "lean" some different

> meaning here from their usual one?—They have a different use.—So ought I really to have used different words? Certainly not that.—I want to use *these* words (with their familiar meanings) *here*. . . .
>
> Asked "What do you really mean here by 'fat' and 'lean'?"—I could only explain the meanings in the usual way. I could *not* point to the examples of Tuesday and Wednesday.
>
> Here one might speak of a 'primary' and 'secondary' sense of a word. It is only if the word has the primary sense for you that you use it in the secondary one.[23]

Wittgenstein sounds remarkably like the sage of Walden Pond when in part 2 of *Investigations* he writes, "Only if you have learnt to calculate—on paper or out loud—can you be made to grasp, by means of this concept, what calculating in the head is."[24] That is, fundamental to our life with language is the certainty that the usual or primary sense of a word informs all the other uses of the word.

The practice of taking a word in its usual or most basic sense, rather than as a metaphor or allegory, appeals to the writer of *Walden*. As Cavell has suggested, the attempt to bring words back from their metaphorical to their everyday use is what drives Thoreau's occupation of Walden. Along the same lines, Barbara Packer proposes that what Thoreau does in *Walden* is "move *himself*, literally, into the world of his own figurative language. The literal woods, pond, and bean field still assume the same classical rhetorical guises in which they have always appeared, but they are suddenly readable in addition as the nonfigurative ground of a naturalist's account of life in the woods. The ground has shifted."[25] Branka Arsić gets behind this view when she argues that just as Thoreau's *A Week on the Concord and Merrimack Rivers* "is premised on the injunction that to understand life as a journey one must start traveling," Thoreau's *Walden* demands that we abandon the desire to express ourselves metaphorically (to use nonliteral language or language "not shaped by a direct 'imprint' of things") and instead attempt to "access literally the life [our] images and concepts represent or symbolize."[26]

However, Thoreau calls attention to the primary and secondary sense of a word (and insists that we can explain the meaning of a word only in the usual, that is to say, primary way) not in order to emphasize "life" at the expense of "language" or to test the limits of figurative discourse. Thoreau wants to show how the figurative use of words is grounded in their literal use because ultimately the lesson of *Walden* is that we have a choice over our words, but not over their meaning. It is because words have meaning beyond our ability to give them meaning that it is possible to keep our bearings as speakers of language. Or as Cavell writes, it is faithfulness to the conditions of language as such that the endless computations in *Walden* are designed to achieve.[27]

The question I wish to raise, then, is this one. Must we understand the "secondary" sense of a word (which Cavell identifies as the "figurations of language") to be its *metaphorical* sense? Does the language we use figuratively condemn us to life among far-fetched metaphors, as some critics call concepts?[28] Are the words we use "nothing but the reservoirs of images," as Arsić writes, deposited "by the history of language, not things"?[29] On this point Wittgenstein's writing is instructive since he makes clear why the secondary sense of a word is different from but never at odds with its primary sense.[30] In the *Philosophical Investigations* Wittgenstein is convinced that "the figurative employment of a word can't get into conflict with the original one."[31] It follows that, for Wittgenstein, the secondary use of language is legitimate and not problematic.[32]

I consider this to be one of *Moby-Dick*'s central lessons. In his narrative Melville feels out the difference between the primary and secondary sense of the word "whale," offers support for the view that the primary and secondary sense of this word are not in conflict, and makes the same pioneering discovery Wittgenstein makes, to wit, that the "experience" language speakers have when we experience the meaning of this word is not an *inner* experience; it is not an impression of material life dematerialized into an idea. As I understand it, the force of Melville's opposition to an essentialist conception of language only adds clout to one of Wittgenstein's most overlooked insights: his conclusion in part 2 of the *Investigations* that the secondary sense of a word "is not a 'metaphorical' sense." This is how Wittgenstein continues his discussion of the primary and secondary sense of words (and his assertion that "it is only if the word has the primary sense for you that you use it in the secondary one"):

> Only if you have learnt to calculate—on paper or out loud—can you be made to grasp, by means of this concept, what calculating in the head is.
>
> The secondary sense is not a "metaphorical" sense. If I say "For me the vowel *e* is yellow" I do not mean 'yellow' in a metaphorical sense,—for I could not express what I want to say in any other way than by means of the idea "yellow."[33]

What Wittgenstein proposes by these important remarks is that when we use a word figuratively we are not applying the word to an object or action to which it is not literally applicable. What Wittgenstein calls the life of the sign, the sign's meaning, can only be explained "in the usual way"—as Wittgenstein says in his "Wednesday was fat and Tuesday lean" example. That is to say, we experience the meaning of a word when we grasp the role the word plays in language and the role the word plays can't be separated out from the primary sense of the word. Wittgenstein's attentiveness to the way we experience the meaning of a word forms part of his argument that we cannot abstract language from the weave of our lives—that "to imagine a language is to imagine a form of life."

Wittgenstein's idea that meaning lies in use is misinterpreted (as Rush Rhees first protested) when it is taken to suggest that use alone gives life to what are otherwise "dead" signs. For instance when we take *without further question* sentences like this one from *The Blue and Brown Books*: "But if we had to name anything which is the life of the sign, we should have to say that it was its *use*."[34] Simply equating a word's "meaning" with its "use" makes the whole process of speaking and being able to understand what is said sound "too mechanical," Rhees argues, because in reality language speakers are not mere operators of a system of signs but experiencing, feeling persons.[35] As Rhees makes clear, speaking and understanding "belong to intercourse with other people. The signs get their life there, and that is why the language is not just a mechanism."[36] For Rhees, Wittgenstein's emphasis on the actual lives and interpersonal dealings of language speakers is vital to the notion that meaning lies in use.

The idea that signs get their meaning in intercourse with other people animates Wittgenstein's investigation of the way we experience the meaning of a word. It also sets the tone of his discussion, in the *Philosophical Investigations*, regarding whether someone who was "meaning-blind" (an expression Wittgenstein associates less with the absence of a sense, as in the case of blindness, than with a certain lack of responsiveness) could, as Rhees, says "get along all right" with other language speakers.[37] The person who is meaning-blind is someone who, "like an automaton," lacks a human being's attachment to his words; it is someone for whom the word "whale" does *not* seem completely filled with its meaning.[38] For his own part, Rhees objects to the idea that someone who is meaning-blind could get along all right with other language speakers—but he notes that on this question he thinks "Wittgenstein was not sure."[39]

I think Wittgenstein is surer than he sounds. In the *Investigations* the idea that someone could *fail* to grasp the role a word plays in language (that someone might be "meaning-blind") is a possibility Wittgenstein takes up as a kind of strategy, a way to radically reorient philosophers' traditional approach to the study of what gives life to signs. For as

Wittgenstein asks, How would we recognize beings who did not experience the meanings of words? His answer: "They would not have an attachment to their words."

> The familiar physiognomy of a word, the feeling that it has taken up its meaning into itself, that it is an actual likeness of its meaning—there could be human beings to whom all this was alien. (They would not have an attachment to their words.)—And how are these feelings manifested among us?—By the way we choose and value words.

The clear contrast between "us" and "them" in this passage (or between human beings and, in effect, automatons) should prompt Wittgenstein's readers to recall that he is in no doubt that the meaning-blind would not get along all right in conversation with beings who feel, as we do, an attachment to words. Here Wittgenstein is critiquing the proposition that "the life of the sign is its use" if by that we mean that life is "breathed into" the sign *by* its use. As Wittgenstein guesses, what gives life to a sign isn't breathed into it by language speakers.[40] As he writes with unaffected perplexity at §432 of *Philosophical Investigations*, "Every sign by itself seems dead. *What* gives it life?—in *use* it is alive. Is life breathed into it there?—Or is the *use* its life?"

In *Moby-Dick*, I've argued, Melville investigates the question of what gives life to a sign. One way to read *Moby-Dick* philosophically, then, is to say that Melville is certain that there are no such things as "human beings to whom all this was alien"—that is, beings who do not feel, as we do, that a word is an actual likeness of its meaning. For Melville, words obviously have a kind of life, but to act as if the life of a word or what Wittgenstein calls its "meaning" hinges (precariously!) on its employment by language speakers turns a word's meaning back into a question of *intention*. Rather than show how signs get their meaning in intercourse with other people, it promotes the fantasy that a speaker's "inner" experience is essential to the meaning of the words she uses. (But how is some inner experience I bring to speaking and understanding essential to the meaning of the word "whale"? Ironically, this well-intentioned effort to protect the variety of experience among individual people only betrays a fundamental anxiety about our relations to others.)

In *Moby-Dick* Melville figures out his own method for explaining the way a word can seem to carry a particular meaning in itself. He explores the broader connections between how people attend to particular phenomena and how they employ words. He does not focus on the relation between words and things; rather, he illuminates the relationship between the lives of language speakers (immersed, perforce, in the material world) and the activity Wittgenstein identifies as experiencing the meaning of a word.[41] In *Moby-Dick*, Melville shows how rightly comprehending the relationship—which is a *two-stage* relationship—between empirical experience and the way we experience the meaning of a word provides an essential key to the puzzle of how we make the world intelligible to ourselves.

In what follows I argue that in *Moby-Dick* it is *Ahab* who effectively expresses the essential features of Melville's vision. Of all the philosophizing characters in Melville's narrative (all the "spiritual personages talking and acting differently from the general business run of the conversation on the decks of whalers," as Duyckinck writes), it is Ahab who is most struck by the concreteness of the word "whale" and who insists on the particularity with which we experience words. It is Ahab who most tenaciously asserts the connection between the literal and figurative sense of a word—and who thus in the end successfully negotiates his grand conclusion: that there are actual things, actual bodies, in our names for things.

Critics have often unfavorably contrasted Ahab's ferocious certainty with Ishmael's characteristic uncertainty, Ishmael's celebrated irresoluteness. Indeed, the reason Ishmael's philosophy of life or conception of the world is thought to serve as a ready substitute for Melville's philosophy (particularly when Ishmael is in a mode of self-examination and illumination, when, for instance, he dedicates himself to communicating the concept of the whale's whiteness) is that all Ishmael's intense efforts to explain himself would seem to end the same way: with Ishmael in a state of undecidedness.

Ishmael's tendency to be of two minds is firmly established in the early chapter "The Counterpane." Here Ishmael—inspired as he says by his inability to tell Queequeg's striated and tattooed arm from the patchwork bedspread on which it comfortably rests (a fabulous possibility that gives birth to the rest of his tale)—recounts a childhood event: waking from a troubled doze to feel a supernatural hand placed in his own:

> For what seemed ages piled on ages, I lay there, frozen with the most awful fears, not daring to drag away my hand; yet ever thinking that if I could but stir it one single inch, the horrid spell would be broken. I knew not how this consciousness at last glided away from me; but waking in the morning, I shudderingly remembered it all, and for

> days and weeks and months afterwards I lost myself in confounding attempts to explain the mystery. Nay, to this very hour, I often puzzle myself with it.

Ultimately Ishmael's summary of this strange event—"Whether it was reality or a dream, I never could entirely settle"—remains his final word. And so it was with much that occurred aboard the *Pequod*.[42] Ishmael's way of settling matters is to not settle them, and that is the chief reason for some critics' very high esteem for him. As Elizabeth Duquette has written, Ishmael's narrative challenges a reader's "naïve faith" not only in systematic knowledge—the taxonomical impulse or futile practice of compiling data represented by that "poor devil of Sub-Sub"—but also in the very idea that something can be true.[43] In other words, truth is something only simple people can believe in. In contrast to Ahab's vow that "Truth hath no confines" (which, for Duquette, indicates a failure to understand the human predicament consistent with Ahab's failure to capture the white whale), Ishmael teaches us to "acknowledge that indeed there *are* limits to our access to 'Truth,' to our ability to understand all aspects of existence."[44] For Duquette and numerous other critics, evidence of Ishmael's trustworthiness as a thinker is provided by his general lament that, in regard to the whale, "I know him not, and never will."

How might the consensus on Ahab and Ishmael change, then, when we advance the view that Ahab is certain only that concepts do not issue from his mind? Ahab's certainty can be understood as no more (and no less) than his confidence that the whale cannot be what Locke would call a "creature of the understanding," an image formed in the mind, an object that exists in name only. To put it another way, Ahab is convinced that he *can* grasp the living whale in his full majesty and significance: the whale as it appears to his senses and as it transpires in his rational life, or as this concept pervades his intelligent relations to the world. That is what Ahab means when he declares that "Truth hath no confines." Ahab's disquieting assertion is that he lives in the world of appearances, as some philosophers call the world we know by means of the senses; however, that does not mean that the whale (or any other hard-to-pin-down concept) isn't an actually occurring fact.

Ahab is unafraid to own the whale—and formally "own" means conceding that something is the case, as in Melville's revelatory line "For unless you own the whale, you are but a provincial and sentimentalist in Truth"—and unapologetic about knowing what he knows. But Ahab's reasoning is sound, I argue, and precipitated by his discerning grasp of the picturing aspect of language, a feature of human life without which our lives would certainly become unrecognizable.[45] (As I aim to show, the picturing aspect of language has to do with the way we see fully realized or three-dimensional objects in the words of our two-dimensional script—a capability Wittgenstein recognizes as "anything but a matter of course.")[46] In "Speculative Cetology," Duquette strongly condemns Ahab's claim to "own the whale," since for her the phrase indicates "intellectual mastery" of a phenomenon.[47] I think this misses the point Melville is making about concepts and how different they are from phenomena, for in Melville's book the phrase "own the whale" means conceding *that* the whale is, not saying precisely *what* the whale is.[48] With Ahab's certainty serving as a desirable model, Melville's extraordinary claim seems to be that our capacity to see a three-dimensional object in the word "whale," and in this special sense to know what a whale "is" (even if we can't *say* what a whale is) is simply an aspect of human life—that is, life with language.

Underlying Ahab's infamous defiance is thus a line of thinking strikingly like the one Wittgenstein lays out in his investigations into the nature of our life with language.[49] Throughout this book I have tried to specify what I understand the force of Wittgenstein's argument to be. It is that language as such cannot be separated from the substratum of practices through which its expressions gain whatever meaning they possess. Language is always already entangled with practical life—the life we enjoy as physical, embodied beings, manipulators of an equally physical world. The impossibility of abstracting language from the weave of our lives accounts for why our words seem to have the power to give organized existence to something; the word "whale" seems completely filled with its meaning because what this word "pictures" isn't a whale's indispensible qualities or intrinsic nature but a sundry chronicle of human activity—what Edward Minar calls the "patterns, connections, and saliences that make up the agreement in judgment in which our understanding resides."[50] Because these patterns, connections, and saliences are "out there" in the world—they are not part of the "inner" life of the mind—we say that what the word whale pictures is real. For Wittgenstein, the meaning of the word "whale" isn't something we discover by way of private impressions or sense-data but something we grasp simply by being speakers of language. In consequence, Wittgenstein's suggestion that the meaning of a word is to be found in the word's function or role in language does *not* lead to the conclusion that words do not have meaning in themselves. Rather, it leads to the conclusion that when we talk about the meaning of a word, "we are not talking about an independent phenomenon," as Hugh Knott writes, "but of a multifaceted *aspect* of this life with words."[51]

As Knott (following Rush Rhees) has observed, many philosophers enamored with Wittgenstein's idea that "meaning is use" have failed to put it together with his related idea about seeing words as pictures—the capacity to see the "meaning" or "the life of the sign" in a sign. Ignoring the picturing aspect of language has led to the conclusion that our words do not have meaning in themselves; that a word's meaning appears *only* in its use. But in addition to holding that meaning lies in use, Wittgenstein is absorbed by the fact that human beings "see 'three-dimensionally' with two eyes" as he writes in part 2 of the *Investigations*—that we see what Melville calls the "fully invested whale" in the word "whale."[52] The picturing aspect of language stirred and puzzled Wittgenstein right from the beginning of his work in logic, for as he wonders in *Notebooks 1914-1916*, "What is the ground of our—certainly well founded—confidence that we shall be able to express any sense we like in our two-dimensional script?"[53] My point is that Wittgenstein did not only want to pull us away from looking inward or looking to mental accompaniments of our uses of words for the source of words' meanings.[54] Sure, he wanted to dislodge the fantasy of the mind as populated with private objects. He wanted us to stop looking for a sign's meaning as though it were an object. But he also wished to throw light on the complicated, interrelated connection between "experiencing the meaning of a word" (to see words in our two-dimensional script three-dimensionally, as it were) and the life we recognize as our own—that is, the kind of life in which various and ever-changing human practices and activities give a word depth or (as Cavell says) turn a word into the assertion of an event.

Hence Wittgenstein's important remark in part 2 of *Philosophical Investigations*:

> But if a sentence can strike me as like a painting in words, and the very individual word in the sentence as like a picture, then it is no such marvel that a word uttered in isolation and without purpose can seem to carry a particular meaning in itself."[55]

For Wittgenstein there is no problem with thinking that a word has meaning in itself. The mistake is when we look for the meaning as if it coexisted with the sign. As he writes in *The Blue and Brown Books*, "The mistake we are liable to make could be expressed thus: We are looking for the use of a sign, but we look for it as though it were an object *co-existing* with the sign."[56] Looking for meaning in this way has created much philosophical confusion. Nevertheless we go too far when we say a word's meaning *only* appears in its use. As Hugh Knott explains, "There is nothing intrinsically illusory in the 'experience of the meaning of a word'; the problems arise when we fail to recognize it for the *kind* of experience that it is, when we fail to recognize the particular sense that 'experience' has in this context."[57] Again, the crucial thing to remember is that "experiencing the meaning of a word" is not an "inner" experience, not an impression of material life dematerialized into an idea. We make a mistake when we talk about the meaning of a word as if we were talking about an inner or mentalistic experience. What we are actually talking about, Knott says, is "our relation to words conceived of in terms of how we choose and value them, the care with which we give expression to their use, how we use them as pictures, and so on." We are talking about "something that is *integral* to their 'use.'" It is mistakes like this one—thinking we are talking about phenomena when we say we know what anything is instead of describing an aspect of this life with words—that Wittgenstein means to point out when he argues that philosophical problems are specially connected with language. Wittgenstein is not saying that there is something amiss with language or that the sign system on which we rely requires special analysis; he is saying, rather, that many of our seemingly intractable difficulties in philosophy are rooted in modes of misunderstanding about our relation to language. For Wittgenstein, understanding the way language belongs to our lives can help with this misunderstanding.

In *Moby-Dick*, Melville also pushes back—hard—against the tradition in philosophy that separates language from life and thus, in the end, can't find Truth in the meanings of words. The belief that the word "whale" has no meaning (or that man's experience of the meaning of this word is intrinsically illusory) is what Melville wishes to repudiate. To this end he manufactures support in the form of Captain Ahab. Of course, understanding how Ahab can be of service in an argument about the nature of discourse depends on what we understand Ahab to accomplish—on what the name "Ahab" means or what we think Ahab's consuming rage amounts to.

To begin with, the reasoning underlying Ahab's infamous defiance sounds less threatening when we encounter it in the writing of certain philosophers. A good example is in the work of Stanley Cavell, who declares that if we have failed to believe that we've learned something about reality when we learn how to use a word or learn what a word means, "it is because we forget that we learn language and learn the world *together*, that they become elaborated and distorted together, and in the same places."[58] As Edward Duffy notes, citing Cavell and thinking of J. L. Austin's close philosophical attention to the way we use familiar words, "unearth the uses and consequences of our words, and . . . 'you seem further to unearth the world.' "[59] When in regard to his capacity to know the whale Ahab argues that "Truth hath no confines," then, he is not simply saying that he knows what a whale is; he is addressing himself to the question of what this thing called knowing is. He is pointing out how *elaborate* a process knowing is. Ahab can insist that he knows the meaning of the word "whale" because the meaning of this word is something his mastery of language affords him. The meaning of "whale" isn't something he has to determine or (even more absurdly) discover by way of his senses. For Ahab it is by the most everyday, run-of-the-mill means—by the attention speakers of language pay to the surface of life, and to the fact that ordinary human life requires expression—that a word like "whale" acquires its measureless depth.

It is therefore possible to think of Ahab's antagonism (toward the profiteering shipowners, for whom the whale is pure matter or quantifiable substance; toward Starbuck, for whom whales exist only for man to make a living by them; even toward Pip, for whom questions about being, knowing, and identity are senseless and obstructive of human intimacy or the bonds of fellowship) as rooted in a safeguarding project. At any rate, framing Ahab's active opposition to the usual way of explaining how concepts have meaning brings Ahab's spiritual landscape closer to Melville's.

It also prompts the recollection that Ishmael is only "Ishmael," a symbol of what it is like to be entirely friendless—to be an isolated, far-driven soul, in D. H. Lawrence's phrase—to the extent that he repudiates the connection between the meaning of any concept or linguistic expression and the texture of life. As Howard P. Vincent reports, the Ishmael image was impressed indelibly on Melville's mind. As the eponymous hero of *Redburn* recounts, "I had found myself a sort of Ishmael in the ship, without a single friend or companion; and I began to feel a hatred growing up in me against the whole crew." As the eponymous hero of *Pierre* testifies, "Fain, then, for one moment, would he have recalled the thousand sweet illusions of Life; though purchased at the price of Life's Truth; so that once more he might not feel himself driven out an infant Ishmael into the desert, with no maternal Hagar to accompany and comfort him." For Melville, Ishmael is a profound symbol of man not merely in exile but deprived of the comforting habits and procedures common to human social experience: the shelterless individual for whom, as Vincent writes, the supports and solaces of family, daily practice, and habit "have been suddenly removed, and the world has been revealed in its instability and unreliability"—an "isolato" or insulated being confronted by the fact of his extreme isolation, a restless and unlaid ghost.[60] In *Moby-Dick*, Ishmael's distinguishing trait might not be his equivocating, in other words, but his tendency to be easily persuaded by the notion that "Life's Truth" is attainable only through the *sacrifice* of life's "thousand sweet illusions"—the distinctively nonepistemic or noncognitive knowledge acquired in relation to concrete, specific socially-constructed practices, what Harrison calls "the numberless theatres which continually form and reform themselves in the course of the detailed working-out of interpersonal relationship and social life."[61] Being an "Ishmael" means being disconnected from the assumptions and certainties that naturally arise through involvement in these practices.

Queequeg, of course, pulls Ishmael back from this logical misstep. Ishmael's friendship with Queequeg becomes his route back to feeling—back, in other words, to the importance of locating sense-making activity in the surface of our everyday lives. From the moment Ishmael decides to "cleave to Queequeg like a barnacle," he has, if he chooses, an anchor in the material world. Eased by Queequeg's "calm self-collectedness" (which gives the lie to the fretfulness and apprehension of dyspeptic philosophers), Ishmael reports feeling "a melting in me. No more my splintered heart and maddened hand were turned against the wolfish world. This soothing savage had redeemed it."[62]

Ahab never requires such salvation. According to his crew he's "hot," or lacks Queequeg's tranquility. ("A hot old man!" Stubb calls him in chapter 29. "I guess he's got what some folks ashore call a conscience.") But unlike Ishmael, Ahab never becomes "disgusted with the carking cares of earth"; he never condescends to empirical life or doubts the very strong influence of corporeal life on the life of the mind. In *Moby-Dick* it is Ahab who knows himself a mind in matter housed. By his own admission, "Ahab never thinks; he only feels, feels, feels, *that's* tingling enough for mortal man! To think's audacity. God only has that right and privilege. Thinking is, or ought to be, a coolness and a calmness; and our poor hearts throb, and our poor brains beat too much for that."[63]

Ahab's defiant honoring of the material world is underscored in chapter 119, "The Candles." For as Ahab swears to the spirit fire (whom he once did worship, till in the sacramental act was burned), "I own thy speechless, placeless power; but to the last gasp of my earthquake life will dispute its unconditional, un-integral mastery in me. In the midst of the personified impersonal, a personality stands here." From his fiery father Ahab came, and to that flaming, supernal power he will return, but there is dust in him, his mother's footprint, and while he earthly lives, that "queenly personality" lives in him "and feels her royal rights." Or as Ahab says even more succinctly, "Thou canst blind; but I can then grope. Thou canst consume; but I can then be ashes."

Ahab's argument here, as I understand it, is that the concept "man," like all concepts, has a material element in addition to its formal element. This is the argument, more generally, that *thought itself* is not purely mental, that there is earthly matter in all God's creations—the things signified by the signs in our language. For Ahab, God may put spirit into dry bones, as in Ezekiel 37, but bone, dust, is the complement to spirit; indeed it is an indispensable aspect of spiritual life. (Melville will make the same argument—that material life is a component of faith—in his long poem *Clarel.*)[64]

What is more, by insisting that there is that in him that's made from coarser stuff than heaven allows—rough matter, bone and soft tissue, so that God might "consume" him, but he must then "be ashes"—Ahab argues that if he is as his Creator made him, mortally indebted, then there *cannot* be a gross discrepancy between reality and his conceptions. If practical effects govern his thinking, or "even the highest earthly felicities ever have a certain unsignifying pettiness lurking in them," then he can take pressure off the impotence of his human intellect simply by allowing that the intellect is enslaved to certain necessities of bodily life.

This is the other side of Ahab's "madness." For a long time Ahab feels humiliated by what he calls that "mortal inter-indebtedness which will not do away with ledgers." (As readers learn in chapter 127, "Ahab and the Carpenter," Ahab is "proud as a Greek God" yet finds himself a "standing debtor . . . for a bone to stand on"; he "would be free as air," but he's "down in the whole world's books.") He struggles cosmically with it. But eventually he finds that what he considered bondage, a mind bound to the limitations of a material existence, is, practically speaking, an opportunity for laying claim to objects that would otherwise be out of reach.

Here is the philosophical basis of Ahab's argument with Starbuck. Ahab bewilders his first mate by refusing to modify his unchanging course, in this matter of the whale: "Come," he goads, "Ahab's compliments to ye; come and see if ye can swerve me." Ahab's fixed purpose is easy to disparage, but in his own provocative way he is drawing attention to a great discovery: that the universe constantly and obediently answers to our conceptions of it; that the track is laid for us. As Ahab's search for the whale reveals, the meaning of our concepts *isn't* something we have a choice about. "Swerve me?" Ahab asks Starbuck, and anyone else unperceptive enough to think the meaning of the concept "whale" is something he might deliberate over; "ye cannot swerve me, else ye swerve yourselves! man has ye there. Swerve me? The path to my fixed purpose is laid with iron rails, whereon my soul is grooved to run." Of course, Starbuck doesn't understand Ahab's argument because he thinks the whale is a thing. As a thing, a whale leaves an impression on those who encounter it. These impressions—call them "ideas," since they are mental images of empirical objects—represent little more than the irrational longings of the mind. Perhaps that is why Starbuck is always trying to urge Ahab to a different course by pleading and coaxing. According to Starbuck, Ahab's conception of a whale is a picture of what he *thinks*, what we might say he has imagined. And since his image or idea of the whale is formed in his mind, there is no reason why he should not find himself mistaken, why he should not change his mind about what he thinks. My point is that Ahab understands what Starbuck doesn't—namely, that our ability to know what a whale *is* is beholden to our inability to decide (as if privately) what "whale" means.

Ahab's speech in "The Candles" might thus be understood as a direct response to the Christian doctrine highlighted in chapter 9, "The Sermon," which features the sermon preached by Father Mapple from the prow pulpit of the Seaman's Bethel. Melville's skillful adaptation of the Old Testament book of Jonah introduces a central theme in *Moby-Dick*, for the lesson that powers Mapple's sermon is that the personal will must submit to the will of God, the personal self must be submerged in the Divine self.[65] As Howard P. Vincent argues, "Father Mapple establishes in whaling language and through a whaling story the Christian paradox that the fullest self-hood may be won only by the annihilation of self."[66]

In its most radical expression, this doctrine supports (what Sharon Cameron calls) the erasure of the interiority of persons. It disturbs the boundaries of personal identities.[67] In "The Sermon," however, the Christian theme most memorably stated by Dante—that "In His will is our peace," or that to be spiritually reborn one must forget self in the service of God—includes a mandate on the body's effacement. In Mapple's story of "the sin, hard-heartedness, suddenly awakened fears, the swift punishment, repentance, prayers, and finally the deliverance and joy of Jonah," Jonah is redeemed when, rather than know his mind embodied, his body is overcome by the purely spiritual unity his mind generates with God.[68] Thus, as Ishmael notes, Father Mapple's act of physical isolation, his ascent to his lofty pulpit by way of a perpendicular side ladder (which he then deliberately drags up behind him, "leaving him impregnable in his little Quebec"), signals his spiritual withdrawal from "all outward worldly ties and connections." Here the isolating prow pulpit symbolizes more than the fundamental isolation of all worshipping persons—a point underscored by Ishmael's account of the waiting parishioners, each of whom "seemed purposely sitting apart from the other, as if each silent grief was insular and incommunicable." It heralds the lesson Father Mapple finds in the story of Jonah, which is that in his *elevated* state man renounces "all the delights of air and earth." Or as Father Mapple thunders, "Woe to him whom this world charms from Gospel duty!" And alternatively, "Delight is to him whose strong arms yet support him, when the ship of his base treacherous world has gone down beneath him . . . Delight,—top-gallant delight is to him, who acknowledges no law or lord, but the Lord his God."

Now, Ahab, like Father Mapple, hopes to confound the identity of the self and the identity of that which lies outside the self. And he, too, is a gloomily "anointed pilot-prophet, or speaker of true things," fated to find in Jonah's story a "two-stranded lesson," a lesson on sin and a lesson on obedience—specifically, that "if we obey God we must disobey ourselves; and it is in this disobeying ourselves, wherein the hardness of obeying God consists." (I say "gloomily" because being a prophet is lonely work, something Mapple reminds his parishioners when he tells them, "Shipmates, God has laid but one hand upon you; both his hands press upon me . . . And now how gladly would I come down from this mast-head and sit on the hatches there where you sit, and listen as you listen, while some one of you reads *me* that other and more awful lesson which Jonah teaches to *me*, as a pilot of the living God.") But unlike Father Mapple, Ahab does *not* think that serving God means abandoning the laws of this earth. In fact, Ahab's speech in "The Candles" can be understood as a direct refutation of Mapple's belief that the earthly world and God's eternal world are irreparably opposed.

If Ahab's defiance in "The Candles" appears in ironic contrast to Jonah's repentance, therefore, it isn't because "in Father Mapple's sermon we behold a man saved by a whale," as Howard P. Vincent writes, and "in Ahab's act we see a man destroyed by one."[69] (For Vincent, as for many readers, "Ahab acknowledges no law but his own; his search will be carried on in self-assertion, not in self-submission.")[70] Ahab's approach diverges from Jonah's for the reason that Ahab remains clear about his dual allegiance to the immortal *and mortal* worlds. In Melville's retelling of the story, Jonah might be spat back on the earth but he is never again *of* the earth; after he is swallowed up, both Jonah's ears are tuned to the sea, the "eddying depths" Melville also calls "living gulfs of doom":

> and 'the weeds were wrapped about his head,' and all the watery world of woe bowled over him. Yet even then beyond the reach of any plummet—'out of the belly of hell'—when the whale grounded upon the ocean's utmost bones, even then, God heard the engulfed, repenting prophet when he cried. Then God spake unto the fish; and from the shuddering cold and blackness of the sea, the whale came breeching up towards the warm and pleasant sun, and all the delights of air and earth; and 'vomited out Jonah upon the dry land'; when the word of the Lord came a second time; and Jonah, bruised and beaten—his ears, like two sea-shells, still multitudinously murmuring of the ocean—Jonah did the Almighty's bidding.

This passage from *Moby-Dick* recalls the celebrated passage toward the close of *White-Jacket* when that story's protagonist, just fallen from the yardarm into the depths of the sea, breaches to the surface. Rising, he hears two sounds in his ears, the one "a soft moaning, as of low waves on the beach; the other wild and heartlessly jubilant, as of the sea in the height of a tempest. Oh Soul! Thou then heardest life and death."[71]

In *The Trying-Out of Moby-Dick*, Vincent recalls the *White-Jacket* passage but then does not make a distinction between the polyphonic experience of hearing *simultaneously* the earthly and the eternal worlds and the very different experience Jonah has of finding both his ears filled with the murmuring sea. To Vincent the submerging or baptism of both men signals what Keats described as "dying into life," a profound renouncement of personal desire and the unambiguous acceptance of the will of God. This reading fails to honor the distinction Melville is making between Jonah's complete capitulation and the experience Ahab famously narrates: owning God's speechless, placeless power but disputing its unconditional, unintegral mastery in him; forging an impersonal personality; feeling himself to be earthly matter animated—matter that includes spirit, which powers it, but earthly matter all the same.

Read in this way, Ahab's insistence that "truth has no confines" isn't the problem we thought it was. Like the very best thinkers in the classical realist tradition, he believes that since the word "whale" is true of something, that which "whale" means is true. So long as he doesn't make the mistake of thinking that the meaning of this sign could be looked for as though it were an object *co-existing* with the sign he has not propagated the worst kind of philosophical confusion.

Perhaps the more germane problem is thus that critics who refuse to believe that there is truth in our words—who contest the proposition that language speakers can know the meaning of the word "whale," or who decline to "own the whale" as Melville says—are the ones who have not gone far enough in their thinking. In the belief that our words are not tools for handling reality (that we might be mistaken in the way we experience a word; that the meaning of a word like "whale" could be determined by reason or will; that the meaning of this word could ever be private, or reflect someone's "inner" experience) lie so many lame answers to badly stated questions that it is hard to know where to begin the effort of dismantling them. The effort must be made, however, because so long as we continue to imagine that someone's intellectual life could determine the meaning of the concepts they use, we fail to see how only the nature of this life with language can do that. And so long as we keep calling concepts the work of the mind, we can keep telling ourselves that a whale is something language speakers have thought up or imagined—that whales aren't really out there crashing into people. On this course, eventually, there will be nothing left to say about the world our concepts classify.

Thinking about *Moby-Dick* in relation to the role language plays in our lives and the question of how our words acquire meaning (and tapping Ahab as a source of intelligibility) should therefore leave us feeling somewhat optimistic. My thought is that in *Moby-Dick* Melville delivers a judicious examination of language and of the misunderstanding, persistent in philosophy, over what language is. As Melville's book makes clear, signification is not an atomistic but a social enterprise. This certainty, in turn, explains how the meaning of a word can be both a human artifact and objectively articulated. All told, *Moby-Dick* offers a strong and defensible notion of objectivity—one that is well suited, moreover, to serve our progressive cultural and political projects.[72] It provides nuanced but stalwart resistance to the thesis (in its particularly influential poststructuralist formulation) that all knowledge is circumscribed or, as Satya Mohanty writes, "tied to the necessary misrecognition of human subjects caught in a network of forces they cannot evade or comprehend."[73] In other words, Melville's whaling narrative resists a pervasive skepticism that seeks to undermine the whole terminology of representation by insisting on the inherent duplicity of language. It opposes the view that all meaning is unstable—that there is no genuine criterion of truth—and the corollary conviction that all reading is a kind of misreading.[74]

What is more, by offering a better understanding of what language is, Melville gives fresh vigor and impetus to Plato's theory of forms—Plato's attempt to talk about how concepts can remain one and the same while also having various subdivisions and many diverse applications.[75] As a handful of philosophers would have us remember, the purpose of such theorizing isn't to posit a world of transcendent forms but to introduce a theory of concepts and concept formation. As I have argued in this book, Melville contributes to this theory when he shows how grasping the difference between merely naming empirical similarities in the world and *concepts*, the means by which we classify the world, provides a key to dealing with "the Problem of the Universe," the problem of thinking we live in two realms, the noumenal and the phenomenal. Understanding how concepts themselves express or carry out an alliance between the general and the particular returns speaking subjects to the one world in which we live and think.

Pointing out the difficulties we can get into when thinking about concepts (the difficulty of the whole idea of making ourselves intelligible or seeing the sense of what is said) is part of this theorizing, but so is coming up with a sufficiently deep and convincing explanation for why it is possible to speak about the meanings of words. In *Moby-Dick*, Melville is able to show why we are not wrong to feel that a particular word has taken up its meaning into itself, that a word "is an actual likeness of its meaning," when he develops a notion rightly associated with Wittgenstein: that meaning isn't something that co-exists with a sign, nor is it a process that accompanies a sign—breathed into it, as it were, by language speakers.[76] What we "experience" when we experience the meaning of the word "whale" isn't a property of the object named by the word because logical notation doesn't register properties but rather what Wittgenstein calls a *Lebensform*, a form of life or a way of living. Understanding Wittgenstein's lesson involves learning to better appreciate the connection between the meaning of our words and the texture of our lives.[77] In *Moby-Dick* Melville develops the notion that—as Wittgenstein puts it—to imagine a language is to imagine a form of life, and so helps to communicate the full significance of Wittgenstein's epigrammatic remark. The result is not only a major work of literature; it is also a highly original study of some central philosophical questions concerning the possibility of discourse.

Finale

✦

The Dust (and the Spirit That Moves It)

> What literature has to offer us—and it is both enough and indispensable—is the extension of our range of responses and, at the same time, their chastening and education.
>
> —Bernard Harrison, *What Is Fiction For?*

I've argued that Melville saw the thinking of his age as stranded between two options. On the one hand an empiricism derived from Locke teaches us that sensory experience shows us things as they really are. On the other hand, an idealism derived from Kant teaches that since the system of concepts in terms of which experience structures the world is provided by the mind, real things are in principle inaccessible to human knowledge. Either the "meanings" in terms of which we interpret reality are mutely proffered to us (as it were by nature herself) in sensory experience or they are inventions of the human mind.

Through the figure of Ahab, Melville calls attention to the deficiency of this logic. For Ahab's pursuit gives a visible or tangible form to the impossible venture: living simultaneously in two very different realms, the realm of things and the realm of ideas—hence Ahab promising to keep with his men "a sharp eye for the White Whale; a sharp lance for Moby Dick." The more explicit Ahab's directive ("to chase that white whale on both sides of the land, and over all sides of the earth, till he spouts black blood and rolls fin out"), the more firmly he sets his sights on what is *in turns* ubiquitous and unique, the more obvious the lesson: that a man with only one foot in the finite world will be torn asunder.

One great pleasure of the novel, then, is that Ahab refuses this splitting. Rather than offer proof of his perverse defiance, Ahab's refusal is in accordance with the indispensable lesson of *Moby-Dick*: that language speakers are able to resurrect events that remain undecidable on their own terms and yet whose identity can be asserted—whose identity is tied to and predicated upon our involvement in a wide variety of socially devised practices, our participation in the life of the society that produced them.

In *Moby-Dick*, Ahab's failed pursuit of the whale is thus buoyed and enlivened by Melville's dissolution of the problem that has haunted man since Descartes first introduced it: that we cannot bridge the ontological chasm between nonspatiotemporal thoughts and spatiotemporally bound thinkers or, as it were, grasp thought; that we are barred from adequate knowledge of anything outside the mind. This phantom menace is what Melville's whaling narrative effectively exorcises.

Of course, seeing *Moby-Dick* as a major work of philosophy as well as literature has much to do with whether we find the story to possess principles of internal organization that are not only entirely coherent but intellectually and morally impressive (as opposed to thinking the book internally contradictory, both in terms of genre and content) and whether we understand Ahab in terms of Auerbach's notion of *figura*, a concordance of personality and the event that is being related (in contrast to the mate Starbuck's view of Ahab: a madman who has chosen to pursue an absurd campaign of vengeance).

Hoping to support the heuristic view of Ahab and the work in which he figures, I've taken as evidence of thoughtful reflection Ahab's declaration not to "fall down and worship" those "malicious agencies which some deep men feel eating at them, till they are left living on with half a heart and half a lung." I've taken seriously Ahab's vow not to venerate that "intangible malignity which has been from the beginning"—the skeptical threat, the denial of the possibility of understanding—but instead and quite self-consciously to pit himself, "all mutilated," against this challenge. The essential content of skepticism's threat (given unforgettable expression in Hume's *Treatise* but frequently in line with a distinctively "modern" point of view) is that evaluation, knowing what anything *is*, seeing something *as something*, is ultimately a function of the mind and sensibility of the individual, and therefore that there is no way in which any concept might be taken to be valid beyond question.[1] Put this way, it is not hard to understand why our great philosophers, including Plato and Wittgenstein, have been concerned about the possibility of discourse.[2]

The skeptic's view of concepts and concept possession is what Melville's story effectively dismantles. Concepts are not metaphorical, mentalistic representations. Concepts do not spring from language speakers' "inner" experience—in fact, it is when concepts (like the concept "whale") are treated like the expression of an inner experience that philosophers start to feel themselves embroiled in the most intractable difficulties. As I believe Melville tries to show, in speaking about the meaning of the word "whale" we are not speaking of some independent phenomenon but of a multifaceted aspect of this life with words. We are addressing the fact that we learn language and the world *together*, that they become elaborated and distorted together.

In *Moby-Dick*, only Ahab articulates this feature of life with language, this certainty that mortal man can know the meaning of the word "whale" and also that the meaning of "whale" is not something we have any choice about—in short, that we have a choice over our words but not over their meaning. There is thus a way to find philosophical significance in Ahab's exaggerated preoccupation with the capacity of material life to move and transform mental life—given expression in his continued assertion that "it was that accursed white whale that razed me; made a poor pegging lubber of me forever and a day!"[3] Ahab's sense that his intellectual or spiritual life is intimately connected to his bodily life, his emphasis on the concreteness and objectivity of even the most abstract, inscrutable, or intangible concepts, serves the account of meaning in language that runs throughout *Moby-Dick*—that meaning goes to ground in practice. Ahab is as riveted as Melville is by, in the words of Branka Arsić, "materiality or, perhaps more precisely, the concreteness of things that includes the spiritual, which moves it."[4]

As Melville's whaling narrative illustrates, the meanings of our words are human artifacts rather than things discoverable in the natural world, but they are artifacts not of "the mind" but of practical life. In *Moby-Dick* Melville makes a case for the concreteness or materiality of thought and its linguistic expressions. He argues that even over our *words* "matter in the end will never abate / His ancient brutal claim."[5] He repudiates the story in which man is an interloper in the realm of third-world objects or the realm of language itself—the realm rightly called real. That our words, too, are real is the claim Melville lays out in his whaling narrative.

Melville's hard-won conclusion is that the word "whale" is objectively articulated not because it suggests an extra quality, *being-a-whale*, that may be present in one object and not in another but because what confronts us in a concept such as this one is an endlessly shifting web of conceptual creation grounded in embodied life. What the word "whale" names is not an imaginary object but real life as expressed through logical representation. This conclusion is of considerable worth to critics in whom, in certain moods, some malicious agencies can take hold—critics for whom the things signified by the signs in our language can come to seem essentially fanciful.

Thinking that words are objectively articulated, however, does not mean that an author can work less hard at the descriptions that make up his fictional narrative. That real life is manifest in words doesn't suggest that the artist's meticulous arrangement of language is superfluous, that is to say, and as Bryan C. Short argues, Melville's writing shows "an increasing involvement with figurative language as a determinant not simply of style but of underlying structural and representational strategies as well."[6] In other words, Melville's trust in the integrity of language only strengthened his commitment to conscious literary artistry, demonstrated, for example, by what I have called *Moby-Dick*'s scenes of mimesis, Melville's lifelike, dynamic pictures of the thing signified by the sign "whale." Such pictures are not stiff *portraits* of the whale—the whale in vacant profile, floated or strung up for the purpose of sober, scientific study. They are, rather, *whaling scenes*—the complex, endlessly branching and subdividing set of practices and situations that make up the leviathanic life: a ship in pursuit of a whale hove to upon the open sea; a vessel in the act of cutting in, a headless whale strapped alongside while boats push off in search of more whales; the smoke of the boiling whale rising in a black cloud; the commotion of excited seamen, or the forced calm of seamen lying in wait, their harpoons and lances leveled for use; a whale entangled in the harpoon line that he tows; the aggregation of whales into immense caravans or extensive herds; nursing whale mothers suspended in becalmed waters, suckling infants at their sides; a singular spout—not the perpendicular twin jet of the right whale, "which, dividing at the top, falls over in two branches, like the cleft drooping boughs of a willow," but the forward-slanting spout of the sperm whale, a "thick curled bush of white mist, continually rising and falling away to leeward."[7]

The painstaking composition of these scenes offers yet another reminder that the meaning of the word "whale" is acquired through participation in the socially devised and maintained practices and institutions in terms of which all words acquire meaning and, as Bernard Harrison writes, come to serve a double function in human life.[8] Words' double function is, on the one hand, to put the speakers of language in touch with the continuous aspects of reality and, on the other, to provide us with some purchase from which those aspects of reality might be better examined and understood. For what language has always offered, in addition to contact with *what is*, what is neither purely sensible nor merely subjective, is the extension of the range of our responses to the complex situations our words signify. Having use of the word "whale" (having linguistic knowledge of the whale, or knowing what is grasped by someone who understands the concept "whale") is also what makes possible an ever more subtle and intelligent response to the situation or state of affairs this word signifies, the living whale in his full majesty and significance. The words we ordinarily use are devices for prompting new kinds of responses in us, their users, just as books of fiction are devices for extending the range of our responses not just to imagined situations but to those we encounter in real life.[9]

Certainty that the word "whale" is objectively articulated, that is to say ("the very thing itself," as Ken Dauber writes, "a referent, as it were one with that to which it refers"), is what permits the full immersion of *Moby-Dick*'s readers into the book's ethical configuration, the propensity everywhere evident in this whaling narrative to help readers swap our self-justifying, self-serving points of view for outlooks more humble and humane.

Consider, for example, the way Melville garners attentive concern for the *Pequod*'s one-legged captain when he tells his readers that "in a pirate, man-of-war, or slave ship, when the captain is rowed anywhere in his boat, he always sits in the stern sheets on a comfortable, sometimes cushioned seat there, and often steers himself with a pretty little milliner's tiller decorated with gay cords and ribbons"—but that the whale boat "has no seat astern, no sofa of that sort whatsoever, and no tiller at all." The result is that the subordinate harpooner or oarsman becomes the steersman, and "the captain, having no place to sit in, is pulled off to his visit all standing like a pine tree":

> And often you will notice that being conscious of the eyes of the whole visible world resting on him from the sides of the two ships, this standing captain is all alive to the importance of sustaining his dignity by maintaining his legs. Nor is this any very easy matter; for in his rear is the immense projecting steering oar hitting him now and then in the small of his back, the after-oar reciprocating by rapping his knees in front. He is thus completely wedged before and behind, and can only expand himself sideways by settling down on his stretched legs; but a sudden, violent pitch of the boat will often go far to topple him, because length of foundation is nothing without corresponding breadth. Merely make a spread angle of two poles, and you cannot stand them up. Then, again, it would never do in plain sight of the world's riveted eyes, it would never do, I say, for this straddling captain to be seen steadying himself the slightest particle by catching hold of anything with his hands; indeed, as token of his entire, buoyant self-command, he generally carries his hands in his trowsers' pockets; but perhaps being generally very large, heavy hands, he carries

> them there for ballast. Nevertheless there have occurred instances, well authenticated ones too, where the captain has been known for an uncommonly critical moment or two, in a sudden squall, say—to seize hold of the nearest oarsman's hair, and hold on there like grim death.[10]

A passage like this one affords readers the opportunity to experience the cumulative effect of Melville's meticulous scene making, to feel how readers are encouraged to change focus or change the direction in which we are looking, as, slowly advancing through a labyrinthine passage, we are repeatedly dislodged by complicated outgrowths of description, additional or supplementary visual aids, with the result that we, too, must always be trying to find our position again in relation to our surroundings.

Chapter 56, "Of the Less Erroneous Pictures of Whales, and the True Pictures of Whaling Scenes," offers Melville's frank account of the superiority of scenes to portraits. As part of his approbation of French painters' facility for painting action and thus, as he says, of "conveying the real spirit of the whale hunt,"[11] Melville describes the second of two engravings by Garneray—engravings identified as "the finest, though in some details not the most correct, presentations of whales and whaling scenes to be anywhere found":

> In the second engraving, the boat is in the act of drawing alongside the barnacled flank of a large running Right Whale, that rolls his black weedy bulk in the sea like some mossy rock-slide from the Patagonian cliffs. His jets are erect, full, and black like soot; so that from so abounding a smoke in the chimney, you would think there must be a brave supper cooking in the great bowels below. Sea fowls are pecking at the small crabs, shell-fish, and other sea candies and maccaroni, which the Right Whale sometimes carries on his pestilent back. And all the while the thick-lipped leviathan is rushing through the deep, leaving tons of tumultuous white curds in his wake, and causing the slight boat to rock in the swells like a skiff caught nigh in the paddle-wheels of an ocean steamer. Thus, the foreground is all raging commotion; but behind, in admirable artistic contrast, is the glassy level of a sea becalmed, the drooping unstarched sails of the powerless ship, and the inert mass of a dead whale, a conquered fortress, with the flag of capture lazily hanging from the whale-pole inserted into his spout-hole.

Melville is by this careful accumulation of evocative details able to express a deep admiration and sympathy—for the dead whale, the oarsmen rocking in their boat, even the powerless ship—without moralizing, or without reflecting on good or bad conduct in some tiresome way. The scene is one of many in which readers' sympathies are turned and turned about, not unlike "a skiff caught nigh in the paddle-wheels of an ocean steamer," until, by the end of some long passage of description, we feel complete solicitude and fellow feeling for objects and events about which, prior to the passage, inspired mild contempt. *Moby-Dick*'s readers are, as a result, "expandingly lifted" by Melville's subject, stretched and enlarged by Melville's style.

As passages like this one show, Melville thinks of fiction as a device for arousing in readers responses not to anything imaginary but to the things of this world.[12] That goal, it seems to me, shapes *Moby-Dick*. Rather than satisfy himself with fiction's capacity to represent real life, however, Melville drew into the orbit of his whaling narrative an exacting account of the way *signs*, words uttered with a specific meaning, the basic unit of discourse, are both manufactured and real; abstractions and codexes of particularity; not coincident with any one person's experience *and reliable gauges of experience*. In consequence Melville's great experimental fiction offers secure footing to anyone who wishes to take a stand against the various incarnations of skepticism fashionable in the present moment; against the idea that people can make up evaluative terms by themselves, at the behest of whatever personal commitments or sentiments happen to animate them; against the idea that linguistic expressions imprison what they manifest and thus are not to be trusted; against the idea that words unhinged from their referents only distance us from the world; against much, in short, that daily works to impair still further our ways of speaking and attending to one another.

NOTES

Introduction

1. In his journals Hawthorne records his impression of Melville's propensity to talk of "Providence and futurity, and of everything that lies beyond human ken," noting that "it is strange how he persists—and has persisted ever since I knew him, and probably long before—in wandering to and fro over these deserts, as dismal and monotonous as the sand hills amid which we were sitting. He can neither believe, nor be comfortable in his unbelief; and he is too honest and courageous not to try to do one or the other" (Herman Melville, *Journals*, ed. Howard C. Horsford and Lynn Horth [Evanston, Ill.: Northwestern University Press / The Newberry Library, 1989], 628). This is not a bad stab at a brief statement of Melville's philosophical stance, and it is handy for critics striving to represent Melville's habits of mind, but even a trenchant observation lends itself to caricature if forced to too much duty.

2. Herman Melville, *The Confidence Man* (Amherst, N.Y.: Prometheus Books, 1995), 206–7.

3. A. D. Nuttall, *A New Mimesis: Shakespeare and the Representation of Reality* (New Haven, Conn.: Yale University Press, 2007).

4. Bernard Harrison, *Reality and Culture: Essays on the Philosophy of Bernard Harrison*, ed. Patricia Hanna (New York: Rodopi, 2014), 20. Harrison's reconstructed realism (from within his provocative reexamination of the interrelations of language and social practice) is a governing influence on this book. For the best summary of Harrison's work on this theme, see his full prologue to *Reality and Culture*, 1–29. See also John Gibson's essay in the same volume, 33–48.

5. Erich Auerbach, *Dante, Poet of the Secular World*, trans. Ralph Manheim (New York: New York Review Books, 2007), 150, 68. *Dante* was published in German in 1923, in English in 1961. For Auerbach, Dante was the first of such writers.

6. Charles Altieri, *Reckoning with the Imagination: Wittgenstein and the Aesthetics of Literary Experience* (Ithaca and London: Cornell University Press, 2015), 105–6.

7. Auerbach, *Dante*, 1.

8. Henry James, *Literary Criticism, Volume 2: French Writers; Other European Writers; The Prefaces to the New York Edition* (New York: Library of America, 1984), 185. "Pen-photography" is what nineteenth-century homiletic novelist Henry Wood (Ellen Price) called writing that imitates temporal reality exclusively, as Gregory S. Jackson reports in *The Word and Its Witness: The Spiritualization of American Realism* (Chicago: University of Chicago Press, 2009), 11. For other recent influential critical attempts to complicate American literary realism or see realist novels as doing something other than recording a naive belief in the correspondence between language and a ready-made material world, see Amy Kaplan, *The Social Construction of American Realism* (Chicago: University of Chicago

Press, 1988), and the introduction in Eric J. Sundquist, *American Realism: New Essays* (Baltimore: Johns Hopkins University Press, 1982).

9. James, *Literary Criticism*, 185.

10. This neat summary of new materialism is offered by Omri Moses in a book that expertly demonstrates, through a close reading of three modernist writers, what may be meant by "a capacious and dynamic view of subjectivity,"—a very useful phrase coined by Charles Altieri. Omri Moses, *Out of Character: Modernism, Vitalism, Psychic Life* (Stanford University Press, 2014), 20; and Charles Altieri, *Reckoning with the Imagination*, 118.

11. Ludwig Wittgenstein, *Tractatus Logico-Philosophicus*, trans. D. F. Pears and B. F. McGuiness (New York: Routledge, 1961), 1.3. My understanding of the way Wittgensteinian "facts" are structured is indebted to David Charles McCarty's atypical reading of the *Tractatus*, invigoratingly portrayed in his long essay "The Philosophy of Logical Wholism," *Synthese* 87, no. 1 (April 1991):51–123.

12. Auerbach, *Dante*, 134.

13. Ibid., 133. Elsewhere Auerbach describes the kind of realist writing Dante produces as "earthly particularity held fast in the mirror of a timeless eye" (68). As Michael Dirda writes in the introduction to the book, Auerbach asks us to regard Dante's great poem "not just as a divine comedy but also as a *comédie humaine*." For Auerbach, Dante "truly is a 'poet of the secular world,' of our fallen earthly realm where people laugh and conspire, love and hate, sin and triumph over sin" (ix). Or as Auerbach himself notes, "In truth the *Comedy* is a picture of earthly life" (133). James I. Porter deftly summarizes the radical interpretive premise of Auerbach's first book in *Time History, and Literature: Selected Essays of Erich Auerbach*, ed. James I. Porter; trans. Jane O. Newman (Princeton, N.J.: Princeton University Press, 2014), xvii and xxi.

14. Auerbach, *Dante*, 1–2.

15. Ibid., 2.

16. Ibid., 2–3.

17. Ibid.,152. The idea of "character" in this original and rich sense has lost ground to the contemporary sense of character as personality, the collection of crucial traits distinctive to an individual. A *person* is what the term "character" now seems to suggest. "Figure" is thus the preferred term for describing a writer's imagined being (if, as in Homer's poetry, he or she is rendered with "reality and dignity," as Auerbach writes). For an illuminating investigation of what we mean, or ought to mean, "when we invoke figures in lieu of persons," see Michael D. Snediker, "*Pierre* and the Non-Transparencies of Figuration," *ELH* 77, no. 1 (Spring 2010): 217–35. For Snediker, a figure is a person who is "ontologically stylistic"—a person who, like Melville's Pierre, "can only be a person to the extent that the terms of his personhood necessarily arise from and negotiate the rhetorical ecosystem in which he finds himself" (231).

18. Auerbach, *Dante*. As Auerbach notes, *manifestazioni plastiche*, "plastic manifestations," is Italian scholar Manfredi Porena's way of describing what Auerbach calls the "real and evident figure" in a work of art.

19. Ibid., 150–53.

20. Erich Auerbach, *Mimesis: The Representation of Reality in Western Literature*, trans. Willard R. Trask (Princeton, N.J.: Princeton University Press, 2003), 137. *Mimesis* was first published in German in 1946, in English in 1953.

21. Altieri, *Reckoning with the Imagination*, 105-6 and 143.

22. Auerbach, *Dante*, 44.

23. Altieri, *Reckoning with the Imagination*, 79.

24. This nimble account of Cartesian dualism is offered by Bernard Harrison in *What Is Fiction For? Literary Humanism Restored* (Bloomington: Indiana University Press, 2015), 125–26.

25. F. R. Leavis, *The Living Principle: "English" as a Discipline of Thought* (London: Chatto and Windus, 1975), 36.

26. Frege's remarks on the third realm are in *Logical Investigations* and quoted in Harrison, *What Is Fiction For?*, 124.

27. This is the valuable description of Cameron's intellectual project offered by Branka Arsić in *American Impersonal: Essays with Sharon Cameron* (New York: Bloomsbury, 2014), 2–3.

28. Stanley Cavell, *The Senses of Walden: An Expanded Edition* (Chicago and London: University of Chicago Press, 1992 [1981]), 33. Though in his study of Thoreau's *Walden* Cavell stages his claim as a question ("Why has America never expressed itself philosophically? Or has it—in the metaphysical riot of its greatest literature?"), it is a question to which *The Senses of Walden* constitutes a full and affirmative response.

29. Stanley Cavell, *Emerson's Transcendental Etudes*, ed. David Justin Hodge (Stanford, Calif.: Stanford University Press, 2003), 65.

30. Branka Arsić develops and extends the Emersonian project as understood by Cavell and Cameron in *Bird Relics: Grief and Vitalism in Thoreau* (Cambridge, Mass.: Harvard University Press, 2016).

31. For a well-known account of the way the Lockean and Kantian projects each in their different ways uphold the view of the mind as a great mirror, see Richard Rorty, *Philosophy and the Mirror of Nature* (Princeton, N.J.: Princeton University Press, 1979). As Rorty suggests in this work, the whole notion of knowledge as the assemblage of accurate representations of the natural world is optional (11). My study of Melville is, however, fundamentally at odds with Rorty's dismissive view of the philosophical concept of "objectivity," which, as he understands it, is a term that describes the mind's accurate representation of the natural world. For Melville, I argue, the notion of objectivity is valid because the term need not imply that which is fixed or immutable—only that which is *intersubjectively accessible.*

32. For philosophers in the empiricist-cum-analytic tradition (the tradition, as I will work to show, Melville sets his writing against) "language" is both *more* and *less* powerful than Melville conceives it to be: more powerful because of the assumed connection between words and the nature of things, and less powerful because concepts and their linguistic expressions are essentially fanciful. My own understanding of how language works has come largely from good readers of Melville, of Wittgenstein, and of Genesis; when one person commands all three, like my teacher Ken Dauber, the effect is exhilarating. See Dauber's account of what he calls ordinary language criticism in "Beginning at the Beginning in Genesis," in *Ordinary Language Criticism: Literary Thinking after Cavell after Wittgenstein*, ed. Kenneth Dauber and Walter Jost (Evanston, Ill.: Northwestern University Press, 2003), 329. See also the introduction in the present work.

33. Cavell, *The Senses of Walden*, 92.

34. In her Introduction to *Bird Relics: Grief and Vitalism in Thoreau* (2016), Branka Arsić calls attention to the follow passage in *Walden*: "It would seem as if the very language of our parlors would lose all its nerve and degenerate into *palaver* wholly, our lives pass at such remoteness from its symbols, and its metaphors and tropes are necessarily so far fetched, through slides and dumb-waiters, as it were; in other words, the parlor is so far from the kitchen and workshop. The dinner even is only the parable of a dinner, commonly. As if only the savage dwelt near enough to Nature and Truth to borrow a trope from them" (Henry David Thoreau, *Walden*, ed. J. Lyndon Shanley [Princeton, N.J.: Princeton University Press, 1971], 244–45).

35. Arsić, *Bird Relics*, 8.

36. *Pierre Hadot, l'enseignement des antiques, l'enseignement des modernes*, ed. Arnold I. Davidson and Frederic Worms (Paris, 2010), 24. As Arnold Davidson notes in his preface to *The Present Alone is Our Happiness: Conversations with Jeannie Carlier and Arnold I. Davidson*, the idea of a philosophy designed to leave the "closed, rigid circle of the school so that it could become accessible and useful to everyone" became fundamental to Hadot's conception of philosophical consciousness. (Stanford: Stanford University Press, 2011), x.

37. The need for an elaborate theoretical framework derived from Melville's own cast of mind was proposed in Bryan C. Short's dazzling study of Melville's rhetorical strategies, *Cast by Means of Figures: Herman Melville's Rhetorical Development* (Amherst: University of Massachusetts Press, 1992). As Short writes, "[Melville's] aesthetic, insofar as he thinks about it—and he thinks about it all the time—combines high self-consciousness with breathtaking rhetorical sensitivity and a passion for dialectical oppositions and departures." To complicate matters further, "Melville has a photographic memory for his aesthetic experiments. Nothing tried is lost. Images, figures, strategies, tonalities, and structural principles get carried along, revised, commented on, combined, turned upside-down, elaborated, and reapplied in a process which often leaves them clotted with multiple layers of rhetorical significance." This "gathering rhetorical significance," as Short writes, drives Melville "not into silence but on to bolder departures. On the one hand, like Tommo in *Typee*, he abhors "a right-about retrograde movement—a systematic going over of the already trodden ground," and on the other hand, he remains obsessively in touch with the accumulating burden of his creative past." For Short, accordingly, Melville's works "reveal him to be a master of the rhetorical tradition, conceptually and in practice, and show him to have derived for himself a theoretical framework that literary criticism has only recently become capable of appreciating" (2–4).

38. This reframing of experience takes its lead from Cavell's reading of Emerson, in particular Cavell's field-changing interpretation of Emerson's provocative remark "but far be it from me the despair which prejudges the law by a paltry empiricism" (Ralph Waldo Emerson, "Experience," in *Essays and Lectures* [New York: Library of America, 1983], 472, and Cavell, *The Senses of Walden*, 126). For a recent and informative framing of what Cavell takes to be Emerson's challenge to both empiricist and Kantian ideas of experience, see also Paul Grimstad, *Experience and Experimental Writing: Literary Pragmatism from Emerson to the Jameses* (Oxford: Oxford University Press, 2013), 3–8.

39. "Being a materialist," as I have framed it here, means eliding entirely the problem, as philosophers have generally framed it, of getting from things to language—of getting from (physical, finite) things to (unbounded, inexhaustible) linguistic constructs.

40. Stephen Mulhall, *The Wounded Animal: J. M. Coetzee and the Difficulty of Reality in Literature and Philosophy* (Princeton, N.J.: Princeton University Press, 2009), 3.

41. Elizabeth Duquette, "Making an Example: American Literature as Philosophy," in *The Oxford Handbook of Nineteenth-Century American Literature*, ed. Russ Castronovo (Oxford: Oxford University Press, 2012), 346.

42. Letter of November [17?] 1851, in Herman Melville, *Correspondence*, ed. Lynn Horth (Evanston, Ill.: Northwestern University Press / The Newberry Library, 1993), 213.

43. Newton Arvin, *Herman Melville* (New York: Norton, 1957 [1950]), 154.

44. John Bryant, "The Persistence of Melville: Representative Writer for a Multicultural Age," in *Melville's Evermoving Dawn: Centennial Essays*, ed. John Bryant and Robert Milder (Ohio: Kent State University Press, 1997), 26.

45. Herman Melville, "Hawthorne and His Mosses," in *The Piazza Tales and Other Prose Pieces, 1839–1860*, ed. Harrison Hayford et al. (Evanston, Ill.: Northwestern University Press / The Newberry Library, 1987), 244.

46. Samuel Otter and Geoffrey Sanborn, eds., *Melville and Aesthetics* (New York: Palgrave Macmillan, 2011), 5.

47. John Bryant, ed., *Melville and Repose: The Rhetoric of Humor in the American Renaissance* (New York: Oxford University Press, 1993), 9. Sharon Cameron critiques this way of bringing *Moby-Dick*'s contradictions into relationship when she writes that such means of interpreting the novel's oppositions "might be expressed in the following formulation: if we understood contradictions properly, we would also be able to reconcile them, to conceive of them simultaneously as a poise or balance, a reciprocal suspension of all one-sidedness." For Cameron, "Such a sanguine interpretation takes account of lucky moments like the one in which Ishmael is able to imagine—without faulting as contradictory—the idea of 'resting at last in manhood's pondering repose of If.' It does not, however, take account of the brutality with which oppositions in the novel customarily fail to recognize each other or, if they do, acknowledge each other for the purpose of doing violence to each other" (*The Corporeal Self: Allegories of the Body in Melville and Hawthorne* [New York: Columbia University Press, 1981], 35–36).

48. Melville, "Hawthorne and His Mosses," 244.

49. The notion of an author's ability to resurrect an event that remains undecidable and yet whose identity is affirmed can be found in Short, *Cast by Means of Figures*, 95.

50. I'm alluding here to the argument that Melville's books are not "wholly or even mainly fictive," as Nina Baym has insisted ("Melville's Quarrel with Fiction," *PMLA* 94, no. 5 [October 1979]: 909–23), and the persisting opinion even among critics who take issue with Baym that Melville "was interested not in 'fiction' but in forms that mixed fiction, autobiography, travel narratives, sailor narratives, ethnology texts, and aesthetic treatises" (Samuel Otter, *Melville's Anatomies* [Berkeley: University of California Press, 1999], 258).

51. See Edgar A. Dryden, *Monumental Melville: The Formation of a Literary Career* (Stanford, Calif.: Stanford University Press, 2004), 1–13. Clarifying the work's meaning in the way Dryden suggests isn't like trying to get behind or beneath writing in order to discover, once and for all, its true import—to bring reading to an end by enforcing what Derridians would call the closure of its interpretive potential. Less reductively, it brings to mind little more than the expected result of reading, so long as "reading" still suggests, as Dryden says, "the painstaking process of examining a primary text with patience and care, taking into account its seemingly unaccountable and inexplicable details with the intention of discovering its law, that which marks it as unique or special" (5).

52. Melville, *Journals*, 628.

53. This view is rather widely championed by Melville scholars of note. However, two particularly convincing or forceful presentations of it can be found in Dryden, *Monumental Melville*, and Jonathan Arac, *The Emergence of American Literary Narrative, 1820–1860* (Cambridge, Mass.: Harvard University Press, 2005).

54. Ronald Mason, *The Spirit Above the Dust: A Study of Herman Melville* (Mamaroneck, N.Y.: Appel, 1972), 20.

55. Arac, *Emergence of American Literary Narrative*, 181–82.

56. Ibid., 140.

57. Daniel Defoe, *Moll Flanders*, ed. J. Paul Hunter (New York: Crowell, 1970), 4, as cited in Edgar A. Dryden, *The Form of American Romance* (Baltimore: Johns Hopkins University Press, 1988), 3–4.

58. Arac, *Emergence of American Literary Narrative*, 122.

59. Ibid., 179.

60. Ibid., 222.

61. Ibid., 127.

62. Ibid., 127, 179.

63. Ibid., 212–17. Arac argues that *Israel Potter* drew on the popular tradition of personal narrative in order to secure its standing as national narrative, and that a similar strategy (namely, the transformation of personal narrative into writing that also supported the ironies of literary reflection) directs the equally well-received tales eventually collected in *The Piazza Tales*. Arac's point seems to be that compared with those texts anchored either in personal narrative or in the tradition of personal narrative, Melville's more determinedly literary narratives seem, like *The Confidence Man*, "marginal and improvisatory," sentenced to a "repeated staging of its incommensurability with itself" (223).

64. Ibid., 179–80.

65. For an extended exploration of this idea, see Harrison, *What Is Fiction For?*. See also Bernard Harrison, *Inconvenient Fictions: Literature and the Limits of Theory* (New Haven, Conn.: Yale University Press, 1991).

66. Melville's well-known line is from *The Confidence Man*, 219. In "Chasing the Whale: *Moby-Dick* as Political Theory," George Shulman, following Eric Bentley's remarks on tragedy, shows how *Moby-Dick*'s foreclosed upon world "does not dictate the lesson of the experiences it performs but releases audiences to the burden and freedom of judgment and action" (*A Political Companion to Melville*, ed. Jason Frank (Lexington: University Press of Kentucky, 2013), 99 and 70.

67. Donald G. Marshall, foreword to *The Unremarkable Wordsworth*, by Geoffrey H. Hartman, Theory of History and Literature, vol. 34 (Minneapolis: University of Minnesota Press, 1987), xiii–iv.

68. The more radical and informed view of the political to which Marshall refers is now widely associated with the writing of Jacques Rancière. For Rancière, notes Samuel A. Chambers, politics "cannot be understood as the making of laws, or the decisions of courts." It isn't "a battle between existent classes." Instead, "politics is that more originary moment of dissensus that brings about the very existence of classes in the first place." Or as Rancière has put it in a celebrated remark, "Politics does not happen just because the poor oppose the rich. It is the other way around: politics . . . causes the poor to exist as an entity." In an orienting comment of particular relevance to readers of Melville, Chambers notes that a useful way of grasping this thinking of politics "is to emphasize that a radical democratic subject of politics does not just appear on the stage; it brings the stage into being" (*The Lessons of Rancière* [New York: Oxford University Press, 2013], 8–9).

69. Jacques Rancière, *The Flesh of Words: The Politics of Writing*, trans. Charlotte Mandell (Stanford, Calif.: Stanford University Press, 2004), 5.

70. Melville, *The Confidence Man*, 218–19.

71. Jay Leyda, *The Melville Log: A Documentary Life of Herman Melville, 1819–1891* (New York: Harcourt, Brace, 1951), 1:437.

72. This vital estimation of what is wanted from a work of fiction appears in chapter 33 of *The Confidence Man*, "Which May Pass for Whatever It May Prove to Be Worth," the second of three chapters in which Melville plays interlocutor to himself. Melville's gloss on the nature of reality appears in the first of these self-reflective chapters, chapter 14, "Worth the Consideration of Those to Whom It May Prove Worth Considering," when he writes that "no one man can be coextensive with *what is*." (Emphasis in original.)

73. Many of Melville's readers have emphasized his disciplined attention to empirical data, his painstaking attention to the natural world and its known operations. However, as Jennifer Baker underscores, the observational rigor in Melville's art does not provide a contrast to but "is a precondition for the experience of wonder." As she notes, the wonders about which Melville writes in *Moby-Dick* "are not simply wonders but 'honest wonders,' which simultaneously hold up as material facts; their wondrousness depends, in part, on their being factual." Or as Thoreau elegantly makes this point in *Walden*, "We are enabled to apprehend all that is sublime and noble only by the perpetual instilling and drenching of the reality that surrounds us." See Jennifer Baker, "Dead Bones and Honest Wonders: The Aesthetics of Natural Science in *Moby-Dick*," in Otter and Sanborn, *Melville and Aesthetics*, 94, 85, 95.

74. *The Early Lectures of Ralph Waldo Emerson: Volume 1, 1833–1836*, ed. Stephen E. Whicher and Robert E. Spiller (Cambridge, Mass.: Harvard University Press, 1959), 79. "The poet loses himself in imaginations and for want of accuracy is a mere fabulist," Emerson writes. "The savant on the other hand losing sight of the end of his inquiries in the perfection of his manipulations becomes an apothecary, a pedant. I fully believe in both, in the poetry and the dissection."

75. Gottlob Frege, *The Foundations of Arithmetic: A Logico-Mathematical Enquiry into the Concept of Number*, trans. J. L. Austen (Evanston, Ill.: Northwestern University Press, 1980), 60.

76. John Milbank, "The Theological Critique of Philosophy in Hamann and Jacobi," in *Radical Orthodoxy: A New Theology*, ed. John Milbank, Catherine Pickstock, and Graham Ward (London: Routledge, 1999), 27. I've referred to this world-transforming insight as the Jobian lesson—though as Neil Hertz justly points out, in the book of Job, "God isn't teaching Job beans." For Hertz, the gist of God's "lesson" to Job is that Job doesn't know what God is talking about. Therefore we might say that it is not Job but readers of the Job who potentially learn something from this scene of instruction, this reminder that our signs have an indisputable validity—we are by necessity creatures who use signs to discern the continuous aspects of reality—but there is nevertheless no direct connection between signs and things in the natural world (conversation with author, July 8, 2016).

77. G. E. Lessing, *The Education of the Human Race*, trans. F. W. Robertson (London: King, 1872), 41–42.

78. "The whole object of the *Critique of Pure Reason*," as Henri Bergson writes, "is, in fact, to explain how a particular order is superadded to supposedly incoherent materials. And we know what price it makes us pay for this explanation according to which the human mind imposes its form upon a 'sensible diversity' of unexplained origin; and the order we find in things is the order we ourselves put in them." The price is epistemology at the cost of metaphysics, as Bergson says, and the human mind "is thus relegated to a corner, like a schoolboy in disgrace; it cannot turn its head around to see reality as it is" (Henri Bergson, *The Creative Mind: An Introduction to Metaphysics* [1946; repr., New York: Citadel Press, 1992], 65).

79. My understanding of the relationship between words and the world is deeply indebted to Bernard Harrison's lifelong engagement of the subject in his many works, in particular his account of the nature of language, founded on an original interpretation of Wittgenstein: Patricia Hanna and Bernard Harrison, *Word and World: Practice and the Foundations of Language* (Cambridge: Cambridge University Press, 2004).

80. Of course, the idea that a certain set of qualities makes something what it is, man's overconfidence in what George Lakoff refers to as classical categorization (the idea that "among the properties that things have, some are essential; that is, they are the properties that make the thing what it is, and without which it would be not that *kind* of thing"), is ridiculed in Melville's *The Confidence Man*. George Lakoff, *Women, Fire, and Dangerous Things. What Categories Reveal about the Mind* (Chicago and London: University of Chicago Press, 1987), 161.

81. Thus for Williams the poetry "registers the affective experience of being in a world that is disarrayed, or which goes through moments of oddity and disorientation; a world characterized by regular prompts to recalibrate our relationship with it, rather than by an ongoing predictability" (Rhian Williams, "Wordsworth and Eco-Poetics," *La Questione Romantica* 3, no. 2 [October 2011]: 31–46). See also Kathleen Stuart, *Ordinary Affects* (Durham, N.C.: Duke University Press, 2007), 2.

82. Hartman, *The Unremarkable Wordsworth*, 29 and 27.

83. Matthew Arnold, *Lectures and Essays in Criticism*, vol. 3 of *The Complete Prose Works of Matthew Arnold*, ed. R. H. Super (Ann Arbor: University of Michigan Press, 1962), 168–69. Thus for Arnold the value of poetic thinking

is as "a means to know the material touch of the ineffable," as Rhian Williams explains in "'Divine Liquidness of Diction . . . Divine Fluidity of Movement': Reading Poetry After Matthew Arnold and the Higher Biblical Criticism," *Literature and Theology* 27, no. 3 (2013): 8.

84. Hartman, *The Unremarkable Wordsworth*, 22.

85. Raymond Williams, *Marxism and Literature* (New York: Oxford University Press, 1977), 132 and 131.

86. Ibid., 134.

87. Ibid., 132. Thus what radically distinguishes Williams's early study of affect from many more recent and more cursory studies of the same is the very serious roadblock it offers aesthetic theorists firmly convinced of the world's fully "administered" quality, as Adorno says. The very word "structure," in Williams's phrase "structures of feeling," will suggest to many readers that language is a structural (in fact a structuralist, "hegemonic") game, an imposition onto the fact of how we think, replacing the fact. This is precisely the *opposite* of Williams's objective in emphasizing affective experience.

88. William Wordsworth, *The Fenwick Notes*, ed. Jared Curtis (London: Bristol Classical Press, 1993), 61. The phrase "reality testing" is from Rhian Williams, "Wordsworth and Eco-Poetics," 1.

89. Raymond Williams, *Marxism and Literature*, 133.

90. Rancière, *The Flesh of Words*, 3.

91. Silvana Borutti and Fulvia de Luise, "Writing and Communicating Philosophy: Consonances between Plato and Wittgenstein," in *Wittgenstein and Plato: Connections, Comparisons and Contrasts*, ed. Luigi Perissinotto and Begoña Ramón Cámara (New York: Palgrave Macmillan, 2013), 132.

92. Wittgenstein, *Tractatus*, 1–1.2.

93. Ibid., 3.221: "Objects I can only *name*. Signs represent them. I can only speak *of* them. I cannot *assert them*. A proposition can say only *how* a thing is, not *what* it is."

94. As Borutti and de Luise note, for Wittgenstein only "life in a linguistico-communitarian horizon appears to be thinkable: there is no life that has not been elevated to its form, that does not become what it is (what it can be) through linguistic form" ("Writing and Communicating Philosophy," 138).

95. Dauber, "Beginning at the Beginning," 329.

96. https://en.wikipedia.org/wiki/Object_(philosophy), accessed March 19, 2009.

97. Melville, "Hawthorne and His Mosses," 244.

98. Auerbach, *Dante*, 5. As is well known, Plato's argument in the *Republic* is that if the empirical world is second in rank, a deceptive copy of the Ideas, which alone have truth and being, then art, which concerns itself with the imitation of appearance, is still lower on the scale, a copy of a copy, third in respect to truth.

99. Ibid.

100. It is worth noting that Plato was a writer, unlike the orator Socrates, and though we can assume that he shared some of Socrates's concerns, it is clear that Plato also recognized the great intellectual advantages writing had over speaking. Eric Havelock, Walter Ong, and other classicists have suggested that in the argument about the value of writing expressed in the dialogues, we see evidence of the strains created by the transition from an oral to a literary culture, and that

when Plato goes out of his way to have Socrates attack "poetry" at the end of the *Republic*, we should understand that Plato's complaint is not with verse per se but with the oral tradition—the tradition of the bard Homer but also the tradition of Socrates. As Eric A. Havelock writes in *Preface to Plato*, the "oral state of mind" (with its dependence on formulaic verse or what we'd now call cliché, common turns of phrase to aid memorization) was Plato's "main enemy" (Cambridge, Mass.: Harvard University Press, 1963), 41. For Plato, writing liberated thought by freeing language from the strictures of individual memory or the rhythmical and formulaic structures required to support memorization and recitation.

101. Frege's innovating suggestion about the two ways a single term can have meaning is from "On *Sinn* and *Bedeutung*," in *The Frege Reader*, ed. Michael Beaney (Malden: Blackwell Publishers, 1997), 151–71.

102. As Auerbach reports, "The first important step in this revision and application to art of the theory of Ideas is Aristotle's aesthetics," for Aristotle, "by his doctrine that the Idea is actualized in the formed particular, rehabilitated the formed particular as an object worthy to be imitated" (*Dante*, 7–8). "Consequently, the notion of mimesis underwent an extreme spiritualization," Auerbach notes, "which, though rooted in Plato's theory of Ideas, produced a result diametrically opposed to Plato's teachings, that is, a belief in the sublimity of art."

103. Ludwig Wittgenstein, *Notebooks 1914–1916*, ed. G. H. von Wright and G. E. M. Anscombe, trans. G. E. M. Anscombe (Chicago: University of Chicago Press, 1979), 2e–3e.

104. Ibid., 3e–4e.

105. In the opening pages of *Notebooks*, Wittgenstein argues that in a well-formed sentence, sense is made possible by what he calls an "internal" agreement in the sentence—that is, by "the logical identity of sign and thing signified."

106. Wittgenstein, *Tractatus*, 5.5303; *Notebooks*, 4e. Thus many readers think that Wittgenstein's solution to this "old old objection" is to deny that identity is a relation. However, I am arguing here that Wittgenstein uses his "study of sign-language," as he calls the *Tractatus*, to try to *understand* the relation of identity.

107. That the symbolic writer's business is with the immanent Idea, the Idea formed in the actualized particular, is what Jean Moréas would seem to be declaring in his Symbolist Manifesto (Le Symbolisme), published in *Le figaro* on September 18, 1886. Moréas announces in it that symbolism is hostile to "plain meanings, declamations, false sentimentality and matter-of-fact description" and that its goal is instead to "clothe the Ideal in a perceptible form."

108. Mason, *Spirit Above the Dust*, 116–25.

109. Ibid., 128.

110. Ibid., 125.

111. Ibid., 83.

112. Ibid., 142.

113. Ibid., 83.

114. Ibid., 125.

115. Herman Melville, *Moby-Dick; or, The Whale*, ed. Harrison Hayford and Hershel Parker (New York: Norton, 1967), chapter 55, "Of the Monstrous Pictures of Whales."

116. Ibid., chapter 45, "The Affidavit"; emphasis added.

117. Auerbach, *Dante*, 22.

118. The idea that Melville "builds up the objects of his attention" and consequently that "the relation of the particular to the general is thoroughly recreated in *Moby-Dick*," is from Kenneth Dauber, *The Idea of Authorship in America: Democratic Poetics from Franklin to Melville* (Madison: University of Wisconsin Press, 1990), 213–14.

119. McCarty, "Philosophy of Logical Wholism," 59–60. This line of thinking is further explored in chapters 3 and 4.

120. Matthew Arnold, "Joubert," in *Lectures and Essays in Criticism*, ed. R.H. Super (Ann Arbor: The University of Michigan Press, 1962), 194.

121. Mason, *Spirit Above the Dust*, 70.

122. Melville, *Moby-Dick*, chapter 55, "Of the Monstrous Pictures of Whales."

123. Hartman, *The Unremarkable Wordsworth*, 11.

124. Genesis 1:21; Melville, *Moby-Dick*, chapter 70, "The Sphinx."

125. The way the character Pip is configured in this scene thus provides useful support for the distinction Ralph Ellison makes between, on the one hand, the use of the Negro stereotype in literature (at large in Hemingway's work, as Ellison notes) and, on the other, a writer's use of the Negro as a symbol of man, which Ellison strives for in his own writing and which he associates with the moral and political depth of nineteenth-century realism. This feature of Ellison's critique—how it is only when an individual's full human complexity is restored that he can be seen, heard, and identified—was brought out by Amanda Anderson in "Bleak Liberalism and the Realism/Modernism Debate" (lecture, Cornell University, Ithaca, N.Y., July 21, 2014).

126. Jonathan Lear, *Open Minded: Working Out the Logic of the Soul* (Cambridge, Mass.: Harvard University Press, 1998), 166.

127. Melville, *Moby-Dick*, 438.

128. Ibid., 436.

129. Mulhall, *The Wounded Animal*, 147.

130. As reported in Andrew Delbanco, *Melville: His World and Work* (New York: Vintage, 2005), 11–13. Rather than offer evidence of a worrying trend, however, Delbanco uses such comparisons to confirm Melville's seeming "ability to renew himself for each new generation."

131. For Melville's clearest account of an "original character," see chapter 44 of *The Confidence Man*.

132. Mason, *Spirit Above the Dust*, 20.

133. Herman Melville, *Mardi: And a Voyage Thither*, ed. Harrison Hayford, Hershel Parker, and G. Thomas Tanselle (Evanston, Ill.: Northwestern University Press, 1998), 283.

134. Melville, *Moby-Dick*, chapter 108, "The Deck: Ahab and the Carpenter."

135. For an account of Melville's reading in Plato, see Merton M. Sealts Jr., "Melville and the Platonic Tradition," in *Pursuing Melville, 1940–1980*, 278–336 (Madison: University of Wisconsin Press, 1982).

136. Matthew Arnold, "Maurice de Guérin," in *Lectures and Essays*, 23.

137. Cavell, *Emerson's Transcendental Etudes*, 63. For a recent excellent account of Cavell's involvement with romanticism, see Edward T. Duffy, *Secular Mysteries: Stanley Cavell and English Romanticism* (New York: Bloomsbury, 2013).

138. Cavell, *Emerson's Transcendental Etudes*, 63.

139. Ibid., 64.

140. Melville, *Moby-Dick*, chapter 125, "The Log and the Line," and chapter 120, "The Deck."

141. As Cavell points out, "Wordsworth dedicated his poetry, in his preface to *Lyrical Ballads*, to arousing men in a particular way from a 'torpor,' [and] the way he sought was 'to make the incidents of common life interesting' " ("Emerson, Coleridge, Kant," 64).

142. Immanuel Kant, *Prolegomena to Any Future Metaphysics*, trans. Lewis White Beck (Indianapolis: Bobbs-Merrill, 1978 [1950]), 61–62.

143. Ralph Waldo Emerson, "Fate," in *Essays and Lectures*.

144. As Merton Sealts has noted, the obvious analogue for the book on which Pierre labors, in *Pierre*, is *Mardi*, and what Melville has to say about Pierre in the self-reflective chapter 21, "Pierre Immaturely Attempts a Mature Work," sounds like a judgment on the role of Plato in his own early writing. Pierre, says Melville's narrator, "did not see, or if he did, he could not yet name the true cause for it,—that already, in the incipiency of his work, the heavy unmalleable element of mere book-knowledge would not congenially weld with the wide fluidness and ethereal airiness of spontaneous creative thought. He would climb Parnassus with a pile of folios on his back. He did not see, that it was nothing at all to him, what other men had written; that though Plato was indeed a transcendently great man in himself, yet Plato must not be transcendently great to him (Pierre), so long as he (Pierre himself) would also do something transcendently great" (Herman Melville, *Pierre: or, The Ambiguities*, ed. Harrison Hayford, Hershel Parker, and G. Thomas Tanselle [Evanston, Ill.: Northwestern University Press / The Newberry Library, 1971], 283–84). *Pierre* is in this sense a narrativization of the greenhorn "standing mast-heads, ashore or afloat," or gripped by the notion that his vision is imperfect.

145. Herman Melville to Nathaniel Hawthorne, April 16, 1851, in *Correspondence*, 186.

146. Melville, *Moby-Dick*, 314.

147. These phrases are from Ishmael's masthead meditation in chapter 35, where he notes that the waves seem to harbor every strange, half-seen, gliding thing that eludes definition, every "dimly-discerned uprising fin of some undiscernable form."

148. Melville, *Correspondence*, 186.

149. In this way Melville would lead readers to the type of evidence, as Borutti and de Luise note, similar "to that of the word that opens, with ease, the lock on a safe that not even force could open" ("Writing and Communicating Philosophy," 144–45). The analogy these authors reference is Wittgenstein's (in "Philosophy," in *The Big Typescript: TS 213*, ed. and trans. C. Grant Luckhardt and Maximilian A. E. Aue [Oxford: Blackwell, 2005], 307e), and Wittgenstein is known to have spoken of the dissolution of problems in philosophy and of the destruction of ways of seeing that have become traps for our thinking.

150. Leyda, *The Melville Log*, 622–23.

151. Melville, *Moby-Dick*, chapter 35, "The Mast-head."

152. "Primal Philosophy" in this way calls to mind the "natural philosophy" memorably described by Emerson in "The American Scholar" (included in *Essays*

and Lectures). The Primal Philosophy is conceivably what enlivens Thoreau's *Walden*, or more generally what characterizes that nineteenth-century American writing charged by awareness, as Jennifer Baker writes, of the way "the imaginative mind can be restricted, but also empowered, by the solidity of hard facts" ("Dead Bones and Honest Wonders," 95).

153. In their winning attempt to characterize Wittgenstein's conception of philosophy, Borutti and de Luise identify this overhauled, feeling-based thinking with the philosophical work of anamnesis or with philosophy "whose task," as they write, citing Wittgenstein, "is to give us back that which is 'always (openly) before one's eyes'—or, more precisely, 'has always been' "; to return us to what "is already there: *da ist*" (Writing and Communicating Philosophy," 142–45). As I understand it, Melville's Primal Philosophy identifies what Borutti and de Luise call the condition "that concerns all human beings," the human capacity for "feeling" thought or "seeing" signs—"our adhesion to sense" (143–44).

154. Melville, *Moby-Dick*, chapter 7, "The Chapel."

Chapter 1

1. Herman Melville, *Correspondence*, ed. Lynn Horth (Evanston, Ill.: Northwestern University Press / The Newberry Library, 1993), 191.

2. Richard H. Brodhead, in his fearless and dazzling introduction to *New Essays on Moby-Dick* (Cambridge: Cambridge University Press, 1986), clearly maintains that what sets the book apart is "the stand it takes toward literature itself—its quite peculiar attitude, registered on every page, toward what literature is and can be, and toward what it can attempt as a work of literary making" (1).

3. For a field-shaping discussion of form in Melville's fiction, see Edgar H. Dryden, "Metaphysics and the Art of the Novel," in *Melville's Thematics of Form: The Great Art of Telling the Truth*, (Baltimore: Johns Hopkins University Press, 1968), 3–29.

4. Richard H. Brodhead, "Hawthorne, Melville, and the Form of the Novel," in *Hawthorne, Melville, and the Novel* (Chicago: University of Chicago Press, 1973), 130–33.

5. Warner Berthoff, *The Example of Melville* (New York: Norton, 1962), 5. Brodhead cites Berthoff and seconds him in *Hawthorne, Melville, and the Novel*, 119.

6. Brodhead, *Hawthorne, Melville, and the Novel*, 126.

7. Richard Chase, *The American Novel and Its Tradition* (New York: Doubleday, 1957), 20.

8. Charles Anderson, *Melville in the South Seas* (New York: Columbia University Press, 1939), 4.

9. Brodhead, *Hawthorne, Melville, and the Novel*, 119.

10. Ibid.

11. Matthew Arnold, *Lectures and Essays in Criticism*, vol. 3 of *The Complete Prose Works of Matthew Arnold*, ed. R. H. Super (Ann Arbor: University of Michigan Press, 1962), 175. See also K. L. Evans, "Emerson as Critic: The Arnoldian Ideal," in *A Power to Translate the World: New Essays on Emerson and International Culture*, ed. David LaRocca and Ricardo Miguel-Alfonso (Hanover, N.H.: Dartmouth College Press / University Press of New England, 2015), 185–201.

12. Brodhead, *Hawthorne, Melville, and the Novel*, 119.

13. Thinking of Dante, Auerbach calls the situation in which an object's outward appearance is not distinct from its idea but contained and transfigured "the ultimate after-life" (Erich Auerbach, *Dante, Poet of the Secular World*, trans. Ralph Manheim [New York: New York Review Books, 2007], 100). But he also argues that it is something "which only poetry can aspire to express"—that "poetry alone is capable of expressing it." For Auerbach, poetry that "raises man to the vision of God" is "more than beautiful illusion; it is no longer imitation, third in rank as to the truth." It is revelation.

14. Branka Arsić, ed., *American Impersonal: Essays with Sharon Cameron* (New York: Bloomsbury, 2014), 4; Paul Hurh, *American Terror: The Feeling of Thinking in Edwards, Poe, and Melville* (Stanford, Calif.: Stanford University Press, 2015), 6–7.

15. Arsić, *American Impersonal*, 2–3. In the conclusion to the present volume, I further investigate the rich implications of Arsić's evocative phrase.

16. Charles Altieri, *The Particulars of Rapture: An Aesthetics of the Affects* (Ithaca, N.Y.: Cornell University Press, 2003).

17. Brodhead, *Hawthorne, Melville, and the Novel*, 126.

18. Empson is writing about Henry Fielding's *Tom Jones* in the essay "Tom Jones," in *Fielding: A Collection of Critical Essays*, ed. Ronald Paulson (Englewood Cliffs, N.J.: Prentice-Hall, 1962), 135; the idea that a great book becomes more interesting when you attend to its thesis is his, though it is to Bernard Harrison's gem of a work of literary criticism—*Henry Fielding's "Tom Jones": The Novelist as Moral Philosopher* (London: Chatto and Windus / Sussex University Press, 1975)—that I owe my most obvious scholarly acknowledgment. Though Harrison is an eminent philosopher, he functions in this book as a literary critic, since, as he says, he is concerned primarily with the question of how Fielding should be read. "If there is rather a lot of philosophy in the book," he explains, it is because he thinks "the discussion of such matters essential if we are to arrive at an adequate reading of Fielding." Harrison's sense that Fielding's intellectual position is philosophically defensible and his thorough reconsideration of Fielding as a moral philosopher have provided the master pattern on which this chapter on Melville has been put together.

19. See "Historical Note," in Herman Melville, *Moby-Dick; or, The Whale*, ed. Harrison Hayford, Hershel Parker, and G. Thomas Tanselle (Evanston, Ill.: Northwestern University Press / The Newberry Library, 1988), 581–85.

20. Herman Melville, *Pierre; or, The Ambiguities* (New York: Harper, 1852), 463.

21. Leon Howard's thesis was first delivered to the Modern Language Association convention in New Orleans in 1939 and was published as "Melville's Struggle with the Angel," *Modern Language Quarterly* 1, no. 2 (June 1940), 195–206, and was later collected in Leon Howard, *Herman Melville: A Biography* (Berkeley: University of California Press, 1951). Duyckinck's mention of the work is in Jay Leyda, *The Melville Log: A Documentary Life of Herman Melville, 1819–1891* (New York: Harcourt, Brace, 1951) 1:385. See also Charles Olson, *Call Me Ishmael* (1947; repr., Baltimore: Johns Hopkins University Press, 1997), 35; George R. Stewart, "The Two *Moby-Dicks*," *American Literature* 25, no. 4 (January 1954): 417–48; Hershel Parker and Harrison Hayford, eds., *Moby-Dick*

as Doubloon: Essays and Extracts, 1851–1970 (New York: Norton, 1970). The history of the mostly unquestioned "two *Moby-Dicks*" theory is nicely laid out in James Barbour, "The Composition of *Moby-Dick*," *American Literature* 47, no. 3 (November 1975), 343–60. All additional citations of Barbour are from this essay.

22. Barbour, "The Composition of *Moby-Dick*," 360.

23. "My dear Sir," Melville writes in a letter to Hawthorne of June 1, 1851, "a presentiment is on me,—I shall at last be worn out and perish, like an old nutmeg-grater, grated to pieces by the constant attrition of the wood, that is, the nutmeg. What I feel most moved to write . . ." (Herman Melville, *Correspondence*, ed. Lynn Horth (Evanston, Ill.: Northwestern University Press / The Newberry Library, 1993), 191.

24. Kenneth Dauber, *The Idea of Authorship in America: Democratic Poetics from Franklin to Melville* (Madison: University of Wisconsin Press, 1990), 202. For an example of writing so showy as to call attention to itself *as* writing, or of the kind of language "difficult to attribute . . . simply to romantic nineteenth-century, or even homoerotic, effusiveness," Dauber cites this unrestrained passage in Melville's letter of November 17, 1851: "Whence came you, Hawthorne? By what right do you drink from my flagon of life? And when I put it to my lips—lo, they are yours and not mine. I feel that the Godhead is broken up like the bread at the Supper, and that we are the pieces. Hence this infinite fraternity of feeling." In this light the fact that none of the letters Hawthorne wrote Melville has survived takes on new significance. "For although it is no doubt too lucky an accident to be credited as evidence for our argument," Dauber argues, "yet surely what we may be credited is a sense, in Melville, that Hawthorne could never write him the kind of letter he really wanted." The idea that Melville cast Hawthorne into the role of soul mate, rather than discovered him to be one, is supported by the fact that Melville did something similar to Dana. As reported by Hershel Parker, in a letter of May 1, 1850, Melville recalled the "sort of Siamese link of affectionate sympathy" he had felt reading *Two Years Before the Mast* (see "Historical Note," in Melville, *Moby-Dick*, 612). As Parker notes, the passage "strikingly presages the rhapsodic language" in Melville's letter to Hawthorne of November 1851—which again should emphasize the literary importance of Melville's letters rather than contribute to some false sense that Melville misunderstood the nature of his friendships.

25. F. O. Matthiessen, in *American Renaissance: Art and Expression in the Age of Emerson and Whitman* (London: Oxford University Press, 1941), assures readers that Melville "had none of Poe's equipment as a theorist" (387), but as Shirley M. Detlaff has shown, the absence of lengthy prefaces or literary manifestos in Melville's oeuvre—the wide dispersal of Melville's theory of art, as it may be discovered throughout his fiction, letters, and reviews—doesn't necessarily validate Matthiessen's view of Melville's aesthetics as derivative or not fully deliberate ("Melville's Aesthetics," in *A Companion to Melville Studies*, ed. John Bryant [New York: Greenwood Press, 1986], 631).

26. Olson, *Call Me Ishmael*, 38.

27. "Genius, all over the world, stands hand in hand, and one shock of recognition runs the whole circle round" (Herman Melville, "Hawthorne and His Mosses," in *The Piazza Tales and Other Prose Pieces, 1839–1860*, ed. Harrison

Hayford et al. (Evanston, Ill.: Northwestern University Press / The Newberry Library, 1987), 249.) Or as Hershel Parker notes, Hawthorne's *Mosses from an Old Manse*, already out for four years, was not an obvious candidate for a review, and that fact, plus the good odds that Melville had not even finished reading the volume when he wrote the essay, further supports the conclusion that Melville used the review as a vehicle for articulating his literary aspirations alongside his delight at having discovered, in Hawthorne's work, hints of what Parker calls the "dark truths that were stirring in his own mind" ("Historical Note," in Melville, *Moby-Dick*, 613).

28. Melville, "Hawthorne and His Mosses," in *The Piazza Tales and Other Prose Pieces*, 244, 243.

29. Olson, *Call Me Ishmael*, 54.

30. By attending to what he calls Melville's wonderfully suggestive sentences, Paul Hurh brings the view of blackness as an atavistic fear back to life in *American Terror*. He explores how the concept of innate depravity could, as an abstract, guiding philosophical concern, contribute to the "terror," as he calls it, that signals epistemological skepticism in certain American writers, a skepticism that, as Hurh frames it, actively contributed to the genius of their writing (161–67).

31. Melville, "Hawthorne and His Mosses," in *The Piazza Tales and Other Prose Pieces*, 244. As I understand it, Melville's most important piece of literary criticism frames a writer's compositional practice as one that makes use of an infinite blackness in order to bring forth the world of his creation. Like original darkness, this "infinite obscure" "gives more effect to the evermoving dawn, that forever advances through it, and circumnavigates the world."

32. Altieri, *Reckoning with the Imagination*, 156.

33. For an extended account of hypotyposis, see Rudolph Gasche, *The Idea of Form: Rethinking Kant's Aesthetics* (Stanford, Calif.: Stanford University Press, 2003), 207.

34. Hawthorne, *The Blithedale Romance*, 27–28. Given the number of times Hawthorne's aesthetics are cited as an influence on Melville's aesthetics, it is worth noting that *The Blithedale Romance* was published in 1852 and Melville's "Hawthorne and His Mosses" appeared in two installments (in Duyckinck's journal *Literary World*) on August 17 and 24, 1850.

35. Needless to say, the more strenuously Hawthorne insists that his romance does not mirror his actual life, the more critics are convinced it does, and very few do not begin their scholarly introductions to *The Blithedale Romance* by sketching the probable likenesses between Hawthorne's characters and his former associates at Brook Farm. In this way scholars have not heeded Melville's warning, in "Mosses," that "the world is mistaken in this Nathaniel Hawthorne" and that readers who locate this writing's expressive possibilities in Hawthorne's real life experience have an "absurd misconception" of his work.

36. The feeling that this view of literature's worth is "un-American" is something Melville notes in his response to a *London Times* editorial of 1863 on the benefit of leisure time to art and scholarship. See Merton M. Sealts, Jr., *Melville's Reading: A Check-List of Books Owned and Borrowed* (Madison: University of Wisconsin Press, 1966), 22–23.

37. Zenobia is what Erich Auerbach calls a "real and evident figure" in a work of art (*Dante*, 150), a person *envisaged* but believable all the same. Henry James

famously credits Zenobia with making *The Blithedale Romance* "the lightest, the brightest, the liveliest" of Hawthorne's novels.

38. Gilles Deleuze, *Essays Critical and Clinical*, trans. Daniel W. Smith and Michael A. Greco (Minneapolis: University of Minnesota Press, 1997), 1–2.

39. Thus the poet's work we could call, with Plato, "Goetia," the sorcerer's art, were it not for Melville's insistence—in marginal comments written in his volume of Shakespeare—that this world making is not sinister or low goetic magic but sacred, elevating "theurgic" magic.

40. Thus Richard Brodhead, one of Melville's most appreciative, ingenious, and subtle readers, notes for posterity that "no other nineteenth-century novelist has so little commitment to the basic storytelling procedures of the novel as Melville has" (*Hawthorne, Melville, and the Novel*, 122–25).

41. If the view that Melville juggled different representational modes is held by formalist critics like Brodhead, the view that Melville sometimes quit fiction altogether is widely associated with Nina Baym, who went so far as to say that in longer works like *Mardi* and *Moby-Dick*, Melville abandoned the fictional genre or even "tried to transcend all genres" and so assemble narratives "written altogether outside the bounds of literature." Announcing her departure from those "apologists for fiction" (Dryden, Brodhead, et al., for whom all of *Moby-Dick*'s heterogeneity exists within the form of the novel or within a fictional rhetoric), Baym argued that these works "have no form" as Melville sets aside the romance for "other more direct forms of utterance" (Nina Baym, "Melville's Quarrel with Fiction," *PMLA*, 94, no. 5 [October 1979], 909–23).

42. Herman Melville, *The Confidence Man* (Amherst, N.Y.: Prometheus Books, 1995), 206–7.

43. Friedrich Schlegel, building on Goethe's work, first made the distinction between conceptual and plot-based fiction when, in "Letter on the Novel" (1799), he extended to the novel (*Roman*), or "romantic book," the privilege that had traditionally been poetry's, or allowed the novel a "higher unity" than the kind of book in which, as Goethe had put it in *Wilhelm Meister's Apprenticeship* (1796), "chiefly sentiments and events are exhibited." Melville read Goethe's romantic novel while writing *Moby-Dick*, and his close reading of key works of romantic literature and criticism is well documented.

44. Chase, *American Novel*, viii–ix. On romance and the American novel, see also Leslie A. Fiedler, *Love and Death in the American Novel* (New York: Criterion, 1960), and Joel Porte, *The Romance in America: Studies in Cooper, Poe, Hawthorne, Melville, and James* (Middletown, Conn.: Wesleyan University Press, 1969).

45. Auerbach, *Dante*, 150.

46. A. D. Nuttall, *A New Mimesis: Shakespeare and the Representation of Reality* (New Haven, Conn.: Yale University Press, 2007).

47. Matthew Arnold, *Lectures and Essays in Criticism*, vol. 3 of *The Complete Prose Works of Matthew Arnold*, ed. R. H. Super (Ann Arbor: University of Michigan Press, 1962), 33.

48. Jonathan Arac, *The Emergence of American Literary Narrative, 1820–1860* (Cambridge, Mass.: Harvard University Press, 2005), 166.

49. Parker, "Historical Note," in Melville, *Moby-Dick*, 635–36. The notion that *Moby-Dick* is rooted in personal narrative is backed by time-honored

authority—for, as Parker notes, "Beginning with Charles R. Anderson in the 1930's, scholars have established that, as in the earlier books, some of the materials in *Moby-Dick* were autobiographical, some borrowed and reshaped from other works, and some invented." Parker also notes, however, that "for *Typee*, *Omoo*, *Redburn*, and *White-Jacket* many documents of several kinds permit a check upon what parts of the books are fictional and what are autobiographical, but the evidence about what is autobiographical in *Moby-Dick* is very slight."

50. William Dean Howells, *Criticism and Fiction* (New York: Harper, 1891), 77.

51. Given its trappings of romance, *Moby-Dick* does not meet the usual criteria for realism as it came to be understood in America, where the term usually characterizes writing (for example, by William Dean Howells or Rebecca Harding Davis) devoted to the accurate representation and exploration of American lives. Indeed, as an erstwhile romance, *Moby-Dick* is regularly charged with *falsifying* reality, as Howells and other advocates of American realism griped about the English romantics, whom they accused of refining and subtilizing sentiment, of modifying human psychology after their own fancy (ibid.). For the kind of realist Howells represents, or for the realist to whom the imitation of "reality" means exclusively the imitation of *material* reality, Melville's book is too disfiguring of the world of the senses to be truthful.

52. Brodhead, *Hawthorne, Melville, and the Novel*, 132. Here I wish to insist that since Melville was in his day unequaled in his observation of the idealist-empiricist debate, as it affected the writer of literature, it is not permissible to explain his *solution* to the problem—that writing he called romance—as an *example* of the problem. I mean that it is not conceivable that the writer of *Mardi* would simply surrender to both Yoomy and Mohi's miscarried attempts to describe reality.

53. Use of the phrase "mixed medium" in regard to Melville's writing can be found ibid., 23. The other descriptions of *Moby-Dick* are from Evert A. Duyckinck's contemporary review, "Melville's 'Moby-Dick; or, The Whale,'" *Literary World* vol., 9 (November 22, 1851): 403–4, and George Ripley's (originally anonymous) contemporary review, "Review of Moby-Dick," *Harper's New Monthly Magazine*, December 27, 1851, 137. In Nina Baym, "Melville's Quarrel with Fiction," *PMLA*, 94, no. 5 (October 1979): 909–23, Baym expresses approval for those contemporary reviewers "more alert to the mixed nature of Melville's genre achievement than later critics have proved to be." Baym then provides her own compendium of contemporary reviews emphasizing *Moby-Dick*'s "strange conglomeration," several of which I reproduce in the next passage (917–18).

54. See, for example, Barbara Hardy's description of the expansive novel, "the massive work which attempts to reproduce something like the spacious scale and range of life itself," quoted in Brodhead, *Hawthorne, Melville, and the Novel*, 14.

55. Ripley, "Review of Moby-Dick," 137.

56. Evert A. Duyckinck, "Melville's 'Moby-Dick; or, The Whale,'" *Literary World* 9 (November 22, 1851): 403–4.

57. Leyda, *The Melville Log*, 438 (November 28).

58. Duyckinck, "Melville's 'Moby-Dick,'" 403–4.

59. As is well known, Melville takes pains in a letter of 1848 to his English publisher, Murray, to distinguish *Mardi* from his two earlier books. Melville's

critics, keen to find in this letter a key to his later behavior, have perhaps been misled by the author's description of what sounds like changing gears midproject—of beginning *Mardi* like a South Seas travel writer only to find himself "suddenly abandoning the thing altogether," as he tells Murray. They have taken "the thing" to be the personal narrative or "narrative of *facts*" Melville no longer wished to finish. That explanation makes sense because we recognize in it a pattern we think Melville guilty of: starting a book in one mood and then growing impatient with the project and abandoning it or changing it midway—more proof of his lack of discipline as an artist. However, I think the thing Melville describes abandoning is a certain *method*, the whole discontenting wretchedness of trying to combine writing that imitates empirical reality and writing that aims to present "more reality, than real life itself can show."

60. Typical summaries of Melville's work, by, respectively, Lorrie Moore, "How to Become a Writer," in *Self-Help* (New York: Knopf, 1985), and Andrew Delbanco, *Melville: His World and Work* (New York: Vintage, 2005), 4, 6.

61. Foster's comment and Milder's can both be found in Robert Milder's hugely intelligent conjunction of biography and literary analysis, *Exiled Royalties: Melville and the Life We Imagine* (Oxford: Oxford University Press, 2006), 35. See, for example, Milder's consideration of Melville's "German streak," as Harrison Hayford names it, an intellectual affinity or feeling of identification Melville's contemporary reviewers "right away recognized," as Milder notes: "They recognized it, named it, and deplored its presence in *Mardi*, *Moby-Dick*, and *Pierre*" (253).

62. Auerbach, *Dante*, 173.

63. Ibid., 160, 161, 163, 171.

Chapter 2

1. Hershel Parker, "Historical Note," in Herman Melville, *Moby-Dick; or, The Whale*, ed. Harrison Hayford, Hershel Parker, and G. Thomas Tanselle (Evanston, Ill.: Northwestern University Press / The Newberry Library, 1988), 620–21. Dana makes his suggestion in April of 1850, and, as Parker documents, in May, Melville makes the first surviving reference to *Moby-Dick* when he writes to say he's anticipated it—is halfway into his "whaling voyage"—though he warns Dana that his whaling book will not be the sort Dana had in mind, for "it will be a strange sort of a book," less factual than the one Dana had in mind, but no less truthful.

2. What Kant calls "objects of sense" are the objects we know only by their appearance—by the way they affect our senses. Objects of sense, phenomena, make up the sensible world. However, "creations of the understanding," noumena, are what make up the intelligible world. As Kant argues, creations of the understanding—whose existence we must grant—cannot be known. See Immanuel Kant, *Prolegomena na to Any Future Metaphysics*, trans. Lewis White Beck (Indianapolis: Bobbs-Merrill, 1978 [1950]), 61–62.

3. The idea expressed here is in accordance with what Charles Altieri identifies as the aesthetics of literary experience in *Reckoning with the Imagination: Wittgenstein and the Aesthetics of Literary Experience* (Ithaca and London: Cornell University Press, 2015). Moreover it is intimately connected with what Altieri rightly calls "a capacious and dynamic view of subjectivity" (118), for as

he shows, it is difficult to make the world a more vital place for habitation—his phrase—without first making the self "feel itself an adequate locus of responsiveness to what the world can offer" (105–6).

4. Auerbach, *Dante, Poet of the Secular World*, 174-75.

5. Ibid., 150.

6. Herman Melville, "Hawthorne and His Mosses," in *The Piazza Tales and Other Prose Pieces, 1839–1860*, ed. Harrison Hayford et al. (Evanston, Ill.: Northwestern University Press / The Newberry Library, 1987), 245–47.

7. Ibid., 246.

8. Herman Melville to Richard Bentley, June 27, 1850, in *Correspondence*, ed. Lynn Horth (Evanston, Ill.: Northwestern University Press / The Newberry Library, 1993).

9. Thomas Carlyle, *On Heroes, Hero-Worship, and the Heroic in History* [1840], ed. Carl Niemeyer (Lincoln: University of Nebraska Press, 1966), 49. As Merton M. Sealts Jr. notes, Melville borrowed Carlyle's book from Evert Duyckinck in June or July of 1850. Merton M. Sealts Jr., *Melville's Reading: A Check-List of Books Owned and Borrowed* (Madison: University of Wisconsin Press, 1966).

10. I think it is not going too far to say that Melville builds his whole whaling narrative on one rhetorical figure, hypotyposis.

11. See Martin Seel's pithy account of Baumgarten's contribution to modern aesthetics in "A Rough History of Modern Aesthetics," in *Aesthetics of Appearing*, trans. John Farrell, 1–18 (Stanford, Calif.: Stanford University Press, 2005), 2.

12. Ibid.

13. In a view that will be developed further in chapters 3 and 4, we can take Melville's refusal to dissociate the inexhaustible significance of the whale from its actual, observable manifestations to be evidence of his belief that, as Julius Kovesi writes, "what a thing or act *is* is not something extra over and above what its material elements amount to" (*Moral Notions* [London: Routledge and Kegan Paul, 1967]. 68). In other words, for Melville the world of conceptual objects or forms is not a *separate* world from the world of physical objects and forces in which, by reason of our physical embodiment, we are immersed.

14. The phrase "visible truth" comes from the transcription of a letter (original now lost) from Melville to Hawthorne. In the letter Melville seems to spell the word "visable," a fact some scholars find suggestive. See Harrison Hayford, "Melville's Usable or Visable Truth," *Modern Language Notes* 74, no. 8 (December 1959): 702–5.

15. Robert Zoellner calls Melville's apprehension of noumenal objects his "analogical rendering of the object as seen intuitively and trans-phenomenally"—another way of suggesting that Melville gives conceptual objects a tangible quality (*The Salt-Sea Mastodon: A Reading of "Moby-Dick"* [Berkeley: University of California Press, 1973], 34.

16. This sentence and much of the passage that follows are indebted to philosopher Stephen Mulhall's wonderfully cogent framing of literature's attempt to put philosophy in question, and vice versa, throughout his close examination of J. M. Coetzee's writings in *The Wounded Animal: J. M. Coetzee and the Difficulty of Reality in Literature and Philosophy* (Princeton, N.J.: Princeton University Press, 2009).

17. Mulhall, *The Wounded Animal*, 4.
18. Ibid., 3.
19. Stanley Cavell, "The *Investigations*' Everyday Aesthetics of Itself," in *The Cavell Reader*, ed. Stephen Mulhall (Oxford: Basil Blackwell, 1996), 373. For an engaging account of the way Cavell keeps the interaction between literature and philosophy open, see David Rudrum, introduction to *Stanley Cavell and the Claim of Literature* (Baltimore: Johns Hopkins University Press, 2013).
20. Mulhall, *The Wounded Animal*, 5.
21. Erich Auerbach, *Dante, Poet of the Secular World*, trans. Ralph Manheim (New York: New York Review Books, 2007), 163.
22. Mulhall, *The Wounded Animal*, 8–9.
23. Herman Melville, *Correspondence*, ed. Lynn Horth (Evanston, Ill.: Northwestern University Press / The Newberry Library, 1993), 186.
24. Here I am drawing on Julian Markels's fine bringing together of Althusser's conception of ideology with Melville's fascinating gloss on "visible truth." See Julian Markel, *Melville and the Politics of Identity: From "King Lear" to "Moby-Dick"* (Urbana: University of Illinois Press, 1993), 11–13.
25. See Samuel Otter and Geoffrey Sanborn, eds., *Melville and Aesthetics* (New York: Palgrave Macmillan, 2011), whose introduction includes this quote, which is from Peter De Bolla's essay "Toward the Materiality of Aesthetic Experience," *Diacritics* 32, no. 1 (Spring 2002): 19–37.
26. Seel, *Aesthetics of Appearing*, 2 and xi. Also, on page 10 of this work appears the following: "Only a finite being is open to the moment of the here and now."
27. H. A. Knott, *Wittgenstein, Concept Possession, and Philosophy: A Dialogue* (New York: Palgrave Macmillan, 2007), xiii. Here Knott is emphasizing that Wittgenstein's expression "form of life," used at five seemingly important junctures in *Philosophical Investigations*, "is not a theoretical construct but is a 'grammatical' device. It is a way of saying that the concepts of language, soul, experience, action and reality are all interdependent. They are *internally* related to each other, which means that they are only intelligible in relation to one another. The problems of philosophy arise out of a failure to see clearly into these relations; and so its work is no more and no less than their elucidation."
28. H. O. Mounce, "Wittgenstein and Classical Realism," in *Readings of Wittgenstein's "On Certainty,"* ed. Danièle Moyal-Sharrock and William H. Brenner (New York: Palgrave Macmillan, 2007), 103–21.
29. Ibid., 104.
30. To Protagoras (490–420 B.C.E.) is attributed the statement that "Man is the measure of all things, of the things that are that they are, of the things that are not that they are not," and in his dialogue *Protagoras*, Plato credits the pre-Socratic Greek philosopher with having invented the role of the professional sophist. However, as with other fragments, the phrase is passed down without any context and so offers less-sure evidence of Protagoras's philosophical commitments than of Plato's use of the philosopher as a foil—a means to emphasize his own commitment to objective reality.
31. Mounce, 'Wittgenstein and Classical Realism," 105–6.
32. Satya P. Mohanty, "Literature to Combat Cultural Chauvinism: Indian Literature to World Literature," interview by Rashmi Dube Bhatnagar and

Rajender Kaur, *Frontline*, April 6, 2012, http://www.globalsouthproject.cornell.edu/literature-to-combat-cultural-chauvinism.html.

33. Ieuan Williams, *Plato: All That Matters* (London: Hodder and Stoughton, 2014), chapters 1–3. See also Hugh Knott's lucid review of this book in *Philosophical Investigations* 39, no. 1 (January 2016): 85–88.

34. This tidy account of realism is offered by the logician C. S. Peirce. Peirce's formulation is reported in Russell B. Goodman, ed., *Pragmatism: Critical Concepts in Philosophy*, vol. 2 (Oxon, U.K.: Routledge, 2005), 212. It is worth noting that Peirce's measure of what it is to be a realist is quite different from the usual measure—namely, that to be a realist about some subject matter is to presume the mind's independence of that subject matter. That is the criterion assumed by Cora Diamond, for example, in her well-known chapter "Realism and the Realistic Spirit," in *The Realistic Spirit: Wittgenstein, Philosophy, and the Mind* (Cambridge, Mass.: MIT Press, 1991), 39.

35. Henry A. Pochmann, entry on Herman Melville in *German Culture in America: Philosophical and Literary Influences, 1600–1900* (Madison: University of Wisconsin Press, 1957), 438. In *Aesthetics of Appearing*, Seel argues that apprehending things and events in respect to how they appear momentarily and simultaneously to our senses constitutes a vital prospect in that it "uncovers a dimension of reality that evades epistemic fixation but is nonetheless an aspect of knowable reality" (17).

36. Patricia Hanna and Bernard Harrison, *Word and World: Practice and the Foundations of Language* (Cambridge: Cambridge University Press, 2004), 357.

37. Ian Watt, *The Rise of the Novel: Studies in Defoe, Richardson and Fielding* (London: Pimlico, 2000); Mulhall, *The Wounded Animal*, 142–43.

38. By this measure, philosophers with evident connections to classical realism include J. L. Austin and Wittgenstein, as well as lesser-known but equally adept readers of Plato like the philosopher Julius Kovesi.

39. Mounce, "Wittgenstein and Classical Realism," 111–12.

40. Charles Altieri usefully takes up the way Wittgenstein's fundamentally anti-epistemic project is related to the aesthetic imagination in *Reckoning with the Imagination*, for example on pages 60 and 80.

41. Kovesi, *Moral Notions*, 40. Kovesi's inspired critique of what constitutes "criteria" and his illuminating distinction between knowing how to use words and recognizing phenomena by means of identifying features (what Kovesi humorously calls "standing around deliberating over the inventory of the universe") is in his breathtaking account of concept formation, *Moral Notions*, 37–44.

42. For Kovesi, as for Plato, the features of a whale that enable us to recognize an object *as* a whale are in fact not the criteria for the proper use of the word "whale." The insight Kovesi imparts is that "the features enable us to recognize the phenomena but they enable us only to do this; they are passive, they do not tell us: 'whenever my features appear use the word *x*,' let alone tell us what else we can or should do with a word" (ibid., 41).

43. John Locke, *An Essay Concerning Human Understanding*, ed. Peter H. Nidditch (Oxford: Clarendon Press, 1975) book 3, chapter 5.

44. Bertrand Russell, *The Problems of Philosophy* (London: Oxford University Press, 1912), 58–59.

45. Hanna and Harrison, *Word and World*, 30.

46. Russell, *The Problems of Philosophy*, 48.

47. This view of Peirce is made available by H. O. Mounce as part of Mounce's persuasive account of Wittgenstein's realism, in "Wittgenstein and Classical Realism," 107 and 121.

48. Ludwig Wittgenstein, *Philosophical Investigations*, trans. G. E. M. Anscombe (Englewood Cliffs, NJ.: Prentice-Hall, 1953), §38.

49. Ludwig Wittgenstein, *Tractatus Logico-Philosophicus*, trans. D. F. Pears and B. F. McGuiness (New York: Routledge, 1961), 5.473; Ludwig Wittgenstein, *Notebooks 1914–1916*, ed. G. H. von Wright and G. E. M. Anscombe, trans. G. E. M. Anscombe (Chicago: University of Chicago Press, 1979), 22.8.14. In *Word and World*, Hanna and Harrison call this maxim or mantra "Wittgenstein's Slogan" (3).

50. Hanna and Harrison, *Word and World*, 113, 296. This point constitutes one of the central pillars of the argument they assemble in their original interpretation of Wittgenstein.

51. Wittgenstein, *Notebooks*, 26.10.14.

52. Hanna and Harrison, *Word and World*, 382.

53. Wittgenstein, *Philosophical Investigations*, §§36–39.

54. See Wittgenstein's example using Excalibur, *Philosophical Investigations*, §39.

55. Ibid., §§37–38.

56. David Charles McCarty, "The Philosophy of Logical Wholism," 53.

57. Of course, many philosophers do not distinguish between realism and realism entangled in empiricism, or do not observe the distinction Melville labors to make between modern realism's obfuscating scientism and ancient realism's illuminating spiritualism. This has presumably made it harder to understand Melville's instinct to recall the key insights of classical realism, an instinct shared by Wittgenstein and expressed by Wittgenstein's enigmatic remark, "Not empiricism, and yet realism in philosophy, that is the hardest thing" (Ludwig Wittgenstein, *Remarks on the Foundations of Mathematics*, ed. G. H. von Wright, R. Rhees, and G. E. M. Anscombe, trans. G. E. M. Anscombe [Oxford: Oxford University Press, 1978], 325).

58. The post-Lockean realist or empirical realist thus succumbs to the desire to "map the realm of Things As They Really Are, Distinct From Our Perception," as Cora Diamond writes (*The Realistic Spirit*, 58). The empirical realist—for instance, Melville's Ishmael, while sitting mastheads—"takes himself to have an idea of what it is to be Absolutely Real, an idea of Existence independent of being perceived" (ibid.). In my view, Melville's "Mast-head" chapter is a brief but lucid excursus on what is fantastic (in the sense of extravagant, absurd) about realism as practiced by the empiricist, as well as what is perilous.

59. Kovesi, *Moral Notions*, 114–15.

60. Bernard Harrison, *What Is Fiction For? Literary Humanism Restored* (Bloomington: Indiana University Press, 2015), 152–53.

Chapter 3

1. Patricia Hanna and Bernard Harrison, *Word and World: Practice and the Foundations of Language* (Cambridge: Cambridge University Press, 2004), 17, 23. Much of my thinking in this chapter comes directly from this extraordinary

book, particularly from Harrison's parts 1–3 and the epilogue. My ambition in this chapter, in addition to defending Melville's philosophical ability, is to make Harrison's reexamination of the interrelations of language and social practice (founded on his singular reading of Wittgenstein) feel like a necessary resource for serious readers of *Moby-Dick*.

2. This doubt has been the source of enduring intellectual anguish. As Harrison notes in a dry understatement, "a good deal of philosophy" has consisted in the attempt to resolve or allay it (ibid., 17–18).

3. Ibid., 17.

4. My own understanding of concept formation is indebted to Julius Kovesi's remarkable *Moral Notions* (London: Routledge and Kegan Paul, 1967) and the valuable recent study of Kovesi's work edited by Alan Tapper and T. Brian Mooney, *Meaning and Morality: Essays on the Philosophy of Julius Kovesi* (Leiden: Brill, 2012).

5. Henri Bergson, *The Creative Mind: An Introduction to Metaphysics* (New York: Citadel Press, 1992), 65. Merleau-Ponty similarly criticizes what he calls the "intellectualism" of most modern philosophy.

6. Tapper and Mooney, *Meaning and Morality*, 6–7.

7. My sense of what is at stake in a conceptual investigation is indebted to Hugh Knott, and the picture I present here is beholden to his luminous Ph.D. dissertation, "An Instinct for Meaning" (University of Wales, 2002), which in general argues that our use of concepts (qua linguistic practice) is more intimately woven into *instinctive* action than is often understood (iv, 14, 10, 28). This dissertation was later published as *Wittgenstein, Concept Possession and Philosophy: A Dialogue* (Houndmills, Basingstoke, U.K.: Palgrave Macmillan, 2007).

8. In chapter 73 of *Moby-Dick*, Melville recounts the unhappy condition in which a right whale's head is hanging to the *Pequod*'s larboard side and a sperm whale's head is hanging to its stern: "As before, the *Pequod* steeply leaned over towards the sperm whale's head, now, by the counterpoise of both heads, she regained her even keel; though sorely strained, you may well believe. So, when on one side you hoist in Locke's head, you go over that way; but now, on the other side, hoist in Kant's and you come back again; but in a very poor plight. Thus, some minds forever keep trimming boat. Oh, ye foolish! Throw all these thunderheads overboard, and then you will float light and right" (Herman Melville, *Moby-Dick; or, The Whale*, ed. Harrison Hayford, Hershel Parker, and G. Thomas Tanselle (Evanston: Northwestern University Press / The Newberry Library, 1988).

9. These readers include moral philosopher Julius Kovesi, professor of mathematics and logic David Charles McCarty, and the "Swansea school" Wittgensteinians—for example, Rush Rhees and H. O. Mounce. But it is Bernard Harrison who most ably translates—and builds on—Wittgenstein's philosophical project for a larger audience. The kind of approach Harrison has taken to reading and writing about Wittgenstein is enjoyably summarized by Harrison himself in the introductory essay to *Reality and Culture: Essays on the Philosophy of Bernard Harrison*, ed. Patricia Hanna (New York: Rodopi, 2014). Following is an excerpt from Harrison's prologue to the work:

> Wittgenstein's work is, notoriously, aphoristic and arcane to an extent that encourages exegetical disagreement on a grand scale. Though

Wittgenstein worried incessantly that his work was misunderstood, his cavalier disregard for the usual means of preventing misunderstanding is brandished with cheerful insouciance in the opening sentence of his Cambridge lectures for the Michaelmas Term of 1934, "What we say will be easy, but to know why we say it will be very difficult."

At the moment, the fashion in Wittgenstein exegesis—pioneered three decades ago by Richard Rorty's celebration of Wittgenstein as an "edifying" rather than a "systematic" philosopher, and now represented by James Conant, Alice Crary, Cora Diamond, and others of the "new Wittgensteinians"—is to read Wittgenstein as a principled opponent of anything in the nature of philosophical "argument." My approach has been the contrary one, which I share with some other recent interpreters, including Danièle Moyal-Sharrock. Its founding impulse is to take it for granted that Wittgenstein's work, like that of any other major philosopher, is rich in arguments and to try to articulate them by a reading that, eschewing pleasing but premature generalities, stays obstinately close enough to the detail of his admittedly difficult texts to stand some close chance of exposing their workings" (9).

10. Ludwig Wittgenstein, *Tractatus Logico-Philosophicus*, trans. D. F. Pears and B. F. McGuiness (New York: Routledge, 1961), 4.1121.

11. Ludwig Wittgenstein, *Notebooks 1914–1916*, ed. G. H. von Wright and G. E. M. Anscombe, trans. G. E. M. Anscombe (Chicago: University of Chicago Press, 1979), 3.9.14, 4.9.14.

12. Wittgenstein, *Notebooks*, 27.10.14.

13. Hanna and Harrison, *Word and World*, 87. "Picture theory" is the name given to Wittgenstein's argument, but his own more precise language—for example, that "the sense of a proposition is what it images" (*Notebooks*, 26.10.14)—is more instructive.

14. Ludwig Wittgenstein, *Philosophical Investigations*, trans. G. E. M. Anscombe (Englewood Cliffs, NJ.: Prentice-Hall, 1953), §43.

15. Hanna and Harrison, *Word and World*, 49. The belief that "meaning is use" has figured "in such a diversity of mutually incompatible philosophical enterprises," Harrison writes, "that one might reasonably despair of attaching to it any clear unitary sense at all, let alone a useful one."

16. Ibid., 72.

17. Bernard Harrison, *What Is Fiction For? Literary Humanism Restored* (Bloomington: Indiana University Press, 2015), xvii.

18. Ibid., 119.

19. Ibid.

20. Ibid., 118. See also Rene Descartes, *Philosophical Writings*, trans. and ed. Elizabeth Anscombe and Peter Thomas Geach (London: Nelson, 1963), 20, and Wittgenstein, *Notebooks*, 3.9.14, 4.9.14.

21. Rene Descartes, *Selected Philosophical Writings*, trans. John Cottingham, Robert Stoothoff, and Dugald Murdoch (Cambridge: Cambridge University Press, 1988), "Rule 13," p. 18. Locke is quoted in Harrison, *What Is Fiction For?*, 118.

22. David Charles McCarty, "The Philosophy of Logical Wholism," *Synthese* 87, no. 1 (April 1991): 51–123. McCarty's long essay "is one installment in a

lengthy task, the replacement of atomistic interpretations of Wittgenstein's *Tractatus* by a wholistic interpretation."

23. McCarty's general arguments against atomism are in the first part of his essay directed toward a specific target, the four aspects of the atomistic reading of the *Tractatus* given in Merrill B. Hintikka and Jaakko Hintikka, *Investigating Wittgenstein* (Oxford: Blackwell, 1986). The phrase "vertical linkage" is employed by the Hintikkas in order to describe this word-to-world connection (McCarty, 65). As McCarty makes clear, however, for a logical wholist like Wittgenstein, the logical role of a sign is *not* "fixed exclusively by the bare fact of its standing in a denotational relation to some bit of the world." Rather, the sign's logical role "consists in the play of the sign against the background afforded by the system of all the signs. This background is in flux; there is 'nothing fixed there' by a denotational relation which coerces the logical role" (McCarty, 65).

24. McCarty, "Philosophy of Logical Wholism," 55–56.

25. Kovesi, *Moral Notions*, 30.

26. Robert E. Allinson, "A Rectification of Terms in the Epistolary Plato: Re-Reading Plato's *Seventh Epistle*," *CUHK Journal of Humanities* 2 (January 1998): 137–41.

27. Kovesi, *Moral Notions*, 43.

28. Or as Bertrand Russell subsequently insisted, as if sentences make sense only because they are "composed wholly of constituents with which we are acquainted" (*The Problems of Philosophy* [London: Oxford University Press, 1912]).

29. McCarty, "Philosophy of Logical Wholism," 55–56; Hanna and Harrison, *Word and World*, 65–69.

30. Harrison, *What Is Fiction For?*, 150.

31. McCarty, "Philosophy of Logical Wholism," 65.

32. Hanna and Harrison, *Word and World*, 50.

33. As Melville writes in a footnote, the Latin phrases translate as, respectively "a penis that enters the female, who gives milk from her breasts" and "from the law of nature, justly and deservedly."

34. That the human world is essentially a system of socially devised and maintained practices, and that words acquire meaning in the context of the roles assigned to them in the conduct of one or another such practice, is the view offered by Bernard Harrison in *Word and World* and in chapters 3, 4, and 5 of *What Is Fiction For?*.

35. Kovesi, *Moral Notions*, 7.

36. Wittgenstein, *Tractatus*, 5.552: "The 'experience' that we need in order to understand logic is not that something or other is the state of things, but that something *is*: that, however, is *not* an experience." See in addition Gilbert Ryle's argument that linguistic knowledge isn't a form of "knowing-that" but of "knowing-how," specifically of knowing how to operate with signs (*The Concept of Mind* [Harmondsworth, U.K.: Penguin Books, 1963], 28, emphasis in the original).

37. Kovesi, *Moral Notions*, 42, 19.

38. Ibid., 42.

39. Ibid., 53.

40. McCarty, "Philosophy of Logical Wholism," 59.

41. Hanna and Harrison, *Word and World*, 51. As Harrison notes, a statement like this one can, in a way, represent Hanna and Harrison's conclusion to the four hundred pages of *Word and World*, a complex, detailed, and groundbreaking study that makes it possible for literary theorists to engage in an informed manner the sometimes convoluted, often quite technical, always contentious philosophical debate on the nature of language. But it also offers an elegant summary of the problem Melville runs up against in his thinking for *Moby-Dick*, and indeed what he discovered regarding its solution.
42. Ibid., 48.
43. Ibid., 348.
44. Ibid., 48.
45. Ibid., 363.
46. Ibid., 50.
47. Ibid.
48. Ibid.
49. Ibid., 348–49.
50. Kovesi, *Moral Notions*, 42.
51. McCarty, "Philosophy of Logical Wholism," 65.
52. Tapper and Mooney, *Meaning and Morality*, 5.
53. Harrison, *What Is Fiction For?*, 171.
54. Wittgenstein, *Philosophical Investigations*, §90, §§37–38.
55. Harrison, *What Is Fiction For?*, 150, 152.
56. Wittgenstein, *Philosophical Investigations*, §182.
57. See Knott, "An Instinct for Meaning," 18. Wittgenstein's emphasis on the logical space of a concept runs throughout the *Tractatus*, beginning at 1.13: "The facts in logical space are the world."
58. Knott, *Wittgenstein*, 82.
59. Hanna and Harrison, *Word and World*, 57.
60. Ibid., 150.
61. Ibid., 96–97.
62. Ibid., 113–14. For another reasoned argument against the view that language or thought enmeshed in language "cuts us off from truth and certainty," see Maurice Merleau-Ponty, *The Prose of the World*, ed. Claude Lefort, trans. John O'Neill (Evanston, Ill.: Northwestern University Press, 1973), 17. As Bernard Harrison notes, *Word and World* offers "a rich series of amplifications" of Merleau-Ponty's views.
63. Bernard Harrison, personal correspondence to author, May 2016.
64. Knott, *Wittgenstein*, 207.
65. Melville, *Moby-Dick*, chapter 36, "The Quarter-Deck."

Chapter 4

1. As B. Scot Rousse reports in "Demythologizing the Third Realm: Frege on Grasping Thoughts," Frege writes near the end of his essay "The Thought" about the "non-sensible something" without which "everyone would remain shut up in his inner world." The phrase "non-sensible something" is a translation of the single German substantive *Nichtsinnliche* (*Journal for the History of Analytical Philosophy* 3, no. 1 [2015]: 1–14). See also Michael Beaney, ed., *The Frege Reader* (Malden, Mass.: Blackwell, 1997), 343.

2. Beaney, *The Frege Reader*, note G, 184–85; 246; quoted in Rousse, "Demythologizing the Third Realm," 1–2.

3. Ludwig Wittgenstein, *Notebooks 1914–1916*, ed. G. H. von Wright and G. E. M. Anscombe, trans. G. E. M. Anscombe (Chicago: University of Chicago Press, 1979), 27.10.14: "The difficulty of my theory of logical portrayal was that of finding a connection between the signs on paper and a situation outside in the world. I always said that truth is a relation between the proposition and the situation, but could never pick out such a relation."

4. Ibid., 3.19.14: "The obscurity *obviously* resides in the question: what does the logical identity of sign and thing signified really consist in? And this question is (*once more*) a main aspect of the whole philosophical problem." Emphasis in original.

5. Beaney, *The Frege Reader*, 246.

6. In his essay "Thought," Frege uses the term "idea" to cover a range of inner states. As Frege writes, "Even an unphilosophical man soon finds it necessary to recognize an inner world distinct from the outer world, a world of sense impressions, or creations of his imagination, of sensations, of feelings and moods, a world of inclinations, wishes and decisions. For brevity's sake I want to use the word "idea" to cover all these occurrences, except decisions" (ibid., 334).

7. Gottlob Frege, *Logical Investigations*, trans. P. T. Geach and R. H. Stoothoff (New Haven, Conn.: Yale University Press, 1977).

8. Beaney, *The Frege Reader*, 246.

9. Alan Tapper and T. Brian Mooney, eds., *Meaning and Morality: Essays on the Philosophy of Julius Kovesi* (Leiden: Brill, 2012), 7. Tapper and Mooney are glossing Kovesi's sense of a given concept's "material elements," which, as Kovesi argues, "are unspecified."

10. Julius Kovesi, *Moral Notions* (London: Routledge and Kegan Paul, 1967), 7–8.

11. Bernard Harrison, "Kovesi's Refutation of Hume," in Tapper and Mooney, *Meaning and Morality*, 37.

12. See J. A. Ward, "The Function of the Cetological Chapters in *Moby-Dick*," *American Literature* 28, no. 2 (May 1956): 164–83, cited in Elizabeth Duquette, "Speculative Cetology: Figuring Philosophy in *Moby-Dick*," *ESQ* 47, no. 1 (2001): 52. In "Speculative Cetology" Duquette argues that in *Moby-Dick* the Ahab narrative "is dependent upon, even secondary to, the cetological sections and their methodological theses" (46).

13. Kovesi, *Moral Notions*, 45.

14. Ibid., 57.

15. On the objectivity of concepts, consult Harrison, "Kovesi's Refutation of Hume," 39, and Kovesi's point about "anybody."

16. Tapper and Mooney, *Meaning and Morality*, 9.

17. Patricia Hanna and Bernard Harrison, *Word and World: Practice and the Foundations of Language* (Cambridge: Cambridge University Press, 2004), 50, 353; Bernard Harrison, *What Is Fiction For? Literary Humanism Restored* (Bloomington: Indiana University Press, 2015), 103–23. These pages, particularly 108–12, contain Harrison's discussion of the necessary indeterminacy of meaning inherent in constituted language.

18. Plato, *Phaedrus*, in *The Philosophy of Plato*, trans. Benjamin Jowett, ed. Irwin Edman (New York: Modern Library, 1928), 311.

19. R. Hackforth, trans., *Plato's Phaedrus* (Cambridge: Cambridge University Press, 1952), 132–33.

20. Harrison, "Kovesi's Refutation of Hume," 42.

21. Ibid.

22. See Shirley M. Detlaff, "Melville's Aesthetics," in *A Companion to Melville Studies*, ed. John Bryant (New York: Greenwood Press, 1986), 625–65.

23. "Ordinary language criticism" represents for many of us a radical paradigm shift away from the kinds of questions that tend to dominate theoretical debate. For a fuller discussion of this position, see Kenneth Dauber and Walter Jost, eds., *Ordinary Language Criticism: Literary Thinking after Cavell after Wittgenstein* (Evanston, Ill.: Northwestern University Press, 2003). However, this practice of not asking certain kinds of questions has contributed to the difficulty of defining ordinary language criticism. As Dauber notes, "in such a place, OLP can't find a place" (Personal correspondence, Dauber-Evans, October 2015).

24. My thinking and language here are indebted to David Charles McCarty, "The Philosophy of Logical Wholism," *Synthese* 87, no. 1 (April 1991): 52–53.

25. Ibid., 64.

26. Rousse, "Demythologizing the Third Realm," 1.

27. Melville, *Moby-Dick*, chapter 26, "Knights and Squires."

28. McCarty, "Philosophy of Logical Wholism," 62.

29. Ibid., 62–63.

30. Ibid., 63–64.

31. Ibid., 64.

32. The view that signs and things signified enjoy a logical and not a natural connection is what Wittgenstein means by his governing claim, in the *Tractatus*, that "logic must take care of itself."

33. McCarty, "Philosophy of Logical Wholism," 64.

34. *Inferno*, xxxii.12, quoted in Erich Auerbach, *Dante, Poet of the Secular World*, trans. Ralph Manheim (New York: New York Review Books, 2007), 154. This line from chapter 32 of the *Inferno* seems even more germane to a reading of *Moby-Dick* when quoted in context. See for example the translation of lines 1-12 in Piero Boitani's "Inferno XXXIII," in *Cambridge Readings in Dante's Comedy*, ed. Kenelm Foster and Patrick Boyde (Cambridge: Cambridge University Press, 1981), 85: "If only I had the harsh and grating rhymes that would match the pit of misery on which all the rocks of the earth bear down, I would squeeze out more fully the juice of my conception; and since I do not have them, it is not without fear that I bring myself to speak. For it is no trifling matter to describe the bottom of the whole universe, and not possible in the language in which children call for their mummy and daddy. But may those ladies come to the aid of my verse who helped Amphion to build the walls of Thebes, so that there may be no discrepancy between the fact and the word."

35. That is what Wittgenstein means when he writes that "the limits of my language mean the limits of my world." What Wittgenstein draws attention to is that words are not images of the states of things. A word, like the word "whale," is, as it were, the thing itself.

36. John Locke, *An Essay Concerning Human Understanding*, vols. 1–2 of *The Works of John Locke, in Nine Volumes*, 12th ed. (London: Rivington, 1824).

37. Harrison, *What Is Fiction For?*, 119.

38. This lesson is given detailed treatment in Harrison, *What Is Fiction For?*, 114, and in Hanna and Harrison, *Word and World*, 184–89.

39. Harrison, *What Is Fiction For?*, 150.

40. Herman Melville, *The Confidence Man* (Amherst, N.Y.: Prometheus Books, 1995), 280.

41. Ibid. As Melville makes clear, commonplace characters are imitations of living people, and the writers who manufacture them are just the kind of writers Plato (rightly) disparaged: "Where does any novelist pick up any character?" Melville asks rhetorically. "For the most part, in town, to be sure. Every great town is a kind of man-show, where the novelist goes for his stock, just as the agriculturalist goes to the cattle show for his."

42. "This distinction is all important," writes Julius Kovesi, "and we must beware of Hume's systematic confusion of perceiving and knowing" (*Moral Notions*, 18).

43. The idea that "language did not emerge from some kind of ratiocination," as Wittgenstein writes at 475 in *On Certainty*, is perhaps the central thesis of that work. (Ludwig Wittgenstein, *On Certainty*, ed. G. E. M. Anscombe and G. H. von Wright, trans. Denis Paul and G. E. M. Anscombe [New York: Harper & Row, 1969]). The idea that the everyday meanings of words are "constituted by, or sedimented out of, long usage in many contexts" is the thesis of Hanna and Harrison, *Word and World*, and an informing principle of Harrison, *What Is Fiction For*.

44. *Phaedrus*, 256e, quoted in Kovesi, *Moral Notions*, 136.

45. This is a generalized interpretation of Spinoza's argument.

46. Kenneth Dauber, "Beginning at the Beginning in Genesis," in Dauber and Jost, *Ordinary Language Criticism*, 337.

47. Hanna and Harrison, *Word and World*, 352.

48. Or as Wittgenstein put it in the *Tractatus*, "A name means an object. The object is its meaning" (3.203). According to the view presented here, Tractarian objects are thus best understood not as starting points but (as David Charles McCarty reasons) *end points* in a process of analysis and of transcendental deduction ("Philosophy of Logical Wholism," 59–60).

49. An argument about something's intrinsic nature is a feeble argument, as Plato worked to show in the dialogues. With his characteristic brevity, Wittgenstein likewise argued that "whereof one cannot speak, thereof one must be silent" (*Tractatus*, proposition 7).

50. Melville's reference to the "Anacharsis Clootz deputation" that "accompanies Old Ahab" concludes the important double chapter "Knights and Squires" (chapters 26 and 27).

51. Harrison, *What Is Fiction For?*, 150.

52. See Melville's letter to Nathaniel Hawthorne, April 16, 1851, in *Correspondence*, ed. Lynn Horth (Evanston, Ill.: Northwestern University Press / The Newberry Library, 1993).

Chapter 5

1. Julius Kovesi calls such concepts "moral notions." Moral notions are, by this measure, not limited to concepts like "good" or "just"—"table" is a moral notion, according to Kovesi, something we can easily see when we compare the word "table" with the word "yellow." For Kovesi, "The important point is that in order for us to judge something to be yellow, that very quality has to be present that we have agreed to call by the word 'yellow.' But for us to judge something to be a table, an unspecified group of properties and qualities have to be present, none of which is that property or quality which we have agreed to call "table" (*Moral Notions* [London: Routledge and Kegan Paul, 1967], 6).

2. This is the view of concepts made available by Gilles Deleuze. As Paul Patton writes in *Deleuzian Concepts: Philosophy, Colonization, Politics* (Stanford, Calif.: Stanford University Press, 2010), the way our concepts "map" or divide up the world "should not be understood as a matter of naming, copying, or tracing the preexisting articulations of the world" (23). For Deleuze and Guattari, what distinguishes "mapping" from tracing or copying is that "it is entirely oriented toward an experimentation in contact with the real" (Gilles Deleuze and Félix Guattari , *A Thousand Plateaus: Capitalism and Schizophrenia*, trans. Brian Massumi (Minneapolis: University of Minnesota Press, 1987), 20, 12).

3. Branka Arsić, *Bird Relics: Grief and Vitalism in Thoreau* (Cambridge, Mass.: Harvard University Press, 2016), 11.

4. Arsić, *Bird Relics*, 15.

5. As Branka Arsić writes of *Walden*, "The promise of recalling actual bodies when we call their name was never actually fulfilled. If I then say that I treat Thoreau's words as if such a promise were fulfilled, it is because his desire to move words in the vicinity of things—to make them literal or to even turn them into what they mean—remains for him a regulative epistemological wish. Even if it is always failing, it is thus nonetheless always consequential in fashioning even his most ordinary acts and perceptions" (*Bird Relics*, 15).

6. For Cavell's comments on the Kantian settlement with skepticism (on which I have put a materialist spin), see "Emerson, Coleridge, Kant" in *In Quest of the Ordinary: Lines of Skepticism and Romanticism* (Chicago: University of Chicago Press, 1988), 31; for the American transcendentalists' search for a materialist epistemology, their attempt to go beyond the philosophical dualism available to them, see Sharon Cameron, *The Corporeal Self: Allegories of the Body in Melville and Hawthorne* (New York: Columbia University Press, 1981), 3, and Branka Arsić, ed., *American Impersonal: Essays with Sharon Cameron* (New York: Bloomsbury, 2014), 3; for a lucid summary of Matthiessen's *American Renaissance*, see Walter E. Bezanson, "*Moby-Dick*: Work of Art," in *Moby-Dick*, Norton Critical Edition, ed. Harrison Hayford and Hershel Parker, 651-671 (New York: Norton, 1967).

7. Cavell, *In Quest of the Ordinary*, 169.

8. Cavell, *The Senses of Walden*, 63.

9. Ibid.

10. Ibid., 34.

11. Henry David Thoreau, *Walden*, ed. J. Lyndon Shanley (Princeton, N.J.: Princeton University Press, 1971), chapter 2, "Where I Lived, and What I Lived For."

12. Ludwig Wittgenstein, *Philosophical Investigations*, trans. G. E. M. Anscombe (Englewood Cliffs, NJ.: Prentice-Hall, 1953), 215.

13. Stanley Cavell, *The Senses of Walden, An Expanded Edition* (Chicago: University of Chicago Press, 1992 [1981]), 44.

14. Ludwig Wittgenstein, *Philosophical Investigations*, 217. By framing Melville's philosophical project in this way I mean to show why Melville's writing, like Wittgenstein's, is fittingly called redemptive and emancipating (better terms, I think, than "therapeutic"). For in a manner akin to Wittgenstein's work in logic, Melville's whaling narrative brings out both how language belongs to our lives and how the way it belongs to our lives has typically perplexed and disoriented us.

15. For a clear-eyed view of Wittgenstein's effort to forestall a "global misunderstanding of his seminal idea that meaning lies in use," see Edward Minar's wonderful essay "The Philosophical Significance of Meaning-Blindness" in *Seeing Wittgenstein Anew*, ed. William Day and Victor J. Krebbs (Cambridge: Cambridge University Press, 2010), 183–203.

16. Ludwig Wittgenstein, *Philosophical Investigations*, §119.

17. Ibid., 218.

18. Ludwig Wittgenstein, *Philosophical Investigations*, 215, 217. Wittgenstein writes that "In a law-court, for instance, the question might be raised how someone meant a word" (214). But as he points out, applying questions of *intention* is not what we are talking about when we talk about the meaning of a word like "whale."

19. Ibid., 215.

20. Ibid.

21. Henry David Thoreau, *Walden*, ed. J. Lyndon Shanley, in *The Writings of Henry D. Thoreau* (Princeton, NJ: Princeton University Press, 1971). For Thoreau, "mother tongue" is the language we learn "unconsciously, like the brutes, of our mothers."

22. Stanley Cavell, *The Senses of Walden,* 16. As Cavell writes, "A son of man is born of woman; but rebirth, according to our Bible, is the business of the father. So Walden's puns and paradoxes, its fracturing of idiom and twisting of quotation, its drones of fact and flights of impersonation—all are to keep faith at once with the mother and the father, to unite them, and to have the word born in us."

23. Wittgenstein, *Philosophical Investigations*, 216.

24. Ibid.

25. Barbara Johnson, "A Hound, a Bay Horse, and a Turtle Dove: Obscurity in *Walden*," in *Walden*, Norton Critical Edition, ed. William Rossi (New York: Norton, 1992), 450.

26. Arsić, *Bird Relics*, 8, 5, 9.

27. Ibid., 62–63.

28. For Arsić, "concepts are metaphors par excellence" (*Bird Relics*, 11).

29. Ibid., 5.

30. Wittgenstein, *Philosophical Investigations*, 215.

31. Ibid.

32. Knott, "On Reinstating 'Part I' and 'Part II,'" 11. As I think Cavell's *The Senses of Walden* makes clear, the idea that the secondary use of language is legitimate and not problematic is also one of *Walden*'s central lessons.

33. Wittgenstein, *Philosophical Investigations*, 216: "The secondary sense is not a 'metaphorical' sense."

34. Wittgenstein, *The Blue and Brown Books: Preliminary Studies for the Philosophical Investigations* (New York: Harper & Row, 1958), 4.

35. The necessity of locating linguistic activities in the textures of our lives is a central preoccupation in the writings of Rush Rhees: see Rhees, *Wittgenstein and the Possibility of Discourse*, ed. D. Z. Phillips (Cambridge: Cambridge University Press, 1998).

36. Rush Rhees, Preface to *The Blue and Brown Books*, (xv).

37. Rush Rhees, Preface to *The Blue and Brown Books*, (xv). Edward Minar offers a thoughtful and stimulating account of these considerations in "The Philosophical Significance of Meaning-Blindness."

38. Wittgenstein, *Remarks on the Philosophy of Psychology*, vol. 1, §198; qtd in Edward Minar, "The Philosophical Significance of Meaning-Blindness," 197.

39. See Rush Rhees's Preface to *The Blue and Brown Books: Preliminary Studies for the "Philosophical Investigations"* (Oxford: Basil Blackwell, 1958), xv.

40. Wittgenstein, *Philosophical Investigations*, §432.

41. Knott, "On Reinstating 'Part I' and 'Part II,'" 9-10. Cf. Rush Rhees, "Wittgenstein's Builders," in *Discussions of Wittgenstein* (London: Routledge and Kegan Paul, 1970), 77.

42. Bezanson, "*Moby-Dick*," 664.

43. Elizabeth Duquette, "Speculative Cetology: Figuring Philosophy in *Moby-Dick*," *ESQ* 47, no. 1 (2001): 33–57.

44. Ibid., 48.

45. For more insight on the picturing aspect of language, see Knott, "On Reinstating 'Part I' and 'Part II.'"

46. Wittgenstein, *Philosophical Investigations*, 213.

47. Duquette, "Speculative Cetology," 36.

48. Duquette uses Melville's subsequent line ("But clear Truth is a thing for salamander giants only to encounter; how small the chances for provincials, then?") to further disparage the whole idea of truth. To my mind Melville's line comes rather closer to a difficult insight Wittgenstein is always trying to get across—namely, that "what expresses *itself* in language, *we* cannot express by means of language" (Ludwig Wittgenstein, *Tractatus Logico-Philosophicus*, trans. D. F. Pears and B. F. McGuiness [New York: Routledge, 1961], 4.121, emphasis in the original).

49. Of course, the idea that it is possible to work out a philosophical point we associate with Wittgenstein by reading Melville's whaling narrative requires some justification, since I am neither arguing that Wittgenstein ever undertook a reading of *Moby-Dick*, nor that we can only understand Melville if we take him to be making the same philosophical point that some readers associate with Wittgenstein. Still, Melville's observations about the way we make the world intelligible to ourselves—and the difficulties we get into when reflecting on such things—seem to me to be remarkably consistent with Wittgenstein's observations. Rather than claim that Melville's narrative is intended to make the same argument Wittgenstein makes, I need only point out that if Wittgenstein's account of our life with language is correct, then any writing having to do with the nature of discourse that hasn't gotten muddled (by the empiricist tradition, for example)

will be consistent with that account—even if an author is not himself attempting to put forward any thesis to that effect. This point was made (and elegantly laid out) by Hugh A. Knott, e-mail message to author, Oct 22, 2016.

50. Edward Minar, "The Philosophical Significance of Meaning-Blindness," 202.

51. Knott, "On Reinstating 'Part I' and 'Part II,'" 12.

52. Wittgenstein, *Philosophical Investigations*, 213.

53. Wittgenstein, *Notebooks*, 26.9.14.

54. Edward Minar, "The Philosophical Significance of Meaning-Blindness," 189.

55. Wittgenstein, *Philosophical Investigations*, 215; Knott, "On Reinstating 'Part I' and 'Part II,'" 10.

56. Wittgenstein, *The Blue and Brown Books* (New York: Harper, 1958), 5.As Edward Minar reports, Rhees was alive to the possibility that Wittgenstein's emphasis on use would be "subject to what amounts to a behaviorist misinterpretation." Minar, 189.

57. Knott, "On Reinstating 'Part I' and 'Part II,'" 10–11; emphasis added.

58. Stanley Cavell, *Must We Mean What We Say?* (Cambridge: Cambridge University Press, 1976), 19–20. Here is Cavell's passage in full (emphasis in the original):

> Now imagine that you are in your armchair reading a book of reminiscences and come across the word "umiak." You reach for your dictionary and look it up. Now what did you do? Find out what "umiak" means, or find out what an umiak is? But how could we have discovered something about the world by hunting in the dictionary? If this seems surprising, perhaps it is because we forget that we learn language and learn the world *together*, that they become elaborated and distorted together, and in the same places. We may also be forgetting how elaborate the learning process is. We tend to take what a native speaker does when he looks up a noun in a dictionary as the characteristic process of learning a language. (As, in what has become a less forgivable tendency, we take naming as the fundamental source of meaning.) But it is merely the end point in the process of learning the word. When we turned to the dictionary for "umiak" we already knew everything about the word, as it were, but its combination: we know what a noun is and how to name an object and how to look up a word and what boats are and what an Eskimo is. We were all prepared for that umiak. What seemed like finding the world in a dictionary was really a case of bringing the world to the dictionary. We had the world with us all the time, in that armchair; but we felt the weight of it only when we felt a lack in it. Sometimes we will need to bring the dictionary to the world. That will happen when (say) we run across a small boat in Alaska of a sort we have never seen and wonder—what? What it is, or what it is called? In either case, the learning is a question of aligning language and the world. What you need to learn will depend on what specifically it is you want to know; and how you can find out will depend specifically on what you already command. How we answer the question, "What is X?" will depend, therefore, on the specific case of ignorance and of knowledge.

59. Edward T. Duffy, *Secular Mysteries: Stanley Cavell and English Romanticism* (New York: Bloomsbury, 2013), 2–3.

60. Howard P. Vincent, *The Trying-Out of Moby-Dick* (Carbondale: Southern Illinois University Press, 1965 [1949]), 58.

61. Bernard Harrison, "Kovesi's Refutation of Hume," 37.

62. As Ishmael notes in chapter 10, "A Bosom Friend," "Here was a man some twenty thousand miles from home, by way of Cape Horn, that is—which was the only way he could get there—thrown among people as strange to him as though he were in the planet Jupiter; and yet he seemed entirely at his ease; preserving the utmost serenity; content with his own companionship; always equal to himself. Surely this was a touch of fine philosophy; though no doubt he had never heard there was such a thing as that. But, perhaps, to be true philosophers, we mortals should not be conscious of so living or so striving. So soon as I hear that such or such a man gives himself out for a philosopher, I conclude that, like the dyspeptic old woman, he must have 'broken his digester' " (Herman Melville, *Moby-Dick; or, The Whale*, ed. Harrison Hayford, Hershel Parker, and G. Thomas Tanselle [Evanston: Northwestern University Press / The Newberry Library, 1988], 53).

63. Ibid., chapter 135, "The Chase—Third Day."

64. For example, consider these lines from the Epilogue to *Clarel*:

> Faith (who from the scrawl indignant turns)
> With blood warm oozing from her wounded trust
> Inscribes even on her shards of broken urns
> The sign of the cross—the spirit above the dust!

By this measure the word "above" in the last important phrase comes closer to "animating" than "higher than."

65. Vincent, *Trying-Out of Moby-Dick*, 72.

66. Ibid.

67. Cameron, *Corporeal Self*, 10; Arsić, *American Impersonal*, 4–5.

68. Arsić, *American Impersonal*, 4.

69. Vincent, *Trying-Out of Moby-Dick*, 72.

70. Ibid., 75.

71. Ibid., 73.

72. For a clear-eyed critique of postmodernism's arguments about the untenability of objective knowledge, and a defense of objective knowledge that serves progressive and cultural politics, see Satya P. Mohanty, *Literary Theory and the Claims of History: Postmodernism, Objectivity, Multicultural Politics* (Ithaca and London: Cornell University Press, 1997).

73. Ibid., 11.

74. For a lucid, jargon-free account of what effect the era of postructuralism, not yet ended, has had upon the study of literature and of literary criticism, see the Introduction, "What Happened to Criticism," to Morris Dickstein's *Double Agent: The Critic and Society* (Oxford: Oxford University Press, 1992), 3-7. Though this book is 25 years old its analysis still feels timely and relevant.

75. Tapper and Mooney, *Meaning and Morality*, 5.

76. Wittgenstein, *Philosophical Investigations*, 218.

77. As Rush Rhees points out, it is the internal or logical connection between speaking and living that Wittgenstein means to emphasize, in the *Investigations*,

when he shows how 'speaking' is not doing one thing, as D. Z. Phillips writes; "it is doing many things." "Editor's Introduction" to Rush Rhees, *Wittgenstein and the Possibility of Discourse*, ed. D. Z. Phillips (Cambridge: Cambridge University Press, 1998), 4.

Finale

1. Bernard Harrison, "Kovesi's Refutation of Hume," in *Meaning and Morality: Essays on the Philosophy of Julius Kovesi*, ed. Alan Tapper and T. Brian Mooney (Leiden: Brill, 2012), 26.

2. This line is taken straight from D. Z. Phillips's "Editor's introduction" to *Rush Rhees, Wittgenstein and the Possibility of Discourse*, 8.

3. Ahab's refrain appears twice in the space of a heartbeat in chapter 36, "The Quarter-Deck," also taking the form, "Aye, Starbuck; aye, my hearties all round; it was Moby-Dick that dismasted me; Moby-Dick that brought me to this dead stump I stand on now."

4. Branka Arsić, ed., *American Impersonal: Essays with Sharon Cameron* (New York: Bloomsbury, 2014), 2–3.

5. Herman Melville, *Published Poems: Timoleon* [1891], ed. Robert C. Ryan, Harrison Hayford, Alma MacDougall Reising, and G. Thomas Tanselle (Evanston and Chicago: Northwestern University Press and The Newberry Library, 2009), 313.

6. Bryan C. Short, *Cast by Means of Figures: Herman Melville's Rhetorical Development* (Amherst: University of Massachusetts Press, 1992), 4. How Melville's investment in literary rhetoric "sustains and renews his creativity in the teeth of both physical and metaphysical woes" is the question for which Short's book seeks an answer.

7. Herman Melville, *Moby-Dick; or, The Whale*, ed. Harrison Hayford, Hershel Parker, and G. Thomas Tanselle (Evanston: Northwestern University Press / The Newberry Library, 1988), 320.

8. Bernard Harrison, *What Is Fiction For? Literary Humanism Restored* (Bloomington: Indiana University Press, 2015), 171.

9. Ibid., 200–201.

10. Melville, *Moby-Dick*, 207.

11. For as Melville writes in chapter 56, "Of the Less Erroneous Pictures of Whales, and the True Pictures of Whaling Scenes," "The French are the lads for painting action. Go and gaze upon all the paintings of Europe, and where will you find such a gallery of living and breathing commotion on canvas, as in that triumphal hall at Versailles; where the beholder fights his way, pell-mell, through the consecutive great battles of France; where every sword seems a flash of the Northern Lights, and the successive armed kings and Emperors dash by, like a charge of crowned centaurs? . . . The natural aptitude of the French for seizing the picturesqueness of things seems to be peculiarly evinced in what paintings and engravings they have of their whaling scenes. With not one tenth of England's experience in the fishery, and not the thousandth part of that of the Americans, they have nevertheless furnished both nations with the only finished sketches at all capable of conveying the real spirit of the whale hunt."

12. Harrison, *What Is Fiction For?*, 201.

INDEX